The Pubs of Bromyard, Ledbury & East Herefordshire

The Pubs of Bromyard, Ledbury & East Herefordshire

by

John Eisel & Ron Shoesmith

Logaston Press

LOGASTON PRESS
Little Logaston Woonton Almeley
Herefordshire HR3 6QH

First published by Logaston Press 2003
Copyright © John Eisel & Ron Shoesmith 2003

ISBN 1 873827 63 6

Set in Times New Roman by Logaston Press
and printed in Great Britain by
Bell & Bain Ltd, Glasgow

Contents

Sources of Illustrations

t-top; b-bottom; m-middle

Hereford Reference Library
11, 19t & b, 21, 29, 38, 50, 61t & b, 63, 64t, 71, 93, 123, 131, 138, 145, 186, 189, 208, 219, 249t, 280t & b, 281, 286

Hereford Record Office
26t, 27, 137

Bromyard Local History Society
52t, m & b, 58, 64b, 65t, 68t, 69, 72, 81, 84, 86, 89, 97, 98, 101, 103, 107, 110t, 119, 141, 142t, 152t & b, 170, 178

Ledbury & District Society Trust Ltd.
192, 210, 254t, 257, 258t

Woolhope Naturalists' Field Club
288t

St Peter's, Bromyard, ringers
45

Frank Bennett
4t, 41t, 43, 44t, 51, 56, 65, 92, 140, 263t

John Hartwright
13, 75, 76, 77, 78, 79

Agnes Jones
126, 132t & b, 133t

Roger Broomfield
251b

Peter Davies
276

Acknowledgments

The preparation of this volume would not have been possible without the cooperation of many people who have spent much time and effort in producing information and illustrations.

Thanks are due to Barry Lawrence for his help with the identification of the Mason's Arms with the Burley Gate Inn, and to Charlie Skerratt for confirming the name of the Ramping Cat and the location of Halfway House in Ullingswick. Peter Garnett was of great help in resolving problems of Ledbury pubs and Allan Wyatt came up with information on the Swan with two Necks in Bromyard. Further information on the pubs of Bromyard was provided by Bill Woodyatt and Jennifer Wheale whilst John Hartwright provided much information on the Rose and Lion and allowed us access to his fascinating archive about the pub. Equally Ted Jones provided information on pubs around Bromyard and allowed us access to his collection of memorabilia. John Thomas helped with Pencombe pubs and Mrs. Lois Edwards provided information about the Frenchman's Inn at Preston Wynne. Desmond Keohane was of help with the Crown Inn at Shucknall as was Janet Parry with the Coddington pubs. Mrs. Agnes Jones and Mrs. Sheila Hince were of considerable help with the Burley Gate Inn.

We are grateful to the many people who provided historic photographs and material including Frank Bennett, Roger Broomfield Agnes Jones and Peter Davies. Katy Shoesmith produced the maps; John Wilson the index — without all their help the task would have been much more arduous.

The volunteer staff in the Bromyard Room of Bromyard Local History Society and the staff in Hereford Record Office and Hereford City Library provided much information and allowed us to copy original material — our most grateful thanks to them all.

Following various requests for assistance through the columns of the *Hereford Times* and the Hereford Family History Society, several people phoned or wrote with information about various inns, both open and closed — our thanks to them all for their encouragement and their permission to use the material.

Andy Johnson of Logaston Press, as always, has been a constant help and encouragement. The sources of many of the illustrations used in this book are listed on a previous page. Others are from the authors' private collections and a few are from unidentified sources.

John Eisel & Ron Shoesmith
September 2003

Introduction

In 1994 a book was published on the pubs of Hereford City and such was the interest that it sold out quite quickly. Not only that, but as a result of the interest generated more material became available and this was incorporated into a second edition, published in 1998. This was followed by several other books including *The Pubs of Leominster, Kington & North-west Herefordshire, The Pubs of Ross & South Herefordshire* and *The Pubs of Ludlow & Neighbouring Villages*. This present book is thus the fifth in the series, and covers the pubs of the eastern part of the county, based on Bromyard and Ledbury. A book of this length cannot possibly include all the information on pubs that is either available or can be found in public and private records, but is designed to give a flavour of each pub that has been identified. Material used includes newspaper reports, deeds, advertisements, census records, trade directories, as well as local memories. Our enquiries seem to have caused much interest, and we are grateful to those who have helped in any way.

Pubs that are still in use are easy to find, but it is those of years gone by that present problems and, while we hope we have located most of these, it is inevitable that some will have escaped the net. We would be pleased to hear of any further information and, who knows, one day there may be sufficient material for a revised second edition!

To present the information gathered merely as a list of pubs would be boring to the reader, and we have tried to organise it in a more meaningful way. Each chapter has a geographical basis, with a definite route that can be followed. The first part of the book, after the two introductory chapters, is based on Bromyard. Inevitably, because of the sheer number of licensed premises, the market towns need several chapters each, so that chapters three, four and five are on different parts of Bromyard, followed by a chapter on pubs in the area around Bromyard, based on the turnpike roads. In order to include all the pubs on the way, chapter seven, which deals with pubs between Bromyard and Hereford, follows a slightly circuitous but scenic route. After chapter eight, which covers the two routes from Bromyard to Ledbury, and chapter nine — the Hereford to Worcester road, the emphasis changes to Ledbury, which merits four chapters (ten to thirteen). The hinterland around Ledbury is covered in chapter fourteen and the final chapter covers the main road from Ledbury to Hereford.

Chapters one and two are a joint effort between us, while John Eisel has written chapters three to nine, and Ron Shoesmith chapters ten to fifteen. As far as the authors are aware, the information in this book is correct at the time of going to press.

John Eisel & Ron Shoesmith
September 2003

CHAPTER ONE

Alehouses, Taverns and Inns

Travelling for work and for pleasure was an essential part of the Roman Empire, and it was during the 350-year period when England and Wales were part of that Empire that a network of roads was constructed and with them a series of guest houses to provide food, drink and overnight accommodation. In the first instance the roads were built for military purposes — to enable Roman troops to travel quickly and safely from one part of the country to another.

During the early Roman occupation, the main road in Herefordshire, which was built by the army to follow the Welsh border and join the legionary fortresses of Chester and Caerleon, probably crossed the river Wye at one of the Hereford fords. After a while their engineers constructed a bridge over the river near *Magnis*, the Roman settlement at Kenchester, and the line of the road was diverted to this, the first Hereford by-pass! Northwards, the road passed through Leintwardine, the *Bravonium* of the Antonine Itinerary, on its way to Wroxeter (*Virconium*).

With its broad main street and large public buildings *Magnis* would, without any doubt, have had guesthouses providing overnight accommodation and places where soldiers, returning from a stint of duty in Wales, could drink and enjoy themselves. Alcoholic refreshments would doubtless have been available to those who required them — the Romans imported wine from other parts of the Empire and made every effort to grow vines in the southern part of England. They would also have made mead from honey and possibly cider from the locally grown apples, and as wheat and barley were both available, some form of ale.

1

The eastern part of Herefordshire was in the civilian zone for most of the Roman period. From *Magnis* a road went eastwards, passing just to the north of Hereford on the now appropriately named 'Roman Road', heading towards the Roman settlement at Stretton Grandison and from there towards Worcester. This road was crossed by two north-south roads; one passing through Blackwardine, Withington and Bartestree, the other through Much Cowarne, Ashperton and the Trumpet — both on their way southwards towards *Ariconium* at Weston-under-Penyard and eventually Gloucester.

With Roman settlements at Stoke Prior (Blackwardine) and Canon Frome, forts at Tedstone Wafer and Canon Frome, and several villas, including Nunnington and Putley, the whole area was well settled throughout much of the Roman period and would have been an important source of crops for producing alcoholic beverages.

The break-up of the Roman Empire in England, which took place following the withdrawal of the Roman troops shortly after A.D. 410, meant that the country descended into the Dark Ages. Although some towns doubtless kept going for a short while, it was to be several hundred years before there were any recognisable new settlements in the whole of Herefordshire. The earliest ones recorded are religious establishments such as St. Guthlac's Priory, which was founded on the area now known as Castle Green in Hereford, and the minster at Leominster, founded by King Merewalh of the *Magonsaete* about 660 A.D.

Shortly afterwards, the foundation of the Hereford Diocese would have encouraged the building of simple churches and the gradual provision of permanent settlements of more than a few houses. The first inns, little more than simple drinking houses, probably date to this period. Indeed, as early as 750 A.D., the then Archbishop of York issued a Canon 'That no priest go to eat or drink in taverns', and there were so many inns by the time of King Edgar (959-75) that he issued a decree limiting their number to one per village.

Immediately after the Conquest the Normans parcelled out their new kingdom and the Domesday survey gives a first indication of the size and importance of the towns and villages in the county. At that time the Welsh were still a real problem, and the whole of western Herefordshire was protected by a series of strategically placed castles, initially of timber but, as their importance grew, they were fortified in stone. The remains of the border castles at Wigmore, Weobley and Richard's Castle, and many others that are now mainly earthworks, testify to this turbulent period. However, the castles generated settlements outside their walls and this would inevitably have resulted in a sizeable increase in the number of inns and taverns within the county.

Following the Conquest there was a gradual growth in the population of the country, as settlers from Normandy were encouraged by tax relief, and with this increase came various measures not just to limit the numbers of drinking houses but to protect the customer. One of the most important of these was the 'Assize of Bread and Ale' in 1266. This enactment accepted the principle that both bread and ale were necessities of life and, for a period of some 300 years, it ensured that the retail price of ale was fixed according to the price of grain. At that time, ale was usually made from malted barley, or occasionally wheat, which was steeped in water and then fermented with yeast.

During the 13th century there was a gradual increase in the sale of wine, and a separation came into being between 'taverns', which sold both ale and wine, and 'alehouses' which only sold ale.

Outside the towns, the principal hospitality for travellers during the medieval period was provided by monasteries — it was only along the more important pilgrim routes that guest houses and wayside inns had been established, and these would have been well beyond the purse of all except the richest of travellers. During the 14th and 15th centuries a gradual change occurred, as merchants began to travel and the influence of the church started to wane. Wayside inns became features of the countryside and hotels providing accommodation and food began to appear in the market towns.

For perhaps 1,000 years ale had been the basic drink for practically everyone, but a fundamental change occurred during the early 15th century. This was due to the introduction of hops, described by the authorities in Shrewsbury at that time as that 'wicked and pernicious weed', and the resultant manufacture of 'beer'. The hop not only gave the new drink a more bitter flavour, it was also of considerable importance for its preservative properties enabling the beverage to be kept much longer than ale before 'going-off'. Of course, there were the adherents of ale:

Though I go bare, take ye no care,
I nothing am a-cold:
I stuff my skin so full within
Of jolly good ale and old.

Back and side go bare, go bare;
Both foot and hand go cold:
But, belly, God send thee good ale enough,
Whether it be new or old.

(part of a 16th-century drinking song by
William Stevenson, 'Jolly Good Ale and Old')

*Hop picking near Ledbury at the beginning
of the 20th century*

*A 14th-century inn from
a contemporary psalter*

Hops have been grown in eastern Herefordshire for many years and the round and square oast houses, with a swinging cowl above, used for drying the hops, are a common sight in the countryside. Charcoal was used for heating, and during the drying process sulphur was added to destroy insect life and fungal and bacteriological infections. Dried hops are still pressed tightly into jute sacks called pockets. These pockets are then marked with the name and address of the grower to identify whose is the tax liability. Apart from their use in beer, hops have other benefits — a bine of hops hung next to the ceiling in the public bars of many an inn in Herefordshire keeps the smoke and smells down, whilst if you can't sleep at night try a pillow stuffed with hops.

For well over 100 years brewers produced both ale and beer, but the popularity of the former gradually declined and beer eventually became the national drink — apart from in Herefordshire where cider reigned triumphant for many years. It was early in the reign of Henry VIII that cider orchards became a branch of the rural economy, but it was the Redstreak, the famous cider apple developed by the first Viscount Scudamore on his Holme Lacy estate near Hereford before and after the Civil War, that revolutionised the trade. It was recommended that the Redstreak:

> was to be preferred for your Plantation to any other apple whatsoever, especially remote from your House. First, because it yields the best of British Drinks. Secondly, because the fruit is harsh and unpleasant, not tempting the Palates of lewd Persons.

The poet John Philips, who died in 1709 aged 32 and is buried in the entrance to the north transept of Hereford Cathedral, wrote of the Redstreak in his poem *Cyder*:

> Of no regard till Scudamore's skilful hand
> Improv'd her, and by courtly discipline
> Taught her the savage nature to forget, —
> Hence styl'd the Scudamore plant.

John Philips' brass in Hereford Cathedral includes a branch of an apple tree

So important was cider to Herefordshire that, in the 14th century, when Nicholas de Hereford was helping Wycliffe to translate the Bible into English, he changed the warning given to the mother of the still unborn Samson which read 'Now therefore beware, I pray thee, and drink not wine nor strong drink' to read 'drink no cider' (Judges, Ch. 13 V. 4). Surely the translation, in the well-known 'Cider Bible', was no more the worse for it.

It was not until the end of the 17th century that there was any serious competition to ale, beer and cider in the retail market. Even then, the cost of the new beverages, coffee and tea, continued to be prohibitively expensive for the next half-century or more.

Although there had been previous attempts at curtailing the number of drinking houses, the first formal licensing law came at the end of the 15th century. It empowered Justices of the Peace to obtain sureties for good behaviour from the landlords and, if necessary, to close alehouses. Some 50 years later the Justices obtained the power, which they still retain, to both licence and suppress alehouses — hence 'licensed premises'.

Legislation continued and 1553 saw an Act of Parliament that curtailed the number of 'taverns', and thus limited the sale of wine. Indeed, the Act also prohibited the sale of French wines. The limits on taverns provide an indication of the size and importance of the towns at that time — London was allowed 40; York, nine; and Bristol, six. Hereford was limited to three, the same as Lincoln, Worcester, Southampton and Oxford. This did not mean that the population of the country was being deprived of places in which to drink — there were approximately 44 alehouses for every tavern in the latter part of the 16th century. This was equivalent to more than one drinking establishment for every 200 persons, a far higher ratio than exists today. These early alehouses were probably little different to the timber-framed and thatched houses that surrounded them. The larger ones would have had sheds at the rear where brewing was carried out and possibly cellars to protect their brew from temperature variations.

Taverns, being of a higher status, were probably of a superior construction. This may well be the reason why the more important towns and cities in the country tend to be well endowed with substantial stone cellars of a late medieval date. They were obviously designed for public use and usually had well-constructed vaulted roofs and entries leading directly from the streets.

Throughout most of recorded history it was a legal requirement that a sign should identify all drinking establishments. Poles, which supported the signs, gradually became bigger and more noticeable. A bush hanging outside the house was a sign of great antiquity, used by the Romans in the form of a bunch of vine leaves to indicate a wine-shop. Poles decorated with evergreens such as ivy were used as signs for early ale-houses. The hanging bush gave rise to the expression

16   99

Whereas by the Laws and Statutes of This Realm

NOTICE

IS HEREBY GIVEN TO ALL

INN KEEPERS, ALEHOUSE KEEPERS, SUTLERS, VICTUALLERS

and other Retailers of

ALE and BEER

AND EVERY OTHER PERSON or PERSONS KEEPING A PUBLIC HOUSE
IN ANY
CITY, TOWN CORPORATE, BOROUGH, MARKET TOWN, VILLAGE, HAMLET, PARISH,
PART or PLACE IN THE *Kingdom of England*

That, as from the 24th day of JUNE. 1700

THEY SHALL BE REQUIRED TO RETAIL and SELL THEIR ALE & BEER

by the FULL ALE QUART or PINT

According to the Laid Standard

IN VESSELS DULY MARKED *with* W.R *and* CROWN

be they made of

WOOD, GLASS, HORN, LEATHER or PEWTER *etc.*

Any Person Retailing Ale or Beer to a TRAVELLER *or* WAYFARER *in Vessels not
signed and marked as aforesaid will be liable to a* PENALTY *not exceeding*

FORTY SHILLINGS

FOR EVERY SUCH OFFENCE

By Act of Parliament ~ at WESTMINSTER
In the Reign of Our Sovereign ~ WILLIAM III by the Grace of God, King,
Defender of the Faith &c

An evergreen bush, indicating an inn, from a 14th-century manuscript

'A good ale needs no bush'. Alfred Watkins, in an article published in the *Transactions of the Woolhope Naturalists' Field Club*, also mentions a 'chequers' sign, which was apparently common in Herefordshire. This consisted of alternate diamonds or lozenges of green and red painted on the door frame on each side of the entrance to the inn. Watkins suggested that the sign originated in the counting board (like a chess board, but used for counting money) and that it was an indication that the innkeeper kept one of these boards for the benefit of his customers. He discovered such a sign at a couple of pubs in Hereford, whilst inns in other parts of the county, including Ledbury and Leominster, took the 'Chequers' name.

Various attempts were made during the Civil War to levy duty on both the manufacture and the sale of beer and ale — attempts which were consolidated following that war and apply to this day. This was the time when beer was brewed in three different qualities: strong, table and small, and each variety attracted a different rate of duty.

It was not until the late 19th century that the duty levied became based on the original gravity of the beer. The specific gravity (density) of the liquor before fermentation gives an indication of the amount of sugars present and therefore the likely alcoholic content of the final brew. Prior to the use of a hydrometer other methods were used to judge the beer's strength, one of which was for the examining officer — the ale conner — to don a pair of leather breeches, pour some of the beer to be tested upon a stone step and then to sit on it. If, at the end of a specified time, he found that he was stuck to the step, then the beer was deemed to be strong!

Although there was a duty on beer, spirits were exempt and towards the end of the 17th century and well into the 18th there was what Monckton in his *History of the English Public House* described as 'one of the biggest orgies of over-indulgence our island history has ever seen'. Every small alehouse in the country was in a position to sell cheap brandy and in particular, gin. The result was that consumption of spirits increased from half-a-million gallons in 1684 to over eight million gallons in 1743 — an increase of well over one gallon per person per year! The various 'Gin Acts' that followed, together with increased duties and a strengthening of the powers of the justices, rapidly changed this trend and by 1758 excise duty was paid on less than two million gallons per year. The 'gin era' was over.

However, means of regulating public houses continued to attract government interest and from 1729 licence renewal had to be made at annual Brewster Sessions, originally held in September, but moved later to February.

Following the closure of the monasteries in the late 1530s, inns began to provide food and accommodation for travellers, the latter often in rooms on several levels around galleried courtyards. By the 18th century most of these establishments had lost their earlier reputation for being rat-infested hovels and were becoming orderly and well-equipped. However, there was still room for improvement as Viscount Torrington's experiences around 1790 show:

> I look upon an inn as the seat of all roguery, profaneness, and debauchery; and sicken of them every day, by hearing nothing but oaths, and abuse of each other, and brutality to horses ... all town inns are so noisy by low company and intemperance.

However, James Boswell in his *Life of Samuel Johnson* gives a totally different picture:

> 'There is no private house', said Johnson, 'in which people can enjoy themselves so well as at a capital tavern ... The master of the house is anxious to entertain his guests; the guests are anxious to be agreeable to him; and no man but a very impudent dog indeed can as freely command what is in another man's house as if it were his own. Whereas, at a tavern, there is a general freedom from anxiety. You are sure you are welcome; and the more noise you make, the more trouble you give, the more good things you call for, the welcomer you are. No

servants will attend you with the alacrity which waiters do, who are incited by the prospect of an immediate reward in proportion as they please. No, sir, there is nothing which has yet been contrived by man, by which so much happiness is produced, as by a good tavern or inn'.

Inns were the base for carriers who delivered goods between the market towns and the surrounding rural areas. As with stage-coaches, each carrier had his own arrangement. The early 19th century was the culmination of coach travel and inns were then at the height of their prosperity. They had an enviable reputation which is well expressed by Washington Irving in *Travelling at Christmas*:

> As we drove into the great gateway of the inn, I saw on one side the light of a rousing kitchen fire beaming through a window. I entered, and admired for the hundredth time, that picture of convenience, neatness, and broad honest enjoyment, the kitchen of an English inn. It was of spacious dimensions; hung round by copper and tin vessels, highly polished, and decorated here and there with a Christmas green. Hams, tongues, and flitches of bacon were suspended from the ceiling; a smoke-jack made its ceaseless clanking beside the fireplace, and a clock ticked in one corner. A well scoured deal table extended along one side of the kitchen, with a cold round of beef, and other hearty viands upon it, over which two foaming tankards of ale seemed mounting guard. Travellers of inferior orders were preparing to attack this stout repast, while others sat smoking or gossiping over their ale, on two high-backed oaken settles beside the fire. Trim housemaids were hurrying backwards and forwards under the directions of a fresh, bustling landlady; but still seizing an occasional moment to exchange a flippant word, and have a rallying laugh with the group round the fire.

Apart from earlier attempts to regulate the marking of drinking vessels to show the capacity, it was during the 19th century that most of the legislation that affects the present-day consumption and sale of alcoholic drink was enacted. The Alehouse Act of 1828 meant that the licensee no longer had to find sureties for his behaviour. However, he was bound to use the legal, stamped measures, not to adulterate his drinks, and not to permit drunkenness on his premises.

The Beerhouse Acts of 1830, 1834 and 1840 followed — the first allowed premises to open for the sale of beer, but not spirits, on payment of a simple excise licence; the second differentiated between 'on' and 'off' licences and made 'on' licences more difficult to obtain; whilst the third ensured that licences were issued only to the occupier of the premises.

Throughout the country as a whole there was a proliferation of beer houses following the Act of 1830, many in the country areas. This Act, pushed through by the Duke of Wellington against a number of vested interests, abolished all duty on beer and enabled any householder to sell beer on the purchase of a two-guinea licence from the Excise. As a consequence, a number of illegal drinking places became legal, and many craftsmen also sold beer as part of their business, naming the beer house after their craft.

The APPRENTICE'S MONITOR.

O R,

INDENTURES

IN VERSE

Shewing what they are bound to do.

Proper to be hung up in all Shops.

EACH young Apprentice, when he's bound, to Trade,
This folemn vow to God and Man has made,
To do with joy his Mafter's juft commands,
Nor truft his fecrets into other hands.
He muft no damage to his fubftance do,
And fee that others do not wrong him too,
His Mafter's goods he fhall not wafte nor lend,
But all his property with care defend.
He fhall not buy nor fell without his leave,
Nor lie, nor injure, nor at all deceive,
Taverns and ALE-HOUSES he fhall not haunt,
Thofe fnares to Youth, thofe fcenes of vice and want,
At CARDS and DICE he fhall not dare to play,
But fly from fuch temptations far away.

O Youth ! remember thou to this art BOUND,
See that no breach of this in thee be found.

Apprentices were not allowed to visit taverns and ale-houses

The effects of the 1830 Beerhouse Act seems to have been variable. In Bromyard there was no noticeable increase in the number of establishments, probably because it was very well provided for anyway, but in Ledbury there was an immediate increase. When the anonymous *Hints of Ledbury* was published in 1831, after a list of inns etc. it stated that 'Several other houses have recently been opened for the sale of beer, since the alterations in the act have taken place'. The effect of the Act in Hereford itself was also commented on in the pages of the *Hereford Journal*. A letter from J. Benbow appeared in its pages on 2 March 1831. He was a glove manufacturer in a large way of business at the Friars in Hereford, and his remarks show an increase in overindulgence in beer among his workforce. This letter was taken up in the editorial, which commented on it as 'one instance amongst many others that have been communicated to us, of the evils the Beer Act is inflicting on the working classes of this community'.

DRUNKARD'S CATECHISM

1. Q. What is your name?
   A. Drunken sot.
2. Q. Who gave you that name?
   A. As drink is my idol, Landlords and their wives get all my money; they gave me that name in one of my drunken sprees, wherein I was made a member of strife, a child of want, and an inheritor of a bundle of rage.
3. Q. What did your Landlords and Landladies promise for you?
   A. They did promise and vow three things in my name; first, that I should renounce the comforts of my own fireside; second, starve my wife and hunger my children; third, walk in rags and tatters, with my shoe soles going flip flap, all the days of my life.
4. Q. Rehearse the articles of the belief.
   A. I believe in the existence of one Mr. Alcohol, the great head and chief of all manner of vice, the source of nine-tenths of all diseases; lastly, I not only believe, but am sure when my money is all gone and spent, the Landlord will stop the tap and turn me out.
5. Q. How many commandments have ye sots to keep?
   A. Ten.
6. Q. Which be they?
   A. The same which the Landlord and Landlady spoke in the bar, saying, We are thy master and mistress, who brought thee out of the paths of virtue, placed thee in the ways of vice, and set thy feet in the road which leadeth to New South Wales.
   I. Thou shalt use no other house but mine.
   II. Thou shalt not make for thyself any substitute for intoxicating drinks, such as tea, coffee, ginger pop, or lemonade; for I am a jealous man, wearing a coat that should be on thy back, eating thy children's bread, and pocketing the money which should make thee and the wife comfortable all the days of thy life.
   III. Thou shalt not use my house in vain.
   IV. Remember that thou eat but one meal on the Sabbath day, for six days hast thou been drinking, and nought else wouldst thou do; but the seventh is the sabbath day, and thou canst have no trust; therefore thou skulketh on the seventh day and abominates it.
   V. Thou shalt honour the Landlords and Landladies and Gin-shops with thy presence, that thy days may be few and miserable in the land wherein thou dwellest.
   VI. Thou shalt commit murder, by starving, and hungering, and beating thy wife and family.
   VII. Thou shalt commit self-destruction.
   VIII. Thou shalt sell thy wife and children's bread and rob thyself of all thy comforts.
   IX. Thou shalt bear false witness when thou speakest of the horrors, saying thou art in good health when thou art labouring under the barrel fever.
   X. Thou shalt covet all thy neighbour is possessed of, thou shalt covet his house, his land, his purse, his health, his wealth, and all that he has got, that thou mayest indulge in drinking, help the brewer to buy a new coach, a pair of fine horses, a new dray and a fine building, that he may live in idleness all his days: likewise to enable the Landlord to purchase a new sign to put over his door, with 'Licensed to be drunk on the premises', written thereon.

An 1850s Temperance Society Tract based on the Ten Commandments

At about the time of the Beerhouse Acts the Temperance Movement was getting under way. Organised temperance societies had originated in America in 1808, crossing to Ireland by 1818 and then to Liverpool, where American ships' captains distributed temperance tracts. By 1830 there were temperance societies in Ulster, Lancashire and Yorkshire having 23,000 paying members, and 60,000 registered abstainers. The main impetus came with the founding of the Preston Temperance Society by Joseph Livesey who, in 1833, instituted the idea of 'the pledge'. The word 'teetotal' was coined by Dicky Turner, a drunkard reformed by Livesey, as a consequence of his stammer! The tracts, distributed by such societies, were often dressed up in religious form: the one on the previous page probably dates from about 1850.

One aspect of the movement was the founding of temperance hotels, the first of which was opened in 1836, and by 1865 there were some 200. Generally these were not a success, being of poor standard and often run by failed landlords or reformed drunkards with no business sense or experience.

At the time of the Beerhouse Acts there were few restrictions on licensing hours. As a whole, the only non-permitted hours were during Divine Services on Sundays, Christmas Day and Good Friday. beer houses could only open between 4 a.m. and 10 p.m. The 1872 Licensing Act tidied up and tightened the complex

BRITISH WINE.

Notice to all persons holding Excise licences authorising the sale for consumption on or off the premises of Foreign Wine or British Wine, or the manufacture of British Wine.

1. The Commissioners of His Majesty's Customs and Excise in pursuance of the Regulations, a copy of which is appended, made by them on the 31st January, 1928, under Section 10 of the Finance Act, 1911, which prescribe, among other matters, that British Wine, to which Foreign Wine has been added by the manufacturer in the course of manufacture, must not be sold or exposed for sale otherwise than under the designation of a British Wine, hereby give notice that :—

(a) Such wine must in all cases be described as a British Wine. If it is desired to indicate that Foreign Wine has been added in the course of manufacture it must be stated that the proportion does not exceed that allowed by the Statutory Regulations, viz., 15 gallons in every 115 gallons of the product.

(b) All bottles in which such wine is sold or exposed for sale must in future bear a distinct and conspicuous indication that the wine has been manufactured in the United Kingdom.

2. The Commissioners also call the special attention of all persons concerned to No. 2 of the Regulations in question, under which a dealer in or retailer of Foreign Wine or British Wine must not mix for sale any Foreign Wine with any British Wine ; and to No. 6 of the Regulations, which states that Foreign Wine includes all wine imported into the United Kingdom.

3. Any person contravening the Regulations is liable to a penalty of £50.

Notice No. 44.

BY ORDER OF THE COMMISSIONERS OF CUSTOMS AND EXCISE.

Custom House, London E.C.3.
February, 1928.

Sec. $\frac{63114}{1927}$

1928 regulations concerning the manufacture and sale of British Wines legislation, but at the beginning of the 20th century public houses were, in general, still allowed to open for some 20 hours each day.

Towards the end of the 19th century and in the early years of the following one, considerable efforts were made to close down inns and public houses by refusing to renew licences, even though this resulted in the payment of compensation to the owners and landlords. This was more common in the towns than in the countryside and in Hereford, by 1919, the Compensation Authority had approved the closure of no less than 35 public houses at a cost of some £16,000.

It is not often realised that the regulations concerning licensed houses, alcohol and children are mainly of 20th century origin. Although the 1872 Act made it an offence to sell spirits to those using licensed premises under the age of 16, it was not until the Children's Act of 1908 that children under the age of 14 were prohibited in licensed premises. It was only in 1923 that it became, in general, an offence to serve alcoholic drinks to those under 18.

Regulations brought in at a time of war often have a habit of staying. It was on 23 November 1914, during the First World War, that limited opening hours were instigated — in Herefordshire this meant that closing time was 9 p.m! Warnings were common and in the *Hereford Times* for 12 February 1916 Mr. Wallis (the magistrate) warned landlords that:

> ... great as were these difficulties, they should set their faces against any drinking by soldiers. To see soldiers about the streets under the influence of liquour was a very sorry sight. The bench also regarded with much displeasure any encouragement of women to spend the money they received from the Army in the public houses of the city. They knew that in the great majority of public houses this would not be allowed.

The Licensing Act of 1921 regularized this situation by defining 'permitted hours' as being eight hours between 11 a.m. and 10 p.m. except for Sunday, which was limited to five hours. In 1934, there was a slight improvement — an extension could be granted to 10.30 p.m. during the summer months, especially in rural areas where evening work was necessary.

The Temperance Movement strengthened during the 1920s and their activities occupied many pages in the *Hereford Times*. Typical is a letter from Charles Smith of Sheffield, included in the edition of 17 July 1920:

Herefordshire devoted over 30,000 acres to the growth of barley, hops, and cider apples wherewith to produce a poison which intoxicates; which lands carters in the street drunk, wounded, and helpless, and leaves the horses straying; and men reeling on horseback, drunk, clamouring for more beer, creating a disturbance, and ending in custody. All this is evil for the community, however profitable to the brewers. I observe that your Herefordshire Fruit Company are using £50,000 value in early fruits, only two-fifths of which are obtained in the county and three-fifths from outside. Why are not the 30,000 acres mentioned above given to the production of fruit wherewith to feed the people, instead of to the production of a drug wherewith to poison them?

Between the wars efforts were made to improve standards of cleanliness in inns throughout the region Thus at the 1936 Brewster Sessions, Col. J.T. Lutley, chair of the Bromyard Licensing Justices, remarked on the unsatisfactory conditions of Bromyard's inns. First, however, he heard police reports that all the licensees had been staying within the law, though four residents had been convicted for drunkenness, three for being drunk and disorderly and one for being drunk in charge of two horses. This was opposed to the previous year, when only one person had been so charged, though on two occasions, both times for being drunk in charge of a horse and trap. He then launched into a tirade in which he supposed this was a clean England and a sanitary country, but he had seen things during his inspections such as he had never seen abroad, be it in Spain, Italy or Africa. 'Even the natives of South Africa were cleaner'. He said that the inns must be put in order to the satisfaction of the Bromyard Rural District Sanitary Authority, with the provision of separate sanitary accommodation for 'each sex — men and women — and that there must be separate accommodation again for the licence-holders'.

After the Second World War there were several minor Acts, which culminated in the one of 1961 that provided for 'restaurant' and 'residential' licences. It also gave the customers' grace — the ten minutes of 'drinking-up time'. A late 20th-century Act restored the situation to more or less what it had been at the beginning of the century by allowing inns to stay open throughout the day if they so wish, most commonly any times between 11 a.m. and 11 p.m., with a somewhat shorter 'window of opportunity' on Sundays. A new millennium has brought new thought and it is most probable that restrictions upon public houses will be further reduced leading to the possibility of 24-hour opening once again.

Map of Herefordshire from an 1805 Road Book used by travellers in the county some 200 years ago

CHAPTER TWO

Brewing & Breweries

At the beginning of the 18th century, Daniel Defoe passed through the county of Herefordshire from north to south and commented that the populace were:

> diligent and laborious people, chiefly addicted to husbandry, and they boast, perhaps, not without reason, that they have the finest wool, the best hops, and the richest cyder in all Britain.

As far as cider was concerned, he went on to say:

> Here it was, that several times for 20 miles together, we could get no beer or ale in their publick houses, only cyder; and that so very good, so fine, and so cheap, that we never found fault with the exchange; great quantities of this cyder are sent to London, even by land carriage tho' so very remote, which is an evidence for the goodness of it, beyond contradiction.

The importance was that both cider and ale were safe to drink at a time when most water supplies were at the best suspect and often could cause serious illnesses.

The production of cider was also an important part of the local economy. When, in 1763, a tax of four shillings was placed on each hogshead of cider, to be levied on the makers, there was an outcry, and as part of the protest Ledbury ringers rang the bells muffled on and off for a whole day. (Muffled ringing is a sign of mourning). The removal of the tax after a short while was a source of rejoicing throughout the county and a pamphlet announcing the repeal was sent to Hereford from London. This contained the following song:

A new SONG, sung by the *Herefordshire* Society

Rejoice, here's welcome News, come let us merry be,
Since GEORGE, our gracious King in his great Clemency,
So kindly has consented his Subjects Wants to ease,
By taking off the CYDER-TAX, which does the Kingdom please.
  Then let the merry Bells all ring
   In every Village round,
  And nought but Joy and Harmony
   In every Place be found.

Come jolly *Hodge*, and *Will*, lay by your Pike and Flail,
For *Susan*'s gone to fetch our largest Milking-pail
Brimfull of brave old Cyder, such, such as B[u]te never knew,
Tis Liberty we'll drink until the Skies look blue.
  Then let the merry Bells ...

It makes each Farmer smile to see the good old Dame
So nimble with her Liquor, which from the Red-Streak came.
Handing it to her Neighbours, by which their Spirits rise,
Rejoicing that their Mills are free from the Excise.
  Then let the merry Bells...

A Health to all our Members let's drink in merry Vein,
To *Rockingham* and *Pratt*, let's fill it up again,
Likewise *Pitt* and *Dowdeswell*, we'll stretch our Throats still wider,
And all the neighbouring Hills shall echo back Old CYDER.
  Then let the merry Bells all ring
   And Musick sweetly play,
  Let shining Bonfires blaze around
   To close this joyful Day.

The better types of cider were considered to be a vintage drink and were allowed to mature like wine. On 22 March 1787 Peter Dickins, a cider merchant of Hereford and to be its mayor in 1791, was advertising cider of the growth of 1784. In the 18th century cider was collected from small wharves along the Wye and stored in warehouses in Hereford for eventual export down the river on barges. The warehouses were often of considerable size, and some at Pearce's Wharf in Hereford, advertised in the *Hereford Journal* in November 1788 as being to let, were capable of holding between 200 and 300 hogsheads of cider. The trade depended on the state of the river. If there was too little water the barges could not float and the movement of trade had to wait for rain. If there was too much water in the river from heavy rain or melting snow, the barges were at risk and had to remain tied up. There was a particularly bad flood in February 1795 caused by a rapid melt, and several bridges across the river were carried away and cider was lost from the warehouses in Hereford.

Not only cider but grain and other commodities were exported down the Wye. On the return journey the barges were filled with a variety of goods, including coal. There was also an import trade in beer and on 26 December 1804 Jonathan Crompton of Pipe Lane, Hereford (now Gwynne Street) was advertising that he had received a large quantity of Bath Porter, Brown Stout, and Taunton Beer. However, the river trade declined and finished by the middle of the 19th century, with other, better and more reliable, means of communication with the outside world.

Ledbury was in some ways more fortunate than Hereford as from 1798

A woodcut celebrating the repeal of the cider tax

A cider press depicted on Taylor's 1786 map of Herefordshire

19

similar goods could travel down the canal to Gloucester, trade that resulted in the price of coal decreasing from 24s. a ton to 13s. 6d. Much of the cider produced in east Herefordshire would doubtless have filled the barges on their return journeys.

Until relatively recently cider was made on almost every farm in Herefordshire. It was sometimes produced as a cash crop, as described above, but was usually made for use by the farmer's family and labourers. Cider is made from bitter-sweet apples, which are richer in sugar but rather unpleasant to the taste as they contain a lot of tannin. The method of making cider was discussed in 1808 by the Rev. Jonathan Williams in his *Leominster Guide*:

> The colours of good cider fruit are red and yellow; of an astringent taste: green colour is to be avoided. Ciders composed of the juices of mixed fruits generally succeed with greater certainty than those made with one kind. In grinding the fruits, care is taken to have as much of the juice of the rinds and kernels as can possibly be obtained. The must or pomage should be suffered to remain about twenty-four hours before it is taken to the press. The quantity of apples sufficient to fill the provincial hogshead of one hundred and ten gallons, varies from twenty-four to thirty bushels. Ciders manufactured from good fruit will retain a considerable portion of their sweetness at the end of three or four years. The best time for bottling cider is when it is from eighteen months to two years old; if perfectly secured from the air, by the tightness of the cork, it may be kept to any age. The annual produce of the fruit, in a plentiful year, is almost beyond conception. Twenty hogsheads of cider have been made from the produce of single acre of orchard ground. This excessive fruitage, however, seldom occurs more than once in four years.

After crushing the apples and pressing to extract the juice, farm cider was produced without the addition of cultured yeast, fermentation relying upon the natural yeasts in the apples to produce a still, cloudy, acidic, invigorating and thirst-quenching drink. This was much appreciated during the heat of the next summer when the farmer would provide bread, cheese and cider for those helping with the hay-making, a practice that continued well into the 20th century. These delights of making hay, and possibly others, are described by Laurie Lee in his best-selling book *Cider with Rosie*.

Where apples grow so do pears, which when processed in the same manner as cider apples are converted from unpalatable varieties of that fruit into the pleasant, heart-warming drink called perry.

Farmhouse cider was not universally acclaimed. In *Hereford in 1892*, the author comments:

> Those who have seen the wretched looking farm-house cider-mills in various parts of the country, the uncleanly surroundings, and the rough-and-ready methods used in the production of this beverage, can only wonder at the good luck that so often favoured the cider maker. All sorts and conditions of apples, some green, some over-ripe, and some half-decayed windfalls, all mixed without care or selection and crushed up in a dirty, lumbering old mill, and the juice left to ferment or mature in something like superannuated water casks or wash tubs, covered with old sacks. Such was frequently the method of making home-made cider.

Rumours also abounded of the addition of dead rats and cats and the use of water from particularly noisome duck-ponds!

Between the wars a former Bishop of Hereford gave evidence to the Licensing Commission and clearly had a poor opinion of his flock,

Early poster extolling the virtues of Herefordshire Cider

21

HELL IN HEREFORDSHIRE

The wild white rose is cankered
  Along the Vale of Lugg,
There's poison in the tankard,
  There's murder in the mug;
Through all the pleasant valleys
  Where stand the pale-faced kine
Men raise the Devil's chalice
  And drink his bitter wine.

Unspeakable carouses
  That shame the summer sky
Take place in little houses
  That look towards the Wye;
And near the Radnor border
  And the dark hills of Wales
Beelzebub is warder
  And sorcery prevails.

For, spite of church or chapel
  Ungodly folk there be
Who pluck the cider apple
  From the cider apple-tree,
And squeeze it in their presses
  Until the juice runs out,
At various addresses
  That no one knows about.

And, maddened by the orgies
  Of that unholy brew,
They slit each other's gorges
  From one a.m. till two,
Till Ledbury is a shambles
  And in the dirt and mud
Where Leominster sits and gambles
  The dice are stained with blood!

But still, if strength suffices
  Before my day is done,
I'll go and share the vices
  Of Clungunford and Clun,
And watch the red sun sinking
  Across the March again
And join the secret drinking
  Of outlaws at Presteign.

for he said that there was much secret cider drinking in Herefordshire. This statement was taken up by the satirical magazine *Punch*, and the poem (opposite) by E.V. Knox was published in its pages.

Late in the 19th and during the first half of the 20th centuries, as well as being produced on farms (which were listed in trade directories as cider producers) cider was made by several larger firms in Herefordshire including W. Evans and Co., H. Godwin & Son, and H.P. Bulmer & Co. all in Hereford. In 1892, William Evans and Co.'s Cider Works on Widemarsh Common were said to produce 'two favourite beverages, namely cider and perry, in greater perfection than any other town in England'. They continued to produce cider in Hereford until well after the end of the Second World War, but eventually closed and the buildings were all demolished by 1975. Godwin & Son had premises at Holmer, but they have also been closed for many years. Bulmer's was founded in 1887 and initially centralised their operations in Ryelands Street, but more recently in Plough Lane. They are now the largest cider producers in the world.

At Belle Orchard in the Homend at Ledbury there was a cider and perry factory which was established about the year 1851. How long this produced these drinks is not certain as in 1885 the owner, Chas. T. Jones, was advertising in Kelly's *Directory* as a cider merchant rather than a cider maker. The premises were demolished in 1891 and the new Cottage Hospital, opened in 1892, was built on the site. The orchard behind the site was subsequently developed for housing by Ledbury Building Society.

In the Southend in Ledbury in 1905 there was the Ledbury Cooperative Cider Co. Ltd. Apart from the cider works mentioned above, there are some 30 cider makers listed in the 1905 Kelly's trade directory. They included J.M. Watkins' Pomona Cider Co. (E.W. Langford, proprietor) of Withington, W.S. Lane of the Farm, Bosbury, and John Parry, of the Old and New Lily Hall farms, Ledbury. The manufacture of cider by small firms declined during the 20th century and the 1941 trades directory records only some 15 makers, including W.R. Symonds of Stoke Lacy, who was the only one in this area.

As well as by the major cider manufacturers, cider continued to be made by a few farmers and inns using traditional methods. However, nearly all cider is now made in plants resembling chemical engineering factories but, technology aside, the process has not changed much and most cider is only made when apples fall off trees, although some are picked and then left to ripen. A major difference is that now the natural yeasts are generally destroyed and replaced by cultured ones, but fermentation is still a batch process and is continued to complete dryness and an alcoholic content of up to 8%. This results in many vats, each containing a slightly different cider, the cider maker's art being in blending quantities from many vats to produce a consistent product. Alcoholic content, sweetness, and colour is adjusted by the addition of water, glucose, and natural colour, the resultant blend being filtered, pasteurised, and carbonated before being marketed under an appropriate brand name and logo. Ciders produced by organic methods do not go through all these processes.

Many processes produce waste-products and by-products: the beer industry amongst other things produces spent malt that may be used as animal food and 'Marmite', that famous 'you either love it or you hate it' by-product. The residue left after pressing the juice from apples is called pommace and may be used in animal feeds or ploughed into the land as a fertiliser and conditioner. It can also be used to produce pectin, a natural gelling agent used in the food industry. Bulmer's used to produce much of the world's requirement for pectin from the residues of Herefordshire apples, but in a global economy things change and pectin can now be produced more cheaply from the residual pulp from the citrus fruit juice industry, meaning pectin is now produced in South America near the sources of its raw material. Thus Herefordshire has lost its pectin plant and on its brownfield site in Ryelands Street, Hereford has given birth to over a hundred houses.

Until the middle of the 19th century most landlords made their own ale and beer in small brewhouses behind their inns. When Mrs. Maile was giving up the Trumpet Inn at Pixley in 1857 she held a sale of her furniture and equipment, including '...beer-coolers, mash-tun, and other brewing requisites; 15 hogsheads, 21 barrels, and other casks;...' Very few of the small breweries in which these utensils were used survive in a recognisable state today — they have either been demolished or converted to become part of the main buildings of the inn.

The brewer, from a 16th-century woodcut

However, many of the smaller inns and beer-houses that opened during the first half of the 19th century had no brewing facilities whatsoever and were totally dependent on other inns or on the growing number of breweries for their supply. This change accelerated as breweries bought public houses whenever they came onto the market, a process that resulted in a substantial decrease in the number of 'free houses' and of independent breweries. This was followed by a series of mergers and takeovers until only a few of the largest breweries survived. In 1941 there were still half a dozen pubs in the east of Herefordshire that brewed their own beer, but by the end of the Second World War the long tradition of inns producing their own beer had completely ceased in Herefordshire.

An early 18th-century brewhouse

Certificate of Analysis

I hereby certify that I have submitted to a very careful chemical Analysis a sample of the Family Ale, brewed by Messrs Lane Bros, and from the results obtained I feel justified in speaking in a highly favourable manner as to its dietetic value.

It has been prepared entirely from Malt and Hops of the best quality, is perfectly pure in composition, & free from all ingredients of an undesirable nature.

The Ale is bright and sparkling in appearance, particularly palatable & refreshing, & in perfect condition.

It possesses, in an agreeable form, invigorating tonic properties, assists the digestive functions, and creates a wholesome and healthy appetite.

Granville H. Sharpe &c.

1892 analysis of a sample of beer from the Lane Bros. Brewery in Ledbury

An advertisement pencil for Lane Bros. & Bastow's Vine Brewery, with an unfortunate spelling mistake

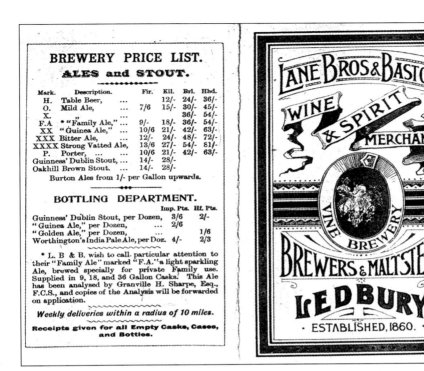

An 1890s price list for Lane Bros. & Bastow Brewery

The Vine Brewery of Lane Bros., in New Street, Ledbury was one that expanded during the second half of the 19th century. It was opened in 1860, and in 1867 Thomas Lane advertised not only as a brewer and maltster, but as a wine and spirit, hop, cider and perry merchant. In the 1890s C.H. Bastow was manager, and on 29 October 1892 the firm obtained a certificate of analysis of a sample of its family ale, certifying its goodness and dietetic value! At about this time the firm became Lane Bros. and Bastow and then in 1919 it was taken over by the Cheltenham Original Brewery. Kelly's *Directory* of 1929 states that this brewery had stores in New Street, so it seems that the brewing had ceased, and even the stores were closed quite soon, as there is no mention of them in Kelly's *Directory* of 1941.

The first brewery of any considerable size to be built in the county belonged to J.C. Reynolds. He had originally started his business at Fownhope, but moved to a new site in Bewell Street in Hereford in 1834 where he established himself as a brewer, maltster and wine and spirit merchant. It appears that he was rather unsuccessful and in 1845 the whole establishment was bought by Charles Watkins, then landlord of the Imperial Inn in Widemarsh Street. Watkins had previously brewed his own beer in a small brewhouse at the rear of the Imperial, but this new acquisition enabled him to put his creative energy to work in increasing output and in finding new sales outlets. He started his new business by changing the name of the firm to the much more imposing Imperial Brewery, capitalising on the name of his inn. The beginnings of his fortune came when he transported vast quantities of his beer a few miles to the north of the city, where the navvies were digging a tunnel underneath Dinmore Hill for the Shrewsbury to Hereford railway. According to his son, Alfred, 'a great deal of beer went into the making of that tunnel'!

Within a few years Charles Watkins was producing 'Imperial Household and Pale Ales', described as 'pure and sound, and unrivalled for excellence of quality and value combined'. Mild and bitter beers were available at 1s. a gallon and pale ale at 1s. 2d.; all being supplied in 9, 18, 36 and 54 gallon casks, delivered free. The brewery grew rapidly and with the profits Charles Watkins was able to buy or lease several public houses in Herefordshire and the surrounding areas. By the end of the 19th century in east Herefordshire the Imperial empire included the Major's Arms at Halmond's Frome, the Wheatsheaf at Frome's Hill, and the Crown and Anchor at Lugwardine together with others that depended on him for their supply of beer. These provided him with the main outlets to sell the beer he was brewing in ever increasing quantities. He also grew his own hops and farmed at Marden, Holmer and Burghill. Charles' son Alfred was brought up in the brewery business and travelled throughout the county on his father's business. At a later date he recorded that:

> I knew well the inside of all these back-street inns and their landlords (almost all of them kindly and decent folk) as I was going to them to sell the ... stout from my father's brewery.
>
> Most of the inns brewed their own ordinary ale in those early days, and bought 'stout' and 'bitter'.

The Brewery included a vat room with a beer cellar underneath, fermenting and racking rooms, and a large, partially covered area used for washing and storing casks. Adjacent buildings contained the

cooper's shop, the wheel-
wright's shop, stables and
harness rooms. The water
used in all the processes came
from the famous Bewell
Spring by means of an
artesian well some 40 feet
deep.

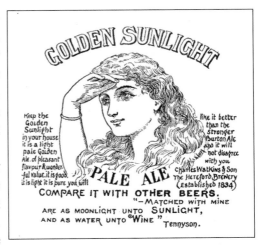

In 1898, a few years after
their father Charles died, the
Imperial Brewery was put on
the market by his two sons.
Included in the sale was the
brewery with its plant and all
the other buildings on the site;
35 hotels, public houses and

Golden Sunlight, one of the Hereford
Imperial Brewery's best selling beers

beer houses in the city and neighbourhood; and branches in
Birmingham, Cardiff and Swansea. The sale was held in London, and
according to the city library copy of the sale particulars £64,000 was
the highest bid for the lot. The new firm became the Hereford and
Tredegar Brewery Co. but by 1950 changes were again in the air.

These changes were also to affect the other main brewery in
Hereford, which had been founded in the latter part of the 19th century.
This was the City Brewery situated on the south side of Maylord Street.
Here, Arnold Perrett & Co., although on a more restricted site than the
Hereford Brewery, produced beer for consumption in the gradually
growing number of inns, both free houses and those belonging to the
company. Arnold Perrett & Co. were eventually associated with the
Stroud Brewery, and in 1924 the Maylord Street premises were
transferred to the Cheltenham Original Brewery Co. Ltd.

The amalgamation of the two Hereford breweries in 1950 produced
the Hereford, Tredegar & Cheltenham Breweries Ltd., although it
continued to make use of the trade names such as the Stroud Brewery
and Arnold Perrett & Co. Brewing continued in Maylord Street until
May 1948 after which the site was just used for storage and
distribution. In 1951 it was put up for sale because the firm was
concentrating all their brewing operations in the city 'at their other

extensive premises in Bewell Street'. The purchase price was £7,600 and the whole area is now part of the Maylord Orchards development.

Following the acquisition of the firm by Whitbreads, brewing operations also ceased in the Bewell Street works, and after a few years all the buildings were demolished. In 1967, a small part of the brewery site disappeared underneath the Relief Road. Eventually, the Tesco supermarket was built on the remainder of the site, the extensive basement car park replacing in part the cellars belonging to the brewery.

Following the closure of the Bewell Street brewery, there was a period of some 30 years when beer for public consumption was no longer produced in Herefordshire. Throughout the country only one or two pubs kept the age-old tradition going, a notable example being the Three Tuns at Bishop's Castle. Convenience beers, in pressurised barrels that did not depend on the skill of the landlord, flooded the market. For a time, it looked as though the old-fashioned beer-engine, used to draw the beer up from the carefully racked barrels in the cellars, would be a thing of the past.

A beer mat from the Royal Oak Brewery

The Royal Oak Brewery in Ledbury boasts that it was founded in 1841, but it is not mentioned in late 19th- and early 20th-century directories and must have had a long period in abeyance. It operated from 1995 to 1997 as the Ledbury Brewing Co. Ltd., producing beers such as Dog Hill Goldings Bitter and Challenger Premium Best. The beer mat is one of a series of eight that was issued in small quantities in 1996.

A welcome change has occurred in recent years and locally produced beer and cider is again available. The Wye Valley Brewery, originally based at the Barrels Inn in St. Owen's Street, now has its beer in inns across the county and has taken over the former Symonds

Cider works at Stoke Lacy as a brewery. In east Herefordshire 'Specialist beers' were formerly produced at the Frome's Hill brewery based at the Wheatsheaf at Frome's Hill, now closed because of a planning dispute, and at the Frome Valley Brewery based at Mayfields, Halmonds Frome, closed in 2003 at the time of writing. It is to be hoped that these reopen in the near future. Locally-made 'single-apple' and 'vintage' ciders and perry have also made a welcome return in Herefordshire with firms such as Olivers at Stanksbridge, Ocle Pychard.

I often wonder what brewers buy
One half so precious as the goods they sell
    (Anon.)

I feel no pain dear mother now
But oh, I am so dry!
O take me to a brewery
And leave me there to die.
    (*Parody of The Collier's Dying Child*, E. Farmer)

O Beer! O Hodgson, Guiness, Allsopp, Bass!
Names that should be on every infant's tongue
    (*Beer*, C.S. Calverley, 1861)

Say, for what were hop-yards meant,
Or why was Burton built on Trent?
Oh many a peer of England brews
Livelier liquor than the muse,
And malt does more than Milton can
To justify God's ways to man.
Ale, man, ale's the stuff to drink
For fellows whom it hurts to think:
Look into the pewter pot
To see the world as the world's not.
And faith, 'tis pleasant till 'tis past:
The mischief is that 'twill not last.
(*A Shropshire Lad*, A.E. Housman, 1896)

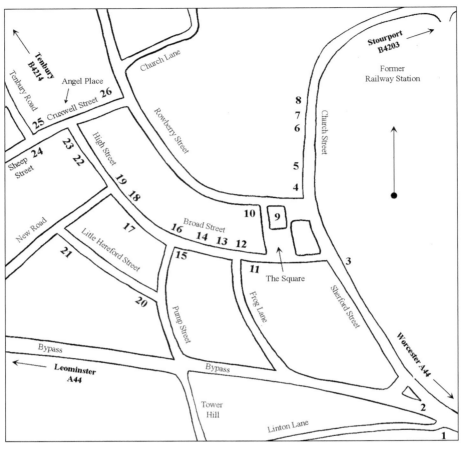

The Pubs of Bromyard

1	Bridge Inn	14	Lion
2	Talbot	15	Falcon
3	Crown and Sceptre	16	T.C.'s Bar
4	Crown	17	Bay Horse
5	Bell Inn	18	The Bull
6	Railway Inn	19	Queen's Arms
7	Red Lion	20	Seven Stars
8	Adam and Eve	21	Rose and Lion
9	Hop Pole	22	King's Arms
10	Nag's Head	23	Green Dragon (1)
11	Swan	24	Royal Oak
12	Fountain Head	25	White Horse
13	Royal Oak	26	Green Dragon (2)

CHAPTER THREE

Bromyard
SHERFORD ST. & CHURCH ST.

Bromyard is a town of considerable antiquity — even its name is Anglo-Saxon and means 'broom or thorn enclosure'. At the time of the Domesday Book in 1086 it was estimated that there were about 80 families in Bromyard and its environs. By 1861 the town and surrounding townships had gradually increased in size and there were 616 inhabited houses with a population of 2,995, although this was a slight decrease from 1851. The description of Bromyard given in Littlebury's *Directory & Gazetteer* of 1867 gives an almost idyllic picture of the town:

> Bromyard is a small market and union town, pleasantly situated on the Hereford and Worcester turnpike road, near to the river *Frome*, and surrounded by scenery exceedingly beautiful, being variegated with woody eminences, teeming orchards, rich meadows, and flourishing cornfields. The town contains several irregular streets, which are lighted by gas. There are two good hotels and posting-houses, a branch of the National Provincial Bank of England, and several good shops and private houses. A small trade is done in tanning and malting. The market is held on Mondays and is tolerably well attended by the agriculturalists of the neighbourhood. Fairs are held as follows: Great Market, last Monday in January; Thursday before March 25th; May 1st (hiring); May 3rd; Whit-Monday; Thursday before July 25th; September 29th (hiring); Thursday before October 29th, and the second Monday in December.

Although the railway had not then reached Bromyard, the London and general mail arrived in Bromyard at 6.42 a.m. each morning and delivery commenced at 7.20 a.m.

As the centre of the district, the magistrates met every week on a Monday, and the county court was held every other month; there was an Inland Revenue Office in the town. The needs of the poorer members of society were met only to a small extent — there were almshouses for seven poor women in Cruxwell Street, and a Union Workhouse a mile outside the town at Linton, serving over 30 parishes. There was also a Working Men's Institute and Temperance Hall in Church Street, which had been erected in 1859. Evidently there was a need for such an institution!

In the days when Bromyard had both a town band and a thriving market on a Thursday (changed from Mondays in the latter part of the 19th century), it was the custom on the market day after Christmas for the band to perform in the town, starting at Cruxwell Street (Top of the Town) and working its way down to the other end of town. It was alleged that the band only performed outside pubs in the hope of free refreshment, but in fairness it must be said that there was hardly anywhere in the town centre that was not in the vicinity of a pub — and often more than one. What was also alleged was that such was the hospitality offered that the band never got as far as the **Railway Inn**! At this time, the town had 13 licensed premises, and there had been more.

The construction of the Bromyard by-pass in the 1960s made a considerable difference to the town, for through traffic now avoids the centre. Approaching Bromyard from Worcester, where the road crosses the river at Petty Bridge, the road originally swung right into Sherford Street just before the present right turn. At the top of the bank the continuation of Sherford Street is Church Street, which passes the church and then heads out of town on the way to Saltmarshe and Stanford-on-Teme. Turning left at the top of the bank brought the traffic into Broad Street, which skirts the Market Square — originally known as High Cross — and then bears right, becoming High Street about half way along. At its end, High Street is crossed by Cruxwell Street, where through traffic turned left. Cruxwell Street is quite short, becoming Old Road at the Tenbury turn. Up this street — formerly called Sheep Street — was the route to Hereford and Leominster, the roads to which separated at the former toll cottage at Flaggoner's Green. Traffic that turned right along Cruxwell Street came to

Rowberry Street — previously Bowberry Street — which ran along the back of the premises lining High Street and Broad Street to join Church Street. Early alleviation of traffic in the town involved the construction of New Road from High Street, running parallel to Sheep Street, taking traffic away from the High Street/Cruxwell Street corner. This 'new' road was constructed in 1835. Sheep Street and New Road converged at the now-demolished toll house at Flaggoner's Green, where the road to Hereford (Pannier's Lane) swung to the left. The present Hereford road, further to the south, is a later construction.

The construction of the by-pass from Petty Bridge up to the Hereford road, where New Road joins it, much reduced the traffic in the town centre. Now, the one-way system means that it is only possible to drive along Broad Street and High Street in a westerly direction, and so the pubs of Bromyard, present and past, are described in this order.

At Petty Bridge, at the start of Sherford Street, was the appropriately named **Bridge Inn**, a fine grade II listed building, dating from the late 16th century (a tie-beam has the date 1577 carved upon it). It is said that Royalist officers were billeted here in 1645 when Charles I was on the way to raise the siege of Hereford. The Land Tax Return for 1812/3 shows that it was then owned and occupied by Benjamin Palmer and attracted a payment of 15s. However, the inn was subsequently bought by James Baggott, and in 1819/20 it was taxed at 12s. A sale by auction was advertised to take place at the **Bridge Inn** on 19 February 1821, and Lot 2 was:

> All that Capital and Well-accustomed INN, and now in full business, called or known by the Name or Sign of THE BRIDGE INN, being a Well-built Dwelling-house, suitable Offices, Stabling, and other conveniences; with a Piece of Hop-ground attached to the same, situate near Petty's Bridge, fronting the Turnpike-road leading to Worcester.

The inference is that the inn had previously been run down. The reason for the sale of part of his property was that James Baggott, described as a Skinner & Wool Dealer, Dealer & Chapman, had become bankrupt and his effects, including his brewing utensils, were sold by auction at the **Bridge Inn** on 12 and 13 March 1821. A trade directory of 1822 records James Baggott as still being at the **Bridge Inn** and his name occurs in the Land Tax Returns for 1822/3, but by the following year it had been bought by one Samuel Gwinn. By 1828 it had been sold yet again, and it was owned by George Kelsey, and occupied by George Clewer, whose name is given in a trade directory of 1830, although in that year the occupier was William Hill. The latter probably witnessed an accident to the mail coach that took place at Petty Bridge, best described in the report that appeared in the *Hereford Journal* of 23 February 1831.

> On Tuesday 15th inst. the Worcester Mail Coach on its way to Leominster, was overturned on the Bridge near Bromyard, the whole of the passengers were injured more or less, but a female servant of Miss Cooke, an inside passenger, was very dangerously bruised by the fall, and had the coach proceeded two yards further before it fell, she and the rest of the outside passengers must have been precipitated into the river below.

By 1835 the inn had been taken over by Thomas Price and had become a posting house, and by 1851 50-year-old Thomas Price was described as a victualler, farmer, and coach proprietor. In 1858 the Royal Mail left the **Bridge Inn** at 10.30 a.m. for Worcester, and 5.30 p.m. for Leominster and Presteigne. Thomas Price was succeeded by Thomas Redding, who was a builder as well as an innkeeper, and then by Edwin Halsey whose name appears (incorrectly spelled as Holsey) in a trade directory of 1867. The last mention in a trade directory was in 1870 and soon afterwards the inn lost its licence and Edwin Halsey

The Worcester Road early in the 20th century,
with the Bridge Inn on the far left

36

moved to the **White Horse**. It was subsequently owned by the Bromyard Gas Company, which offered it for sale by auction on 29 October 1919. The auctioneer's advertisement described it as: 'The Old Bridge Inn, a very commodious House with Stables and Coachhouse, &c., &c., let at present to Mr. S. James at a yearly rent of £13. The premises are well suited for a coach builder or garage'. At the auction bidding for this and three cottages started at £300 — they were sold for £420.

The Bridge Inn in 2003

There was another pub close to the **Bridge Inn**, called the **Talbot**. In 1804 James Baggott (mentioned previously) bought a property in the Square for the then considerable sum of £203 19s. This, together with other property, was leased out in November 1815, and included:

> ...a messuage, tenement or inn called by the name or sign of the Talbot with the stables, outbuildings, garden and fold thereunto adjoining situate, lying and being near Petty's Bridge, Bromyard, and which inn with a large stable on the north side of the road is now converted into a dwelling house and shop. Together with a piece of land behind the same now or late in the possession of Benjamin Palmer. And which messuage, tenement or inn, stables and hereditaments some time since were converted to two messuages or dwelling houses one of which with the stable and outbuildings adjoining was in the possession of Samuel Chalinor and now of Samuel Baggott and the other was with the stables, building and yard and garden and hopyard in the possession of ... Wall.

This is the only mention of the **Talbot**, which was not the same as the **Bridge Inn**. Local legend has it that cottages that were demolished when the ring road was constructed had formerly been a pub — this may well have been the **Talbot**.

Turning right from the ring road into Sherford Street, on the left is a pair of cottages, the left-hand one with very pretty latticed windows, while the windows of the other one have regretfully been replaced. Half way down is the very grand Sherford House, built in about 1770. Pevsner describes it rather ungraciously as 'Georgian, red brick, five bays, two and half storeys, alas with an incongruous long porch'.

On the opposite side of the road and slightly higher up is the old police station. In 1843 it was decided that the two small cells at the magistrates' court in Dumbleton Hall (in Church Street) were inadequate and it was decided to have a 'Lockuphouse', for which purpose a piece of ground was bought. A substantial police station was built, the courtyard behind having walls 12 feet high. It was only used as a police station for about 30 years until a larger one was built next to Dumbleton Hall, and it then became a private house.

Further up the street is the former Congregational chapel. Established in 1696, a building had been erected in 1710, but the present splendid chapel dates from a rebuilding in the early 19th century. It has a pyramidal roof, recently re-roofed, and a doorway with Tuscan columns.

BROMYARD, HEREFORDSHIRE.
FREEHOLD INN, WITH YARD, GARDEN, AND
BUILDINGS ADJOINING.

MR. F. W. OAKLEY will SELL by AUC-TION, on the PREMISES,

On TUESDAY, the 22nd day of OCTOBER, 1878,

At four for five o'clock p.m., subject to conditions to be then produced,

All that old licensed INN known as the "CROWN AND SCEPTRE," situate at the top of Sherford-street, Bromyard, about three minutes' walk from the Railway Station, and now in the occupation of Mrs. Rogers.

The House is substantially built and in good repair, it has a brick front of 50 feet, with slated roof, and contains Bar, Smoke-room, Sitting-room, large Parlour, small ditto, tap-room, kitchen, 10 bedrooms, pantry, and excellent dry Cellars.

The Outbuildings are good, and comprise 3 loose Horse Boxes, a three-stall and two open Stables, Lofts, Gig-house, Brew-house, Coal-house, Granary, Cider Mill and Press; also a lock-up Yard, with Pump of excellent water, and a capital Garden, from which pleasing views are obtained.

The whole forms a valuable and compact Property, in a good situation, and is very desirable either for occupation or investment. Possession will be given on completion of the purchase.

Further particulars may be had of the Auctioneer and Messrs. Wm. West and Allen, solicitors, Bromyard. [8005

Sale of the Crown and Sceptre in 1878

Towards the top of Sherford Street, on the right hand side, is the **Crown and Sceptre**. The front of the building dates from the early 19th century, although it conceals a timber-framed structure behind. Beneath it is a cellar cut in the bedrock, through which the Bibble Brook flows, a trickle that comes in at one side and exits through a hole in the other. Interestingly, recent excavations at the rear of the building exposed a well some 40 feet deep, still containing plenty of water at a level well below that of the Bibble Brook. There is firm evidence that shows that the pub has had at least one previous name. An indenture dated 15 June 1789, referring to the **Queen's Head** in Sherford Street, was found when the attic was cleared out, and this is a reference to a pub on the present site; this indenture is on display inside the pub. The **Queen's Head** occurs in a trade directory of 1822 when William Bridgewater was given as the licensee, but the Land Tax Returns for 1822/3 only state that he owned and occupied a house, and did not give it a name. By 1828 the owner and occupier was Thomas Lewis, and the name was given as the **Crown and Sceptre**. It is quite likely that the building was refronted at this time. In the 1830s the stables to the rear were used as a base for Nathaniel Derry Morris's wagons, which left for Hereford every Tuesday and Friday evening, and for Worcester every Monday and Thursday. Thomas Lewis was still there in 1851, aged 60, and the census shows that he was a native of Presteigne, and was a victualler and maltster. By 1858 John Lewis had taken over. In 1867 Richard Rogers, a later landlord, was also a shopkeeper. It seems that after the death of Richard Rogers, his widow

The Crown and Sceptre in 1999

ALL THAT messuage or dwellinghouse called "The Crown and Sceptre" with the gardens stables buildings and yard thereto adjoining and belonging situate on the East side of Sherford in the Town of Bromyard in the County of Hereford.

The 1960 sale of the Crown & Sceptre

took over, for when the pub was put up for sale in October 1878 it was stated to be in the occupation of Mrs. Rogers. A report in the *Hereford Times* of 2 January 1892 recorded that Charles Partridge, former landlord of the **Crown and Sceptre**, was charged with assaulting his wife Caroline and was sentenced to three months hard labour.

In 1891 Josiah Bridges held the pub, and when his widow Mrs. M. Bridges held the licence in 1902 she advertised that she kept wines and spirits of the finest quality, while in 1917 Percy Burgess advertised that the **Crown and Sceptre** has 'good accommodation for visitors'. The pub was sold by Spreckley Bros. to the Cheltenham and Hereford Brewery in 1960.

A later licensee was a Tommy Green who had played professional football for West Ham and West Bromwich Albion in the early 1940s. Many years later, when his son Phil was asked why he did not go into football, he replied that 'the sight of my father's cartilage muscle in a jar on the bar convinced me that there must be an easier way of making a living'. The **Crown and Sceptre** continues to serve its customers into the 21st century.

Sherford Street leads on to Church Street, and on the corner with Rowberry Street was a pub called the **Crown**. A deed of 8 December 1764 refers to the premises as:

All that messuage or tenement called or known by the sign of the Crown, with barn, stable, buildings, backside and garden belonging, now in occupation of Thomas Taylor, having Church Street on the East and Bowberry Street on the South, being the corner house.

In 1834 a deed referred to the premises as 'hitherto the Crown Inn', inferring that it had closed before that time, and indeed many years before this the name was being used for another establishment further along the street. The corner site was bought for £170 in 1843 by the Rev. William Cooke, vicar of Bromyard, who had a market hall

The Bell in the early 20th century

Old Bell; new sign

erected on it. This was not successful, and by 1867 it was disused and in 1886 his daughter made a gift of the market hall to the town of Bromyard on the condition that the town purchased the reversion of the market tolls, of which she was the lessee.

A few yards further north from the **Crown Inn**, on the same side of the road, was the **Bell Inn**; the building is now identified by a small plaque. In 1851 it was called the **Three Horseshoes** being named after the trade of the occupant Edward Moss, who was both blacksmith and beer retailer; the blacksmith's shop was on the south side of the premises, fronting on to Church Street. The next year Edward Moss contracted to buy the premises for £210, when it was described as 'All those two newly erected messuages or tenements now converted into a beer house and called the Three Horse Shoes, with the smith's shop, yard and garden ground … bounded … on the south by the newly erected market hall'.

41

Edward Moss soon sold his interest, but stayed on as tenant. Elizabeth Cropp bought the premises for £370 in March 1868 and it was at about this time that the name was changed to the **Bell Inn** (occasionally referred to as the **Blue Bell**). On her death in 1880 Elizabeth left the pub to her friend Mrs. Ann Knight who sold it to the Cheltenham Brewery in 1890 for £700. The last licensee was Tom Drinkwater — an unfortunate name for a publican — who held the licence for at least 20 years. His constant wearing of a bowler hat is well remembered by older inhabitants, as is his work as an amateur vet.

At the 1936 Brewster Sessions Superintendent J. Edge objected to the renewal of the licence for the **Bell** on the grounds that it was not required, being redundant. This recommendation was advertised in the *Hereford Times* of 18 April 1936 requesting anyone to come forward who considered the licence should be renewed; evidently no one did, for the licence was formally revoked. There was presumably enough provision of public houses in Bromyard, for the *Bromyard News and Record* of 14 May 1936 stated that there was one public house for every 98 inhabitants! The premises were offered for sale, but not enough was bid at auction and the property was withdrawn. In recent years the render has been stripped from the front of the house and the stonework repointed. The outline of the former front door of one of the two houses from which the pub was converted can clearly be seen.

Further northwards, on the same side of the street was the **Railway Inn**, another closed establishment, this time from the 1970s. It still has its sign and is clearly a former licensed premises, whose architectural merit is recognised by being grade II listed. This is another pub that has had several names, including those of its nearby competitors! In the *Hereford Journal* of 25 September 1811 it was described as the **Crown Inn**, situated in Church Street, Bromyard. It was advertised as being to let, and it was stated that further particulars could be obtained from Mr. Maund of Bromyard. This is enough to identify this **Crown Inn** with the **Railway**, as the name of Andrew Maund occurs both in the deeds of the **Railway Inn** and in the Land Tax Returns. It continued to be called officially by this name until at least 1824/5, during which time John Harris was the tenant, but by 1828 it was recorded as the **Bell** in the Returns.

Church Street and the Railway Inn about 1910

However, in a trade directory of 1822, John Harris is given as the licensee of a pub called the **Bell Inn**, whilst the return for that year calls it the **Crown Inn**, so it evidently took a while for the official record to catch up with the change of name! It was taken over by Thomas Price in 1831 and a deed of that year states that it was called the **Barley Mow** (but still called the **Bell Inn** in the Land Tax Return for that year). By 1835 the landlord had become Joseph Robertson, who had changed the name to the **Mason's Arms**, the change reflecting his trade as a stone-mason. Like many of the pubs in Bromyard the stables in the rear indicate its connection with the carrying trade. In 1858 Joseph Booton, a beer retailer on the Downs, advertised that he was a carrier to Worcester, departing from the **Mason's Arms** on Tuesdays and Fridays at 5 p.m. and returning on Wednesdays and Saturdays. By 1861 the name had been changed to the **Carrier's Arms** and then, by 1877, to the **Railway Inn**, the sixth name in less than 60 years!

This final change of name was to celebrate the connection of Bromyard to Worcester by rail. When Parliament approved the construction of a railway from Worcester to Leominster via Bromyard in 1861, it could not have been expected that the line would take 36

Bromyard station shortly before its closure in September 1964

years to complete. After some ten years the Great Western Railway (its initials — G.W.R. — humourously said by some to stand for God's Wonderful Railway) agreed to work the section from Bransford Road (on the Worcester to Hereford line) as far as Bromyard. By 1874 the line had reached Yearsett, but the money ran out, and for three years this was the terminus for Bromyard and the last 3¾ miles had to be covered on foot. The line to Bromyard was finally opened on 22 October 1877 and Yearsett station was closed.

This was not the end of the story, for the Leominster to Bromyard link was still missing. A start was made in 1884, when the four-mile section between Leominster and Steen's Bridge was completed. Even then the two sections remained isolated for another 13 years until the

LEOMINSTER & WORCESTER LINE--G.W.R. (Week days only)

	a m	a m	p m	p m	p m	
LONDON (Padd.) ... dep	...	5 40	9 50	1 40	4 45	...
WOR'STER (Sh'b Hill) ,,	8 20	1030	2 40	5 10	8 0	...
,, (Foreg'te St.) ,,	8 23	1033	2 43	5 13	8 3	...
Henwick ,,	8 28	1038	2 48	5 18	8 8	...
Leigh Court ,,	8 38	1048	2 58	5 28	8 18	...
Knightwick ,,	8 45	1055	8 5	5 35	8 25	...
Suckley ,,	8 49	1059	3 9	5 39	8 29	...
Bromyard { arr.	9 1	1111	3 20	5 51	8 41	...
Bromyard { dep.	9 4	1114	3 22	5 54	8 44	...
Rowden Mill ,,	9 12	1122	3 30	6 2	8 52	...
Fencote ,,	9 22	1133	3 39	6 13	9 3	...
Steens Bridge ,,	9 29	1140	3 46	6 20	9 10	...
LEOMINSTER ,,	9 37	1148	3 54	6 28	9 18	...

	a m	a m	p m	p m	p m	p m	
LEOMINSTER ... dep	7 20	8 55	1230	3 57	...	7 45	...
Steens Bridge ,,	7 31	9 6	1241	4 8	...	7 56	...
Fencote ,,	7 40	9 21	1251	4 17	...	8 5	...
Rowden Mill ,,	7 47	9 28	1258	4 24	...	8 12	...
Bromyard { arr.	7 54	9 35	1 5	4 31	...	8 19	...
Bromyard { dep.	7 59	9 50	1 20	4 33	...	8 42	...
Suckley ,,	8 11	10 2	1 32	4 45	...	8 54	...
Knightwick ,,	8 15	10 6	1 36	4 49	...	8 58	...
Leigh Court ,,	8 22	1013	1 43	4 56	...	9 5	...
Henwick ,,	8 31	1022	1 52	5 4	...	9 13	...
WOR'STER (Forgt St.),,	8 35	1026	1 55	5 8	...	9 17	...
(Sh'b Hill) ar.	8 40	1031	2 0	5 16	...	9 22	...
LONDON (Padd) ...	1215	2 33	5 50	8 45	...	...	...

The railway timetable for 1899

44

whole line was completed and opened on 1 September 1897. The railway was never really a success — the section from Leominster to Bromyard survived the two world wars but closed in 1952; this left Bromyard at the end of a rural line and the Beeching axe eventually fell, the line to Worcester closing in 1964.

The inn, satisfying the thirst of railway commuters, thrived during the railway age. In 1875 James Loxley, who then held the licence, bought the premises, selling them to Emma Halsey in 1883. She, in her turn, sold them in 1889 to the Cheltenham Original Brewery. In 1902 the publican was William James, but by 1917 Mrs. Rosalind Roberta Preece was there. Margaret Eisel (wife of the co-author) recalls her grandfather, Will Gibbs, telling how he used to stable his horse at the **Railway Inn** when he came to market from Harpley, but falling out with the Preeces who held the pub, he then changed to the **Bay Horse**. Right up until closure the **Railway Inn** was used as the local for the band of ringers from St. Peter's church, after which the street was named. The last landlady was Mrs. Flo Preece, who referred to the ringers as 'Her boys'. In the years between the two world wars, she and her husband Les had a five-

Flo Preece's 'boys' — St. Peter's church bellringers in the Railway Inn

45

The Railway Inn in 1999

piece band with Flo on the piano and her husband on the violin. It is said that the band did not always play to the same rhythm, one might be playing a waltz and another the quickstep. After she retired from the **Railway Inn** until her death she sent a Christmas card and present to the ringers. A photograph of the ringers, taken in the bar of the **Railway Inn**, hangs in the ringing chamber of the church and is reproduced opposite.

On the north side of the **Railway Inn** is a pair of cottages, on a large site that was later sub-divided. In the 18th century it was occupied by a pub called the **Red**

The Red Lion was next door to the Railway Inn,
where there is now a pair of cottages

Lion, described in a deed of 1768 as 'ALL THAT messuage ... formerly called or known by the name or sign of the Red Lyon'. It was then in the possession of Elizabeth Chip, who kept it until her death in 1812. However, she does not seem to have run it as a pub and there are no further

At one time this attractive building was the Adam and Eve Inn

references. Similarly, little is known of the **Adam and Eve**, which occupied what is now 33 Church Street, immediately to the north of the site of the **Red Lion**. In the mid-18th century the property was in the hands of the Holbrook family, but in 1796/7 a dispute about inherited interests in the property led to it being sold by auction at the **Hop Pole** on 24 April 1797, when it made £100. When it was conveyed to the successful bidder on 7 November 1797 it was described as 'All that messuage with a large garden on the back side or West part thereof and being in the Church St. or Sherford St. formerly used as a public house and called the Adam & Eve'. Curiously, the Land Tax Returns still refer to it as the **Adam and Eve** until at least 1824/5, although it is unlikely that that it had continued to be run as licensed premises and it was not mentioned in the 1822 trade directory.

Just across the road from the former **Adam and Eve** and a few yards further north was the Working Men's Institute and Temperance Hall. It was built in 1859 and used for lectures, penny readings etc. By the end of the century it was owned by a solicitor from Worcester, who employed Vincent Weeks of Bromyard as agent. Weeks was a member of a well-known local family, which will be met with again in connection with the **(Red) Lion** in Broad Street, and at that time was the proprietor of the *Bromyard Record*, with offices in Rowberry Street. It was at about this time that the name was changed to the Public Hall.

In March 1904 the Medical Officer of Health recommended to Bromyard Urban District Council that 'the owner of the Public Hall in Church Street be called upon to whitewash the inside of the house attached to the hall and have the closets made into a proper water closet'. This clearly upset Mr. Hill, the owner, and he wrote offering to sell the hall to the Council for £650. On 21 June 1904 the *Bromyard News and Record* reported that no action was to be taken by the UDC on the offer, despite it being understood that Mr. Hill intended to knock down the hall and build cottages on the site. Concern was expressed that there would then be no public hall except for the one at the **Falcon**, which was thought to be unsuitable in many ways.

The threatened demolition did not happen, and at about this time the hall was leased to Edward J. Cuff, landlord of the **Falcon**, who eventually bought it. In 1922 it was fitted out as a cinema, called the *Electric Theatre*, and this opened at the end of October. The cost of admission ranged from 5d. to 1s.10d. The following year Cuff leased it to Thomas Diacoff and it reopened in May 1923. However, it was only a cinema for a few years as in April 1931 it was gutted by fire, a packed audience fortunately managing to get out in time. Mr. and Mrs. R. Diacoff — Thomas Diacoff had died by this time — lived in the house attached to the hall and lost their home and so, in May 1931, a benefit dance was held for them. Later that year the Electric Theatre was sold by auction and subsequently a new house was built on the site, set well back from the road.

CHAPTER FOUR

Bromyard
THE MARKET SQUARE & BROAD ST.

The left turn at the top of Sherford Street leads into Broad Street, and the Market Square where, from 1774 onwards, hiring fairs for servants took place initially three times a year. At that time there was a small market hall, removed in 1844. By the side of the market hall were the stocks and whipping post, and the town weights and measures were probably kept in the upper story of the market hall. The standard bushel measure used in Bromyard, which was cast in bell-metal by a Worcester founder in 1670, subsequently passed into private hands and was later found doing duty as a water butt in a garden. In 1819 Hereford Corporation adopted the smaller Winchester bushel measure, and it may be that the same happened in Bromyard and the old standard measure was made redundant. After the Bromyard bushel measure was rediscovered it was given to Dr. W.W. Davies who lived at Tower House, and he used it as a log basket. When he left Bromyard in 1936 he presented it to the parish church, where it can still be seen.

The stocks were in use, or at least their use was contemplated, in the early 19th century. On 14 June 1819 Thomas Jones, a baker, appeared in front of Bromyard magistrates to answer 'Informations' laid against him, that he had a quantity of bread deficient in weight, that such bread was not marked 'agreeable to Act of Parliament' and that he had unlawful ingredients in his possession. He was convicted with penalties of £11 4s. and a large quantity of bread was ordered to be confiscated. This conviction obviously enraged Thomas Jones and 'Mr. Jones's conduct before the Magistrates was so very violent and outrageous, that they ordered him into the custody of a Constable, and committed him to the public Stocks'. Friends, not wanting him to be made a public spectacle, interfered and solicited the magistrates to overlook his misconduct, which they did upon his public acknowledgment of his offence and agreeing to pay £5 towards the poor of Bromyard. A statement was drawn up and signed by Mr. Jones, three magistrates and various other persons, and this appeared in the *Hereford Journal* of 23 June 1819. However, a week later Thomas Jones placed another advertisement in the *Hereford Journal*, denying that the incident ever took place. In response, George Badham, the Clerk of the Court, inserted a long advertisement in the issue of 14 July stating the facts of the case, and there the matter rested.

At present the Square comes into its own in the third weekend in September when the Folk Festival is held. This was first held in 1968 and has grown in popularity ever since. Although based on a site just outside the town on the road to Saltmarshe, the activity both in music and dance spills over into the town, mainly based on the Square, with both formal and informal events. The latter include impromptu groups of musicians that form and play in and around the pubs.

The market hall in front of the Hop Pole in 1842

Where there was a market a licensed establishment is normally found, and the first one in the Square of which there is record was called the **Nag's Head**. In 1765 this was taken over by Edward Williams, being previously held by Thomas Williams, a barber, who had moved to Worcester. The lease states that it was near the Market Hall and High Cross. Another lease of 1767 states that the inn was then in the possession of Edward Williams. In the *Hereford Journal* of 20 January 1774 there is an advertisement for an association for the prosecution of felons that had been established in Bromyard, and one of the signatories was Mr. Edward Williams, Innholder. There is no information about when the **Nag's Head** closed, but Edward Williams later took over the **Hop Pole** and it is possible that he did so when this inn was built in the late 18th century. When Thomas Payne leased the **Hop Pole** in 1826, the lease also covered '…the messuage called the Nags Head formerly a public house, now in the occupation of William Wildsmith…'. Evidently the building that had been the **Nag's Head** was still in existence, but when the **Hop Pole** was conveyed to John Hawkins in 1834, the conveyance also included '…those three newly erected messuages built on the scite of the Nags Head, two being in the tenures of John Warburton and William Weaver, which said messuages being near the Market Place and the Cross…'. On the west side of the Square, separated from the **Hop Pole** by a narrow road called Twyning

A quiet market day in front of the Hop Pole in the early 20th century

51

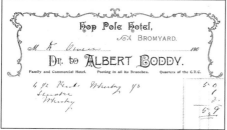

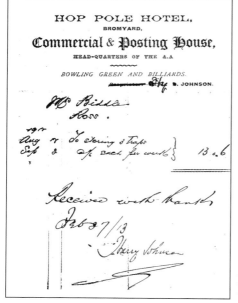

Various billheads from the Hop Pole

Street are three houses of this period — the only houses in the street — and this seems to be the most likely site for the **Nag's Head**.

When the market hall was removed in 1844, the **Hop Pole Hotel** came into full view across the square. Its close proximity to the market hall suggests that the building was a substantial encroachment on the market square, but no record of this has so far come to light. Dating from the 18th century but with 19th-century alterations to the front, it is built of brick with roughcast and colourwash. Its merit is recognised by being grade II listed as is the 18th-century stable block associated with it, to the rear and on the opposite side of Rowberry Street. Behind the stable bock there was formerly more stabling.

An early reference to the **Hop Pole** occurs in an advertisement that appeared in the *Hereford Journal* of 26 February 1794, which stated that an auction of land would take place 'at the sign of the Hop-pole, in Bromyard…'. In that same year the rules of a Friendly Society of tradesmen, which met at the **Hop Pole**, were printed, but no copy is known to survive. Parliament passed a Friendly Societies Act in

1794 and as a result many Friendly Societies, which were usually based on public houses, overhauled their rules.

From some uncertain date the **Hop Pole** was held by Edward Williams, described in 1794 as an 'innholder, maltster, dealer and chapman of the Hop Pole', and by 1822 was in the hands of Thomas Payne, referred to in a lease of 1826 as a butcher. In February 1834 the property was conveyed to John Hawkins, whose name appears in a trade directory of 1835. By 1851 the **Hop Pole Inn** was in the possession of Daniel Cottrell, a native of Suffolk then aged 32. Subsequently he changed the name to the **Hop Pole Hotel**, marking its superior status. In 1867 it was stated that it was a 'Family, Commercial, and Posting house, and Inland Revenue office'. Not all of its landlords appeared in a good light, and in 1890 Mr. Nathan Faulkner appeared in court to answer a charge of being drunk in charge of a horse and carriage and with furious driving. In 1902 the proprietor, Albert

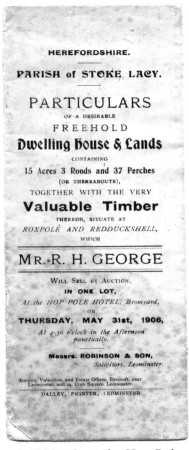

A 1906 sale at the Hop Pole

Boddy, advertised 'Posting in all its branches' and at this period there was a bowling green associated with the hotel. Also at this period there was a lot of trouble in the area from tramps and travelling families, and one incident affected Mr. Keene, a visitor to Bromyard who was staying at the **Hop Pole**. In September 1906 the *Bromyard News and Record* reported that he was cycling along Avenbury Lane when he was pestered by a number of tramps to give them money. He refused, whereupon they attacked him, his injuries necessitating medical attention. Occasionally there were more unusual visitors, and the *Bromyard News and Record* of 25 August 1933 recorded that, as a consequence of their transport having broken down, a case of sea lions had spent the night at the **Hop Pole** 'making the night hideous with their noises'. In 1964 bed and breakfast in one of the 14 rooms then let cost 18s. 6d. per night, with lunch at 7s. 6d. and dinner at 10s. 6d.

The **Hop Pole,** including the stabling and car park across the road, was sold by auction in London on 5 December 2002, fetching £180,000.

1960s advertisement

Leaving the square, on the left-hand side of Broad Street, at No. 34, was the **Swan Inn**, first mentioned in the early 1820s. In 1822 the **Swan Inn** was owned and occupied by Thomas Smith. His name occurs again in the records of the manor of Bromyard on 31

The Hop Pole in 1999

October 1836 when Thomas Smith, of the **Swan with Two Necks Inn**, Broad Street, was appointed ale conner (see p.8) for the borough for the ensuing year. This is the only mention of this form of the name, which is derived from the phrase 'swan with two nicks', the mark of ownership of the Worshipful Company of Vintners placed there during the swan-upping ceremony that takes place on the Thames in July each year. But the evidence is confusing, as directories of 1830 and 1835 record Samuel Wilcox as being at the **Swan Inn**, and perhaps Thomas Smith was living there in retirement. Be that as it may, in 1851 the landlady was 53-year-old Lucy Wilcox, Samuel's widow. The pub does not seem to have survived long after this and does not appear in Cassey's *Directory* of 1858.

On the opposite side of the road at what is now 29 Broad Street was the **New Inn**. In 1812/13 this was owned by John Amiss but tenanted by John Fox. Within a few years it had been taken in hand, and from about 1819 John Amiss was running the **New Inn** himself. His name appears in the directory of 1822, but he became bankrupt in that year, and the notice of his bankruptcy that appeared in the *Hereford Journal* of 1 May 1822 stated that he was a 'Victualler, Draper, Grocer, Dealer, and Chapman'. As a consequence of the bankruptcy his assignees put up his property for auction at the **Bay Horse Inn** on 8 July 1822, the first lot being stated as:

> ALL that FREEHOLD and Well-accustomed PUBLIC-HOUSE called the NEW INN, with the Brew-House, Stable, Garden, and Pump, thereunto belonging, Situated and being in the High-street, in the Town of Bromyard, aforesaid.

There was an error in this advertisement, as the property was — and still is — in Broad Street. The pump was a valuable selling point, as at this time water was in short supply in Bromyard. What happened at the auction was, as usual, not reported, but the Amiss family remained at the **New Inn**, but probably as tenants rather than owners. Hannah Amiss was there by 1835: she may not have been too popular as a landlady, as in November 1851 she was fined £1 with 8s. 6d. expenses for having two quart and five pint measures that were deficient. Hannah Amiss was still there at the age of 80 in 1858, but in 1861 the **New Inn** was being run by Catherine Amiss, her unmarried

Broad Street looking west about 1910.
The Fountain Head was on the right-hand side behind the vehicle

daughter. John Wilson had taken over by 1867. After this the name disappears from trade directories but seems to have subsequently reopened as the **Fountain Head**, no doubt a reference to the important pump. In 1890 H. Scarlett Davies of 'Ye Fountain Head' was advertising ales, wines and spirits, and he ran the business for a number of years, his retirement being advertised in the *Bromyard News* of 3 February 1899. The business was sold to Messrs. Ind Coope and Co. and John Haynes, from the Bull's Head, Worcester, took over as tenant, the business then being called the **Wine Stores**. In 1902 he advertised that he was a 'wholesale and retail wine & spirit merchant'. By 1912 it had become known as the **Wine Vaults**, and the *Bromyard News and Record* of 4 January 1912 recorded that Percy Rooker, of the **Wine Vaults**, celebrated the New Year by entertaining 100 of his customers to supper. By 1917 it was held by Walter Spreadborough and was being called the **Liquor Vaults**. On 29 October 1925 a sale of furniture was advertised to take place at the **Wine Vaults**.

At the Bromyard Petty Sessions in 1938 there were objections to the renewal of the licence of the **Fountain Head** on the grounds of redundancy — the name had reverted to the former one — but it was reprieved as the tenant, a Mr. Pugh, said that he was making a living. In May 1941 an application to suspend the licence for the duration of

Broad Street looking west. The Falcon is centre left

the war was granted. The premises were requisitioned by the Ministry of Works and the Ministry was still in occupation in 1948 when the licence was suspended for yet another year. In 1949 the renewal of the licence was opposed, the premises then being occupied as offices by the Ministry of Food, the Ministry of National Insurance and the Ministry of Works. At that time it was stated that there were ten licensed houses in the Urban District and as the last census had given a population of 1,585 this meant that there was one licensed premises for every 158 persons, including women and children.

That was the end of the **Fountain Head**, and the premises continued to be used as a food office until about 1957. Because they were on a long lease the premises were then shut up and not entered for about twenty years. They were subsequently renovated, with the ground floor being used as commercial premises and the upper floor becoming part of Bromyard Masonic Hall. There is little sign that it was ever a pub except that in a shed in the back yard is a disused gentlemen's slate urinal.

Seventeenth century deeds relating to a pub called the **Royal Oak**, are thought to relate to buildings on the site of the premises of Gilbert's Fruit and Vegetables, a brick-fronted building further along the north side of Broad Street. In 1673 a house of this name was bought by one Stephen Northern who immediately passed it on to his son John Northern. In 1692/3 this was in the ownership of Edward Clarke and John Northern, then described as being of St. Martins in the Field, Co. Middlesex, who appointed William Beck of Bromyard, an ironmonger, to collect the rent. A year later John Northern sold 'that messuage known by the sign of the Royal Oak' for £100. The last in this series of documents is dated 1701, and there is no later mention of this pub.

Yet further along is another former pub, the **Lion**, now being used by Age Concern and others, the timbered front of which has been exposed in recent years. In the late 18th century it was bought by the tenant, Richard Weeks, for £235. At that time it was called the **Red Lion**, the name being changed officially to the **Lion** in the 1850s. It seems likely that the earlier name post-dates the closure of the **Red Lion** in Church Street in or before 1768, but it is not known whether the pub opened at that time or whether it had a previous name. The 19th-century Land Tax Returns refer to this as the **Lion Inn**, although the deeds call it the **Red Lion**.

Vincent Weeks had taken over the inn by 1835 and held the licence for several years, being still there in 1867, but by 1870 he had been succeeded by Edward Weeks. The property remained in the ownership of the Weeks family until 1877, when the new owner, from Worcester, rented

The Lion about 1900

the pub to James Tarbath, except for the malthouse and rear premises (still in existence), which were leased to Joseph Burrow Weeks who previously had traded as a maltster in Sherford Street.

Broad Street was the place of the butter and poultry markets, and in a newspaper report that appeared in the *Bromyard News and Record* of 13 February 1890 Joseph Burrow Weeks stated that he could remember live poultry being bought in the street opposite the **Falcon** some 30 years previously. James Tarbath, who had been born at Bedlam, Bringsty, had started as a carrier and mail-cart contractor, working from Sherford Street, and he rented the former **Bridge Inn** to provide stabling for his horses. He carried on this business after he took on the tenancy of the **Lion** in 1877. Two years later he was advertising that he had horses and carriages for hire and that he was a carrier to Worcester, leaving at 7 a.m. on Saturdays, returning the same day. On 10 July 1884 he advertised that he would be running a brake to catch an early train from Leominster to Shrewsbury Flower Show. A story about his transport business was told by a local resident, Miss Annie Roberts, in a letter that she wrote in 1969 and which was published in 1989 in the Bromyard Local History Society *Journal* No. 12. She wrote:

The house which is now the Book Shop was owned by a man named Tarbeth (*sic*) who kept a livery stable. There was no transport to the outlying villages, he used to take his brake to meet the train in case anyone needed his help.

Now the church had to supply Grendon Bishop and the Rev. Martin had to employ him (Tarbeth) to take him there every Sunday and so they were good friends. This is a bit of fun. One day Rev. Martin was going to the station to meet his daughter and Mr. Tarbeth overtook him and said 'Oh good morning Bishop of Bromyard' to which Rev. Martin said 'Oh good morning publican and sinner you are'. You see Mr. Tarbeth kept a public house.

James Tarbath was also involved in other local affairs and in 1906 was elected as Overseer of the Workhouse. He was succeeded as licensee just before the First World War by his widow, Mrs. Agnes Louise Tarbath, and she was still there just before the Second World War, when she was said to be the oldest licensee in the country; in 1938 she would have been 91. She clearly looked after her younger customers as it is reported that she refused to serve them more than two half pints of beer as the beer was too strong! Her name disappears in 1938, and the assumption is that she either died or retired at that time, but there was no mention of either event in the *Bromyard News and Record* of the previous 12 months, and she was not buried in the cemetery.

The renewal of the licence was objected to at the Brewster Sessions in 1938 and the pub closed, the premises became a bookshop, as mentioned by Miss Roberts, which it remained for many years, and it since has had a variety of uses. In 1932 the Royal Commission on Historical Monuments stated that at the rear there was an original window of three lights with moulded mullions that was then blocked. Inside, the room to the south-east has an original plaster ceiling with moulded panels enclosing fleur-de-lis, roses and birds. At the stair head there is a re-set elaborately-carved acanthus bracket. The names of certain of the Weeks family were engraved on panes of glass in what was the upstairs sitting room, all dated 1853.

Next door but one to the former **Lion** at 1 Broad Street was, until recently, **TC's Bar.** Many years ago this was a draper's shop run by John S. Foot, and later by his widow until the 1950s. It had a very fine shop front, taken out one Sunday morning about 30 years ago, but regretfully no proper photograph of the front before its removal has

TC's bar in 1999

been found. Subsequently it became a steak bar called **The Fox and Badger**, with a table licence, but it eventually became **TC's bar** with a full licence about 10 years ago. It closed in autumn 2002.

Opposite the former **Lion** and **TC's Bar** is the **Falcon Hotel**, certainly the largest licensed premises in Bromyard and occupying a prominent position. The front of this 17th-century timbered building was later Georgianised, with sash windows and the timberwork rendered over. As early as 1883 it was reported in the *Bromyard News* that the Falcon Hotel was beginning to lose its plaster coat and that it was hoped that it would be restored to its timber frontage again. Despite this, it was not until 1933 that the rendering was finally removed to expose the timberwork once more. Inside, some of the first floor rooms are lined with 17th-century panelling, partly with a frieze of jewel ornament.

Clearly such an impressive building played an important role in the town, and during the 18th century some of the manorial courts were held here. At Courts Leet held in the manor of Bromyard the lord of the manor, the Bishop of Hereford, laid a pain (penalty) of £1 19s. upon all victuallers and innholders that did not sell full measure.

The first publican at the **Falcon** of whom we have any detail was William Blew, who took over the property in 1760. On 14 March 1771 an auction was advertised to take place here '...at the Dwelling-House of William Blew, at the Sign of the Falcon...', while from 30 August 1772 William Blew's name appears on the front of the *Hereford Journal* as the local agent for advertisements to be placed in the *Hereford Journal*.

The **Falcon Inn** was also where meetings about the Bromyard Turnpike Trust took place and an advertisement appeared in the *Hereford Journal* of 5 May 1774. Evidently there was difficulty in getting a suitable bid, for the auction was postponed, first to 6 July 1774 and then to 15 August 1774.

William Blew was clearly in a good way of business, and in 1783 he acquired several properties from John Freeman of Gaines, including two dwellings called Piccadilly and three parcels of land. By his will of July 1786 William Blew left all his property to his wife Elizabeth. She made her own will in July 1789 and left Piccadilly to her son William, and the **Falcon**, which was in her possession, to Joshua Blew, another son. On 1 January 1794 an advertisement in the *Hereford Journal* stated that an auction of the **New Inn** in the chapelry of 'Grindon' Bishop would take place at the **Falcon Inn**, Bromyard, at that time in the hands of Joshua Blew. He was succeeded by Richard Lockley, who married Margaret Edwards in 1799 and in a pre-nuptial settlement agreed to sell the **Falcon** to Thomas Havard for £2,600. But, curiously, the name of Richard

Letting the turnpike in 1784

Concerns about protecting game in 1785.
Both meetings held at the Falcon

Lockley later appears in the Land Tax Returns as owner as well as occupier. His advertisement in the *Hereford Journal* of 6 August 1800 reads:

FALCON INN, BROMYARD
R. LOCKLEY

Returns his sincere Thanks to his Friends the Public, for the great encouragement he has received from them, since his commencing business at the above Inn; and informs them, that he has made such alterations at his House, as will make it much more comfortable to those who please to honour him with their favours, which he will endeavour to merit by every attention.

N.B. the Road from Hereford to Worcester, through Bromyard, is four miles nearer than any other road, and much better.

Good HORSES and careful Drivers.

As the main establishment in the town, when peace was proclaimed in 1814, after Napoleon's exile to Elba, it was decided to have a Wellington Ball at the **Falcon** 'to commemorate the blessings of Peace, and the return of the Duke of Wellington to his Native Land, after all his glorious Victories'. Entry was by ticket, costing 3s. for ladies but 6s. for gentlemen. This was a resounding success, and on 20 July 1814 the *Hereford Journal* reported:

The Ball at the Falcon Inn, Bromyard, on Thursday last in honour of Lord Wellington, attracted a very numerous and respectable company. At nine o'clock the dancing commenced; tea, coffee, and a cold collation, were introduced about twelve, and the lively dance was afterwards resumed and kept up with unabated spirit, till four o'clock in the morning, when the assembly separated, highly delighted with the polite attentions of the Stewards, and the excellent arrangements of the entertainment. We understand it is contemplated to renew the Winter Dancing Assembles (*sic*) at Bromyard, a measure which we doubt not will be warmly patronised and supported by the families in the neighbourhood of that town.

In 1826 Richard Lockley and his wife lent Thomas Havard money against the security of the **Falcon**, but by 1831 Thomas Havard had become bankrupt and forfeited his property. Richard Lockley died in 1832 and in March of that year the **Falcon** was advertised in the *Hereford Journal* 'To be sold or let (with immediate possession) ...

with about 60 acres of land. For particulars apply to Mr. Jones, Huntlands, or to Mr. Wm. Eckley, Bromyard'. The amount of land calls attention to the fact that this was a posting inn. In the 1830s the *Royal Mail* called there daily on its way from Kington to London, and on the return journey. How many coaches of the same name were needed to operate the service is not known, but it was probably several. Similarly, the *Sovereign*, operating between Aberystwyth and Worcester, called at the **Falcon** on Mondays, Wednesdays and Fridays, at seven in the morning on the way to Aberystwyth and seven in the evening on the way to Worcester. It is not surprising that the new landlord, Moses New, advertised in 1836 that it was a commercial and posting house as well as the excise office.

In the same year the **Falcon** was conveyed to William Plumtree Grape. Moses New was succeeded as landlord by Harcourt Noake, and by 1850 John Devereux had taken over, probably related to the family of the same name at the **Bay Horse Inn**. In 1851 the landlord was John Hawkins, a native of Staffordshire, who was then aged 61, and it seems that he had moved from the **Hop Pole** to the **Falcon**.

The importance of the **Falcon** in the life of the town is emphasised by the entry in Cassey's *Directory* of 1858 which states that 'The Manor courts are held quarterly, and the County court monthly, at the Falcon hotel'.

Meanwhile, in 1856 the property was conveyed to William Baggott, nephew of the William Baggott who had held the licence of the **King's Arms** and who died in the same year, leaving property in the Market Square to his nephew. The nephew was not as

HEREFORDSHIRE.
ELIGIBLE INVESTMENTS.

MESSRS. OAKLEY will SELL by AUCTION at the FALCON HOTEL, BROMYARD, on MONDAY, the 13th of AUGUST next, at four o'clock in the afternoon,—

All those seven pieces or parcels of Meadow and Arable Land, and Fold-yard, adjoining Pool Hall, containing 15a. 3r. 27p. or thereabouts, in the occupation of Mr. Cave.

All those six pieces or parcels of Arable land situate and being near the Avenbury Lane and Burley, containing 16a. 1r. 15p., or thereabouts, and in the several occupations of Mr. Thomas Price, Mr. John Williams, and Mr. Thos. Tyler.

Four pieces or parcels of Arable Land, with a cottage and garden, situate at Burley, containing 25a. 0r. 3p. or thereabouts, in the occupation of Mr. Wm. Smith.

A piece of garden ground and quarry of excellent building and paving stone, adjoining Bromyard Church-yard, containing 1a. 0r. 32p., or thereabouts.

The whole of the foregoing property is situate in the townships of Linton and Norton, close to the market town of Bromyard, and is free of tithe rentcharge.

Also the Great Tithes of the township of Linton, commuted at the annual rent charge of £138.

The whole being held on lease for lives of the respective ages of 24, 23, and 24.

Also two several policies of Assurance for £1000 each, payable on the death of the survivor of such lives subject to a small annual premium.

Also three Freehold Cottages, and about 1a, 1r. 3p. of land, called Stiles Acre, situated on the Hundred Bank, in the parish of Little Cowarne, in the occupation of Mr. Drew and others.

Particulars and conditions of sale may be obtained of Mr. West, solicitor and the auctioneers, Bromyard, Messrs. Davies and Edwards, solicitors, Leominster, Mr. W. H. Apperley, surveyor, Hereford, where a plan can be seen; the Crown Hotel, Worcester, and Mr. G. F. Cooke, solicitor, 17 Chancery Lane, London. [6239

A sale at the Falcon in 1855

successful as his uncle and was declared bankrupt in 1861, losing his property in the Market Square. It was probably as a consequence of the bankruptcy that the **Falcon** was advertised to be let, to be entered on 20 February 1862.

Subsequently the hotel changed hands and in 1867 was owned by the Falcon Hotel Company Ltd. Thos. H. Wheeler was the company secretary and Mrs. Humphries was manageress. The hotel was sold again in 1868 and then in 1875 to Henry Bennions. At this time Frederick Baker took over as the landlord, and it cost him 6d. to have his name painted on the licence plate over the door (as recorded on the account below left). The hotel was sold yet again in July 1888.

For many years at the end of the 19th century and the beginning of the 20th century the landlord was Edward Jackson Cuff. He was there in 1891 and still there in 1917. There were notable visitors to Bromyard in his time, and when in November 1899 a party from Birmingham, including the Lord Mayor, visited the town, it stayed at the **Falcon**. In the summer of 1909 Lloyd George visited Bromyard and took tea at the **Falcon**. In 1899 E.J. Cuff had a dispute with the Great Western Railway over a lost dog. This was sent to London in the care of the railway company but was lost, the railway claiming that the dog slipped its collar and ran away, leaving the porter holding the lead and collar. Cuff sued the railway for the value of the dog, which he claimed was worth £8 8s., a claim accepted by the jury. Unfortunately for Mr. Cuff the contract stated that the limit of compensation was £2 and that was all he was awarded. In 1902 the Falcon was stated to be a 'Commercial and Family Hotel & Posting House. Headquarters C.T.C. [Cyclists Touring Club] and Cricket Club. Every description of posting'. There were later advertisements for horses and carriages for hire in 1911 and 1914.

Despite the size of the building, in 1964 only seven bedrooms were to let, with bed

BROMYARD, HEREFORDSHIRE.
FALCON HOTEL.

TO be LET, and entered upon on the 20th day of FEBRUARY, this old-established HOTEL and POSTING-HOUSE.—For particulars and to treat for the same, apply to Mr. THOMAS WEST, Angel-street, Worcester, and Mr. WILLIAM WEST, Solicitor, Bromyard.

Top: To Let — The Falcon in 1862

Bottom: The tattered remains of an 1875 account for work done for Mr. Baker

and breakfast costing £1 10s., with lunch at 10s. 6d. and dinner at 13s. 6d., much more than at the **Hop Pole**.

About 10 years ago the **Falcon** became a drinker's paradise, but only for a day. The landlord had departed and the inn was being run by his wife, Maria Brown. One Sunday night she emptied the cigarette machines of coins, collected all the other cash in the place, and said to those persons in the bar 'I'm off, help yourself to drinks', and departed. The **Falcon** remained open and unattended for at least 24 hours.

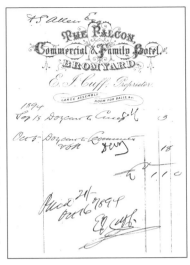

Account for a 1894 hire of a dogcart from the Falcon

When the inn was advertised for sale early in 2002 the particulars stated that it had three bars, a restaurant seating 40, a ballroom with a capacity of 200, a conference room for 60 and 8 *ensuite* letting rooms. The price of £235,000 for the freehold property and its contents seemed quite modest.

The mention of a ballroom calls attention to the assembly room at the side of the **Falcon** which made this a focal point in the town. The first mention of a Bromyard Assembly was in the *Hereford Journal* of

Outside the Falcon on an early 20th-century market day

11 October 1770. However, in this and later advertisements the place of the Assembly was not given, and it was not until 1781 that the advertisement in the *Hereford Journal* stated that it would take place at the **Falcon.** When the **Falcon** was offered for sale in 1888 the assembly room was used as a butter market and drill hall. It was also the scene of weekly dances in the 1930s and an advertisement of 17 May 1935 states that Les Preece would be performing. His name has already been met with in connection with the **Railway Inn.** At the rear of the Falcon and fronting onto Pump Street is a long building which was used as a cinema. First called the Rio, and then the Plaza, it opened in August 1948, and closed in 1963.

The Falcon in 1999 with the render stripped off.

Pump Street leads down the side of the **Falcon** and a few yards along there is the area known as Nunwell. On the opposite side of the road to the **Falcon,** on a prominent corner site, is the imposing Nunwell House. There was pub called the **Seven Stars** on this site for many years. It was bought in 1782 by one William James, and had previously been occupied by Stephen Bridges — the name of the latter occurs in the Land Tax Return of 1777. It was mortgaged for £70 in 1787, repaid in full in 1789. How long it survived as a pub is not known — the name still appears in the Land Tax Returns as late as 1812/13, but it may have been like the **Adam and Eve,** with the name continuing long after the pub closed.

CHAPTER FIVE

Bromyard
HIGH ST., CRUXWELL ST. & SHEEP ST.

After the junction with Pump Street, the name of the main street changes from Broad Street to High Street. The next pub along, on the left-hand side, is the **Bay Horse**, a fine building dating from *c.*1620. Like the **Falcon**, the façade, which is clearly two separate parts, was formerly plastered over. The original entry was from the large yard at the rear, evidence of its former use as a coaching inn. It was also noted for its connection with the turf.

The **Bay Horse** was formed by the amalgamation of two adjacent inns, both owned by the Freeman family of Gaines. On the left-hand side was the **Black Swan**, which was mentioned in a will of 1765, while on the right-hand side was the **Castle Inn**. In 1796 the **Castle Inn** was occupied by Edward Cook who paid 9s. in Land Tax. Cook was still there in 1801 when he is mentioned in a deed which refers to:

> Also all those two messuages with the appurtenances situate and being in the Town of Bromyard in the County of Hereford, then converted into one being the Castle Inn in the occupation of his tenant Edward Cook.

William Devereux appears in the 1802 Land Tax Returns as holding property in Bromyard and although not specifically named, it seems that this was when he took over the **Castle Inn** as tenant. He probably changed the name to the **Bay Horse** at this time. In June 1815 a two-day racing event was advertised to take place on Bromyard Downs on 26 and 27 July. The horses were to be shown and entered at the **Bay Horse Inn** on or before 24 July, and the entrance fee was one

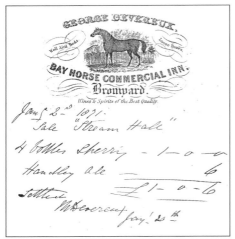

Sale prices at the Bay Horse in 1871

guinea and half-a-guinea to the clerk of the course — William Devereux of the **Bay Horse**. Devereux was still Clerk of the Course in the 1820s but by 1835 the **Bay Horse** had been taken over by Anne Devereux and by 1841 John Devereux had succeeded her.

For many years in the middle of the 19th century the landlord was George Devereux, who died in November 1878. An ostentatious monument to his memory and to those of other members of his family is just inside the Church Street entrance to the churchyard. George Devereux was noted for the stud of thoroughbred stallions that he kept. In the 1920s William Madders, an old native of

The Bay Horse in 1999

68

Bromyard, published in the *Bromyard News and Record* his reminiscences of Bromyard in the 19th century. He could remember two of the horses owned by George Devereux, Scotch-finder, which was a rich gold in colour, and Double X, which was nearly black, being paraded around the block by one Coldrick, the groom.

George Devereux's successor, a Mr. Holloway, was not successful — in 1884 W. Alkins, a butcher, applied for a licence for the **Bay Horse**, stating the pub had been conducted in a 'very improper way' by Holloway. The mention of a butcher applying for a licence for this pub is not so surprising as it may seem — there was a slaughterhouse directly to the rear. In January 1933 it was reported that the Sanitary Inspector had inspected four slaughterhouses in Bromyard, not including the one at the **Bay Horse**, which was apparently then in regular use by country people who slaughtered and sold their own meat. In 1902 the licensee, Chas. M. Evans, advertised that he had good accommodation for travellers and the best covered-in yard in the town. In recent years it was closed and neglected, but has now been restored and reopened and forms an asset to the town.

A few yards along, on the opposite side of the road and almost directly opposite New Road is the **Queen's Arms**, in the 18th century and early 19th century called the **Leopard**. It started as private residence, and it was said that about 1760 or so it was an 'old ruinous piece of building' and that a house was then erected on the site; this is incorrect and probably

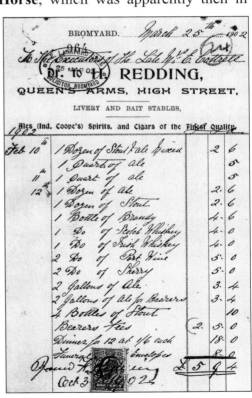

The account for a wake, held at the Queen's Arms following the death of Mrs. E. Cottrell in 1902

69

indicated that the building was re-fronted at that time. It was then used as a private residence, but about 10 years later became an inn—the **Leopard**. At this time the adjacent building just before this was called the **Bull**, and this may also have been a pub. There was also a school in a room on the first floor of the **Leopard,** kept by a Mr. Hirdman, who later built a school house on the rear of the plot, fronting on to Rowberry Street. The present entry to the rear through the **Queen's Arms** was formerly through the **Bull**.

The **Leopard** was offered for sale several times. When it was advertised in the *Hereford Journal* on 15 November 1781 as being for sale by auction at the **Falcon** on 3 December 1781, it was said to be:

> a Freehold Messuage or Tenement, situate, standing, and being in the town of Bromyard aforesaid, and used as a Publick Inn, and known by the name or sign of THE LEOPARD, together with the stable, buildings, garden, and appurtenance thereunto belonging, now in the occupation of George Morris.

In 1787 an agreement was made between James Eckley and John Lane for the sale of Leopard House, Bromyard, with its gardens and buildings and this was probably the inn. For a while the premises ceased being an inn and were used as a bakery. An advertisement in the *Hereford Journal* of 20 January 1802 stated that it was:

> lately known by the name or sign of the LEOPARD INN, but now in the possession of a person in the Baking and Malting Business.

It was for sale or to let.

In 1808 the **Leopard** was leased by Thomas Thornes of Bromyard, victualler, from George Hill of Worcester, gentleman, so it would appear that it was once again licensed premises. When the **Leopard** was advertised on 20 October 1813 the details were much more specific:

BROMYARD – HEREFORDSHIRE.
FREEHOLD INN.
TO BE SOLD BY PRIVATE CONTRACT.
All that capital and most desirable well-accustomed INN, called THE LEOPARD, in the centre of the Town of Bromyard, in the County of Hereford, being an excellent situation, and the business well established, now in the occupation of Mr. William Jones, whose term expires at Lady-day next.

The House consists of Two good Parlours, Two Kitchens, Bar and Pantry, in the ground floor; Five good Lodging Rooms on the second; and Two good Attics; Two good Cellars, Brewhouse, Scullery, Garden, and Piggery; Three substantial and convenient Brick built STABLES, fit for upwards of Thirty Horses, and every other necessary convenience.

The whole of the Premises have lately been put into complete repair, at a very considerable expense, and are well adapted for an Inn, as at present occupied, or for any Person wishing to carry on a Wholesale Wine or Liquor Trade, which is greatly wanted in and about the neighbourhood of Bromyard.

Part of the Premises, called *The School House*, are also well situate for being converted into a separate Dwelling-house, or for a Stable unconnected with the other part of the Premises.

For a view of the Premises apply to Mr. Bradford, Shoemaker, Bromyard; and for further Particulars, and to treat for the same, apply to Mr. Thomas Smith, of Tenbury, in the County of Worcester; or at the Office of Messrs. Robinson and Wheeler, Solicitors, Tenbury aforesaid.

WELLINGTON ARMS INN,
BROMYARD, HEREFORDSHIRE.
To be Sold by Auction,
By GEO. WINTON,
(Son of and Successor to G. Winton, Auctioneer, deceased),
At the FALCON INN, Bromyard, on Tuesday, the Seventeenth day of August, 1824, precisely at Four o'Clock, subject to Conditions then to be produced,
ALL the said INN, lately called THE LEOPARD, and now the WELLINGTON ARMS, in the Centre of the Town of Bromyard, and now in good Business.
The Premises have lately been repaired at considerable expense, and comprise every convenience for a Public or any other Trade, and Possession may be had at Lady-day next.
The Tenant Mr. Lewis, will show the Premises, and for further Particulars apply at the Office of Messrs. Robinson and Cowburn, Solicitors, Tenbury.

Leopard / Wellington sale in 1824 from The Hereford Journal

Subsequently the pub was owned by a Mr. R. Evans whose name appeared in 1818/19. By 1819/20 it was still called the **Leopard**, but the ownership had changed to a Mr. Robinson — no doubt the solicitor mentioned above. By 1822/23 the tenant was Thomas Lewis, and the name had been changed to the **Wellington Arms**. When the property was advertised for sale by auction at the **Falcon Inn** on 17 August 1824 it was stated that it was 'lately called The Leopard, and now the Wellington Arms …'.

This sale by auction was apparently unsuccessful and the property was later bought privately by Henry Tomkins, and the Land Tax Return for 1828 shows that he was running the **Wellington Arms** himself. It may well be that the Thomas Lewis from the **Wellington Arms** was the person of the same name who took over the **Crown and Sceptre** at this time. Tomkins later changed the name from the **Wellington Arms** to the **Grey's Arms,** another version of the name being the **Earl**

BROMYARD.

TO BE SOLD BY AUCTION, BY

BENTLEY, HOBBS & MYTTON

At The Queens Arms, Bromyard,

On TUESDAY, 5th JULY, 1921,

AT 3 P.M.

THE WELL-FREQUENTED OLD-ESTABLISHED FULLY-LICENSED
FREEHOLD COMMERCIAL INN AND MARKET HOUSE,

Known as

"The Queen's Arms,"

With extensive Stabling, Yard and Offices, situate in High Street, in the centre of the Market Town of Bromyard and extending to Rowberry Street, within a few minutes' walk of the Railway Station and Cattle Market, at present let to Messrs. IND, COOPE AND COMPANY LIMITED, on lease expiring 29th September, 1921.

The Accommodation comprises, on the Ground Floor:—Entrance Passage; Front Bar with Bay Window 21ft. x 12ft. 9in., with Fireplace and Cupboard enclosed Folding Doors; Smoke Room with Bay Window 21ft. x 7ft. 9in. with Fireplace; Back Passage with Wine Cellar; Tap Room 14ft. 9in. x 9ft. 3in. with oven grate; Sitting Room 14ft. 6in. x 10ft. 10in. with two Cupboards enclosed Folding Doors and Shelves over and Fireplace; Old Bar with two Cupboards enclosed Folding Doors; Larder with Shelves; Kitchen with Range, having Sink with Tap of Water over, Double Cupboard enclosed Folding Doors and Plate Shelves; Wash House and W.C.; Large Store Room about 17ft. 5in. x 17ft. 5in.

On the 1st Floor.—Club Room 29ft. 2in. x 19ft. 4in., having one side panelled with old oak with handsomely carved frieze and two antique firegrates; Anti Room adjoining; Two Back Bedrooms with Fireplaces; and Box Room.

On the 2nd Floor:—Two Front Bedrooms with several pieces of Old Oak panelling and Small Cupboard; and two small Back Bedrooms.

The SPACIOUS YARD has two approaches from High Street and Rowberry Street and comprises Lean-to Store Shed; Stable to tie Eight Horses with Loft over; two-stall Stable with Loft over; Stable to tie 14 Horses with Loft over; and usual appurtenances.

THIS PROPERTY is situate in a good position in the centre of the Market Town of Bromyard, and is well worthy of the attention of Brewers, Licensed Victuallers and Capitalists, having a frontage to High Street of about 30ft. 6in. with Driving Way to Back Yard, and extending to Rowberry Street at which there is a Frontage of about 33ft. 6in.

Town Water and Gas laid on.

The Lessees claim certain fixtures—a list will be supplied at the sale.

Sale of the Queen's Arms in 1921

Grey, which appeared in a directory of 1835. This is a reference to the second Earl Grey who was Prime Minister from 1830 until 1834, during which period Wilberforce's Act abolishing the African slave trade went through Parliament.

In 1833 Henry Tomkins closed the entry at the side of the **Grey's Arms**, and advice was taken from counsel about the legality of this. Depositions were taken from a number of elderly residents and from these the history of the building in the 1760s can be deduced. It also shows how hearsay evidence can be unreliable. In this case part of the evidence gathered stated that the premises were unsuccessfully offered for sale by auction in about 1819 or 1820, when notice of the right of way was given by the vendor, a Mr. Robinson—actually, the unsuccessful sale was in 1824, and a check of the *Hereford Journal* for the period 1819-22 shows that the pub was not offered for sale in that period. The statements showed that when the entry was constructed it was used as a means of going to church. Memories inevitably varied, but it seems that the entry was open during the day but was usually closed at

night. The outcome was not recorded, but the entry remained open.

The name had been changed to the **Queen's Arms** by 1851, when George Morris, victualler, held the pub, the fifth name for the pub in less than 50 years. It is most likely that the queen referred to was the young Queen Victoria. George Morris's widow still held the pub in 1858.

Despite all the changes of name, the entry at the side was still known as the 'Leopard entry' in the first part of the 20th century. In the *Bromyard News*

The Queen's Arms in 1999

An early 1970s advert for the Queen's Arms

and Record of 30 December 1915 it was reported that the entry had been closed for a day to indicate private ownership. There were changes in ownership in the early years of the 20th century. As a result of the bankruptcy of Edward King, the landlord, in 1906, the pub was sold and a tenancy granted to Ind Coope & Co. The lease expired in September 1921 and the property was put up for auction again. In 1941 the licensee was Edward Oakley.

In 1969, when John Tate was in charge, the *Hereford Guide* sang its praises, commenting on the specialities of roast duck and steak portugais or rossini. The inn prided itself on good English cooking and 'eschews hot cupboards and reheating of food'. Clearly this was well before the microwave oven came into general use!

Early in the 21st century the pub was closed, awaiting a new tenant, but it reopened under new management at the end of May 2002. Another half-timbered building but with a more recent front, it was built in the late 16th century and has a contemporary staircase with round newel post and steps.

Making a slight detour up the not-so-new New Road, on the corner with Little Hereford Street is the **Rose and Lion**, which seems to have been established after 1835, and was a beer house under the 1830 Act. In 1851 the landlord was Joseph Partridge, described in the census as a beer-shop keeper, aged 32, from Cradley. He was still there in 1861, while just along the road lived Elizabeth Cropp, described as an 'Innkeeper, (out of business)'. By 1867 Elizabeth Cropp was at the **Lion** in New Road, and this seems to refer to this pub, but she was not there long as she bought the **Bell Inn** in the following year. She was succeeded at the **Rose and Lion** by Henry Lane, who was also a wholesale fruit dealer and a carrier to Worcester. By 1877 John Edward Turbill had taken over and in November 1905 he complained to the Bromyard

74

Urban District Council that the new main drain constructed near his property had damaged the foundation of his house. A committee was formed (in the usual local authority manner!) and this reported back to the U.D.C. that it was because Mr. Turbill did not have his property properly spouted that had caused the damage, rather than the new drain.

In 1918 Mr. Turbill put the pub up for auction and in the advertisement it was described as 'a noted and old-established Inn'. At the auction it was bought by Mr. W. James, a builder and contractor, for £625, but he seems to have sold it on to Harper Hitchmans Ltd. of Lowesmore Brewery, Worcester. George Royall took over as tenant and on 1 May 1918 Mr. Turbill made over his interest in the licence to him. A tenancy agreement between George Royall and Harper Hitchmans Ltd. was dated 24 June 1918, and provided for a rent of £20 per year. In 1921 (and perhaps before) a market licence was obtained allowing the pub to remain open all day on Thursdays.

It seems to have been during George Royall's tenancy that the custom of having a coach outing for regulars of the pub began, and on those occasions plenty of liquid refreshment was taken—the stoneware bottles and jars which were used still survive. The outings continued

A coach outing from the Rose and Lion in 1933

75

FINANCE (1909-10) ACT, 1910.

No. 354.

N⁰ 18266

ENGLAND AND WALES.

BEER AND WINE RETAILER'S ON LICENCE AND TOBACCO LICENCE.

[stamp: COLLECTOR OF CUSTOMS & EXCISE — CUSTOM HOUSE — 2 OCT 1934 — NEWPORT, MON.]

.... *New Port Mon* .... Collection. *Loss 6/40*

I, the undersigned, duly authorized by the Commissioners of Customs and Excise, hereby grant Licence to *Henry Reginald Starwright*

to exercise and carry on the trades or businesses undermentioned at premises situate at* *Rose & Lion Inn New Road*

in the Parish of *Bromyard*   in the

County of *Hereford*

from the date hereof, until and including the Thirtieth day of September next ensuing,   he having paid for this Licence, being† *an ordinary* Licence, the undermentioned Duties :—

	£	s.	d.
Retailer of Beer for consumption on or off the premises	10	,,	,,
Retailer of Wine for consumption on or off the premises	6	,,	,,
Dealer in Tobacco	,,	5	3
Compensation Levy under the Licensing (Consolidation) Act, 1910	1	10	,,
Total ...£	17	15	3

Dated the *17* day of *October* 193*4.*

.... *J. S. Dawson.* ....

Collector of Customs and Excise.

A person holding the Licence to be taken out by a Retailer of Beer may sell Cider and Perry, as well as Beer.

A person holding a Licence to be taken out by a retailer of Wine may sell by retail Sweets as well as Wine.

" Wine " means imported wine.   " Sweets " includes British Wines, Made Wines, Mead and Metheglin.

Wt12669/52   203 Bks   6/33   W. H. & S.   125/264   [OVER.

This 1934 licence to sell wines and tobacco for consumption on and off the premises at the Rose and Lion cost £17 15s. 3d. for 12 months when the **Rose and Lion** was taken over in 1932 by Henry Ronald Hartwright, a member of a well-known local family and the son-in-law of George Royall.

In 1934 wine and tobacco was added to the beer and cider licence —by definition a wine licence allowed the licensee to sell 'sweets', which included British wines, 'made' wines, mead and metheglin. Curiously, during the paperwork for this addition to the licence, it was stated that the owner of the premises was John Edward Turbill, who had sold the property about 16 years before. In 1936 Mr. Hartwright applied to the Shropshire, Worcestershire & Staffordshire Electric Power Company for an electricity supply to be connected to the **Rose and Lion**, this supply to be for two electric lamps of 50 watts each!

Along the New Road frontage of the property is a stone wall, at present capped by a row of stones set on edge, but previously there used to be one section where the top of the wall was flat. Formerly barrels were collected from Bromyard station, and these used to be hauled up through the town by a drayman. It was customary for the drayman to give the horses a breather outside the **Rose and Lion**, but as the drayman could not leave his horses, he stopped by the flat-topped section of wall where Mr. Hartwright would serve him.

After the outbreak of war in 1939 the **Rose and Lion** was registered as a catering establishment. Mr. Hartwright was called up for military service in 1943 and the licence was transferred to his wife, Mrs. Ivy Lizzie Hartwright, but was transferred back to him in 1946 after his discharge.

Registration No. CR 20.

FOOD CONTROL.

CERTIFICATE OF REGISTRATION

Catering and Residential Establishments and Institutions.

The Food Control Committee for the district of

BROMYARD AREA.

hereby certify that

" Rose & Lion " [H.B. HARTWRIGHT]

New Road

Bromyard

has been duly registered as

A Catering Establishment

Signed on behalf of the

BROMYARD AREA. Food Control Committee.

Signature John W. Jackson
Food Executive Officer

Date 27 NOV 1939

The Rose and Lion was registered as a catering establishment in November 1939

THE SHROPSHIRE, WORCESTERSHIRE & STAFFORDSHIRE ELECTRIC POWER COMPANY.

CENTRAL OFFICE:
MUCKLOW HILL, HALESOWEN.
NR. BIRMINGHAM.
TEL. No.
WOODGATE 2271.

DISTRICT OFFICE:
New Street, LEDBURY.

Bromyard and Ledbury Rural Electricity Special Order, 19

THIS PORTION
TO BE RETAINED
BY APPLICANT

F.R.

APPLICATION FOR SUPPLY OF ELECTRICITY.

Full Name of Applicant (Block Letters)....*MR HENRY KENALD HAINTWRIGHT*....
(State whether Mr., Mrs., or Miss.)

I hereby request the Company to provide a Supply of Electricity (herein called "the Supply") to the premises named below of which I am the owner and/or occupier. Upon the Company commencing the works necessary to make the Supply available to me or where no further works are necessary upon the commencement of the Supply a contract shall thereby be concluded between the Company and myself (hereinafter called "the Consumer") **on the Terms and Conditions here following and as set out on the back hereof,** but the Company shall not be bound to provide the Supply until expiry of a reasonable time from the date hereof.

I hereby agree to make payment in respect of the Supply in accordance with the published Flat Rate Tariff for the time being in force under the above-mentioned Act or Order and as respectively charged by the Company for Domestic, Office, Shop and/or other purposes in the district in which the premises named below are situate. I also hereby agree to pay, if required by the Company, and whether or not the Supply is taken (a) the appropriate meter rent for meter(s) hired from the Company and (b) either the periodic charge embodied in the appropriate published tariff for the time being in force (not exceeding the maximum quarterly charge enforceable under the said Act or Order) or a sum of...........................per annum whichever shall be the greater.

The Supply is desired in respect of the installation described in the Schedule hereto which shall be deemed to declare the maximum power required, and I agree to give reasonable notice before connecting any additional apparatus.

Date.................193

Applicant's usual Signature...................

Occupation of Applicant...................

Witness to above Signature...................

Address of Witness...................

Address of Premises to be supplied...................

Description of Premises to be supplied ....

Date supply desired.................193

Wiring Contractor's Name and Address..... THE SHROPSHIRE, WORCESTERSHIRE AND STAFFORDSHIRE ELECTRIC POWER CO.

SCHEDULE OF INSTALLATION.

	No. to be installed.	Total Watts or H.P.	Rate Number and/or Tariff Selected.
LAMPS	2.	50 watt	F 1 A — 3
HEATERS			
COOKERS			
WATER HEATERS			
MOTORS			
OTHER APPARATUS, VIZ.—			

The Company's Tariff Leaflet gives tariffs in operation and rate numbers.

The declared system and constant voltage of the Supply are as follows:
Alternating current 50 cycles either (a) 3-phase 4-wire at a pressure of 400/230 volts or (b) single-phase 2-wire at a pressure of 230 volts. The neutral wire is in all cases earthed.

It is apparent that the landlord of the Rose and Lion in 1936 did not really trust electricity. His application was for a supply sufficient for two 50 watt bulbs only

There is little change to the Rose and Lion from this photo of the 1960s

There was, of course, a gradual increase in the annual rent and in 1961 it was raised from £52 to £80. After the death of Mr. Hartwright in 1965, his widow carried on until her death in 1975. By this time the **Rose and Lion** was owned by Bass Ltd. of Burton-on-Trent.

Just up the road from the **Rose and Lion** is the fire station. During the Hartwrights' time the firemen used to practise on a Thursday night and then retire to the **Rose and Lion** for bread and cheese, washed down with a couple of pints. One night, while they were taking their refreshment, the siren sounded, warning of a fire. All except one of the firemen immediately rushed out of the bar, leaving Bert Berry finishing his pint. When asked why he hadn't gone, he replied that it was OK—they would have to wait for him because he was the driver!

A later tenant of the **Rose and Lion**, Fran Herdman, made a story in the *Hereford Times* in January 1997. It was reported that the pub had been bought by Peter Amor, owner of the Wye Valley Brewery, and that in order to protect the garden from development he was letting it out for an annual rent of 1lb. of parsnips, grown in the garden, to be paid in December each year. Early in 2001 her daughter Phillipa took over the tenancy and within 12 months the pub had won the award of Herefordshire Pub of the Year 2001, an award made by the

Campaign for Real Ale (CAMRA). A certificate for this award was presented in January 2002.

New Road seems to have had a good reputation. In May 1915 the *Bromyard News and Record* reported the opening of the Picturedrome in New Road, describing it as 'The fashionable quarter of Bromyard'. This early cinema had tip-up seats and electric light. Stalls were 1s., second seats 6d. and (ordinary) seats 3d.

Returning to the High Street, on the left-hand side was the Central Temperance Hotel. This seems to have been established in the later 19th century but by 1902 it was being advertised as the Central Dining Rooms—'Hot dinners on Market days. Good accommodation for cyclists and commercials'.

Next door was the **King's Arms**. The front of the building has been largely refaced, but behind this the front block dates from the early 17th century, and the south-eastern part is about 100 years older. A pub for many years, in 1733 it was mortgaged for £260. It was described in an indenture dated 7 October 1745 as: 'All that messuage, Mansion house, tenement or burgage, commonly called or known by the name of the Kings Arms, being in the town or burrough of Bromyard, in a street called the High Street or Beast Market.' As this suggests, this part of High Street was used as a cattle market. Towards the end of the century the **King's Arms** was held for many years by Mrs. Joyce Taylor. In the *Hereford Journal* of 9 March 1796 Joyce Taylor advertised that, unless it was claimed, a brown 'Poney' which had been left at the **King's Arms** would be sold to pay expenses. After her death the pub was taken over by her daughter, as the following advertisement from the *Hereford Journal* of 11 December 1799 shows:

KING'S ARMS, BROMYARD

The Public are most respectfully informed, That the KING'S-ARMS, in Bromyard, so many years kept by the late Mrs. JOYCE TAYLOR, deceased, will continue to be kept by her Daughter MARY BRAY, who will make it the study of her life to procure the best Liquors and Provisions of every kind; and having provided good Beds and Stabling, she humbly hopes for the continuance of the Favours of her Friends and the Public in general, which it will be her constant study to merit.

Dec. 10 1799.

PARTICULARS.

The well-frequented, old-established, FREE and FULL-LICENSED FREEHOLD

COMMERCIAL AND MARKET HOUSE

KNOWN AS

"The King's Arms,"

TO BE SOLD BY AUCTION BY

BENTLEY, HOBBS & MYTTON

At the King's Arms, Bromyard,

On Thursday, 31st October, 1907,

At **2-30** for **3-30** p.m. punctually, by direction of the Executors of the late Mrs. ANN PARTRIDGE.

The Accommodation comprises—ON THE GROUND FLOOR: Capital large Bar, Dining Room, 22ft. by 12ft. 4in., Commercial Room 17ft. by 11ft., Back Parlour, Tap Room with Fire Place, Kitchen with Range and Sink, Pantry with Store Room over and Coal House.

ON THE FIRST FLOOR: Large Front Dining Room with bay window, 25ft. by 16ft. 8in., and 4 Bedrooms.

ON THE SECOND FLOOR: 6 Bedrooms.

IN THE BASEMENT: Large Wine and Beer Cellars.

THE SPACIOUS YARD has two approaches, from Cruxwell Street and the New Road, and comprises BREWHOUSE with Two Furnaces and large Soft-water Tank, WASHING HOUSE with Furnace and Sink, extensive range of STABLING, 2 LOOSE BOXES with SADDLE ROOM and Loft over, Lean to Shed, Pigstye and Offices, Pump and good Supply of Water.

There is a LARGE KITCHEN GARDEN planted with Apple, Pear and Plum Trees, Poultry House with wire run, Pigstye and Offices.

THE PROPERTY is situate in a good position in the centre of the MARKET TOWN of BROMYARD, and is well worthy the attention of BREWERS, LICENSED VICTUALLERS and CAPITALISTS, a most LUCRATIVE BUSINESS having been carried on by the late Mr. and Mrs. Partridge for nearly FIFTY YEARS, and is now sold owing to their decease.

THE BUSINESS is being carried on by the Executors of the late Mrs. Partridge. POSSES-SION WILL BE GIVEN ON COMPLETION OF THE PURCHASE.

The Purchaser will be required to take to all Trade and other Fixtures and Fittings, Stock-in-Trade, proportion of the Licenses, Assessments and other Payments at a valuation to be made in the usual way.

Sale of the King's Arms in 1907

In 1812/13 the **King's Arms** was owned and run by Philip Bray, who later let it out. Philip Bray sold the inn for £1,000 in 1819 and it seems to have been as a result of this that the tenant, William Wells, was given notice to quit. The sale by auction of his household furniture was advertised in the *Hereford Journal* of 31 March 1819 and the large amount of furniture indicates that he was in a good way of business. The **King's Arms** was bought by William Baggott, who ran it for many years. He died on 4 August 1856 and in his will he left a property in the Market Square, which he had inherited from James Baggott, to his nephew William Baggott of Manchester. The year before William Baggott died the **King's Arms** had been sold for £805, and it was sold again for the same price in 1858. In 1890 it was bought by Joseph Partridge, the licensee, for £1,200. He may have been the publican of the same name who was formerly at the **Rose and Lion**. His widow, Mrs. Ann Partridge, was licensee in 1902, and after her death in 1907 the property was sold by auction. The property was again offered for sale by the local auctioneers Bentley, Hobbs and Mytton in 1913, but was withdrawn at £2,050. In 1920, when it was offered for sale yet again, it fetched £2,400.

On 18 January 1923 the *Bromyard News and Record* reported that electric lighting was being installed in Bromyard, and that a wireless was being installed in the **King's Arms** for the benefit of the customers.

The large yard at the rear, now used as a car park, was being used as a poultry and produce market before the Second World War. This thriving market had superceded

The King's Arms in 1999

82

the old custom of selling produce in Broad Street. At the beginning of the war, when Mrs. Florence Emily Pengelly was licensee, it had some unusual inhabitants. In the 1930s there was a circus owned by Miss Ada Chapman which, at the beginning of the war, she moved *en masse* to Bromyard. The elephants were housed initially in the yard behind the **King's Arms** but were also used on the land at The Tack Farm, Edwyn Ralph. Security was not good behind the **King's Arms** and the elephants used to get out and roam through the High Street, stealing cakes and other goods. A Mrs. Lock had clothes eaten from her washing line and, clothes being rationed, she had difficulty explaining the circumstances to the authorities in order to get the necessary coupons to replace them. Old inhabitants of Bromyard still remember the elephants being taken down to water in the river by Petty Bridge, where there was a watering place, now covered and fenced off, by Linton Park. Unfortunately the elephants died during their first winter in Bromyard. One died in the corrugated iron building that housed the market and the body stiffened up before it was removed, necessitating it being dismembered before it could be extracted. The market itself continued during the war but on a reduced scale, with a good demand for rabbits and poultry. It expanded again after the war. However, in 1969 there were objections from some of the town's tradespeople about the Thursday open-air market and as a consequence it was closed.

Next door but one to the **King's Arms**, in the premises now used as a butcher's shop, was a pub called the **Green Dragon**. In 1777 it was owned by William Madders, but it may not have outlasted the 18th century. A deed of 1835 referred to it as 'formerly known as the Green Dragon' and so it had certainly closed by this time. Evidence relating to a pub called the **(Green) Dragon** in the 19th century almost certainly relates to the later pub of the same name (described below).

At the top of High Street, Cruxwell Street forms the cross-piece of the junction, referred to by old inhabitants as 'Top of the Town'. To the right was another pub called the **Green Dragon**, the name no doubt being taken from its predecessor in High Street. In 1812/3 William Gard(i)ner (the name is spelled various ways) owned and ran an establishment called the '**Draggon**', referred to later as the **Green Dragon**. Within a few years William Gardner was letting the pub, in the early 1820s, to Henry Tomkins, and a cross-check with directories

BROMYARD.

IMPORTANT TO BREWERS, WINE AND SPIRIT MERCHANTS, AND OTHERS.

MR. GEORGE GREEN

Is instructed to SELL by AUCTION,

On THURSDAY, the 14th day of APRIL next, 1881, ·

AT THE DRAGON INN, BROMYARD,

At THREE o'clock in the Afternoon, subject to Conditions;

THE FOLLOWING

Freehold & Leasehold Property.

LOT 1.

All that old-established and full-licensed Inn and Premises, with large and productive Garden attached, called

"THE DRAGON INN AND VAULTS,"

situate in Cruxwell Street, in the Town of BROMYARD, and for some years in the occupation of the present Tenant, Mr. WILLIAM PRICE.

LOT 2.

A pleasantly-situated and substantially-built

DWELLING-HOUSE,

With a GARDEN attached, situate in Church Street, Bromyard, now in the occupation of Mr. JAMES HARRELL.

LOT 3.

AN EQUALLY DESIRABLE DWELLING-HOUSE,

With GARDEN attached, adjoining Lot 2, for some years in the occupation of the present Tenant, Mr. THOMAS REDDING.

Lot 1 is FREEHOLD; *Lots 2 and 3 are* LEASEHOLD *for the residue of a term of 200 years. Lot 1 is excellently situated for a good out-door business; and Lots 2 and 3 are suitable for a retired couple or small family, being in a very dry and healthy situation, fronting Church-street, and close to the Church and Railway Station.*

For further particulars apply to the AUCTIONEER, Hardwicke House, Bromyard; or to Mr. E. LASHFORD CAVE, Solicitor, Bromyard.

Sale of the Dragon and two dwelling-houses in 1881

shows that Tomkins called it the **Unicorn**, but when it was tenanted by John Harris, and Elizabeth Harris by 1835 it had reverted to the **Green Dragon**. In 1850 it was run by William Gard(i)ner, of a later generation, as the 1851 census shows that he was aged 32 and had been born at Martley. At that time, Elizabeth Harris, then aged 72, was living in retirement further up Sheep Street.

On 14 April 1881 the pub was sold by auction on the premises. At that time it was called **The Dragon Inn and Vaults**, and the tenant was Mr. William Price who had been there for a number of years. When it was advertised as being to let in the *Bromyard News and Record* in October 1901 the licensing valuation was stated to be £130, there was stabling for 14 horses and there were wheelwright, smiths and paint shops—all for a rent of £29 *per annum*. Henry Andrews, a carpenter, took it over. In 1960 this was one of the Spreckley Bros. pubs taken over by the Cheltenham and Hereford Brewery which then sold it on to Bromyard R.D.C. It was then demolished and the site used as part of a car park.

---

12. BROMYARD—GREEN DRAGON INN.

ALL THAT messuage or dwellinghouse called The Green Dragon Inn (formerly called The Dragon Inn) with the buildings yard garden and appurtenances thereto adjoining and belonging situate on the North side of Cruxwell Street in the Town of Bromyard in the County of Hereford.

Spreckley Bros. sale of the Green Dragon in 1960

Adjacent to the **Green Dragon** on the east side was the Victoria Café and Hotel. This was built in 1889 by a Mr. Phipp to provide good food and drink—of a temperance type, however, and so it was not a licensed premises. It is better known to older residents of Bromyard as The Dairy.

Close to the **Green Dragon** and looking down the High Street was Angel Place, where then is said to have been a pub, and although this is quite likely, if this was so then it was a very long time ago. No firm evidence has so far come to light. There were two houses, of different sizes, one being larger because of rooms over a driving way that led to a yard at the rear where there was a separate blacksmith's shop. There was another house between the driving way and the

Green Dragon. The buildings on the site were demolished in 1957 to make way for a car park. Later the whole area, including the site of the **Green Dragon**, was developed as the Leisure Centre, which was opened in October 1991. There is a fully licensed bar in the Leisure Centre, so all is not entirely lost.

The other pub in Cruxwell Street is the **White Horse**, on the corner of Cruxwell Street and the Tenbury Road, in 2002 closed and shuttered up, and for sale for redevelopment. Compilers of trade directories in the 19th century couldn't make up their minds whether it was in Cruxwell Street or in Sheep Street (the continuation of Cruxwell Street). The 18th-century brick front hides a 17th-century building, and it may be this building that was referred to in a deed of 1669, when Ann Capper, a widow, made over the **White Horse** to her son Edward Capper of Bromyard, a slaughterman, and Rebecka his wife. Christopher Capper, of the same family, was bailiff of the town in 1678.

Sheep Street was so named because, during markets and fairs, sheep that were being offered for sale were penned up here, the hurdles used for this being stored in the **White Horse** yard when not in use. By 1818/19 Edward Harris was the tenant, and he held the

A late 19th-century photograph of Sheep Street
with the White Horse on the right

The boarded-up White Horse in 1999, with its sign (below) still swinging

licence through the 1820s, although he was only the tenant. Joseph Harris had taken over by 1835, while Edward Wilkinson, a local man, had taken over by 1850. Pigott's *Directory* records that in the 1830s waggons conveying goods to London, Presteigne and Rhayader, and Worcester, all left from the **White Horse** at varying times during the week. In 1867 the landlord, Mark James Hodnette, was also listed as a grazier and hence had connections with the stock trade. This sale of stock in the street continued until towards the end of the 19th century, when the stock sales were removed from the streets and held in the large yard at the rear of the **White Horse**. Earlier in the century this yard would have been used as a base for the carriers on this side of the town. Mrs. Jane Ann Park was here in 1902. The extensive range of stables to the rear of the **White Horse** were demolished after the closure of the market in the 1960s.

A short way along the Tenbury road and off to the left was **Ballhurst**, where there was a cider house. In June 1900 the licence was transferred from Mrs. Payne to William Harris who was described in 1902 as a farmer. It still had a cider licence in 1926 when the tenancy of the smallholding and cider house was taken over by W.E. Williams of Stanford Bishop. The land has since provided a better cash crop in the form of houses.

Sheep Street, in former days, was the unhealthiest part of the town. When Benjamin Babbage visited Bromyard in 1850 to report back to the General Board of Health about the sanitary state of the town, he was told that, in the previous two years, there had been 27 deaths from typhus in Sheep Street. Rising up the floor of a valley, all the water naturally flowed downwards into a drain along the centre of the street. Not only this, but the sewage from the privies of the houses lining the street emptied into the drain, and when the drain overflowed this was only too evident.

Despite this generally insanitary state, at the time there were at least two pubs in Sheep Street. One of these was called the **Royal Oak**. In 1673 a house of this name was bought by one Stephen Northern who immediately passed it on to his son John Northern. In 1692/3 this was in the ownership of Edward Clarke and John Northern, then described as being of St. Martin's in the Field, Co. Middlesex, who appointed William Beck of Bromyard, an ironmonger, to collect the rent. A year later John Northern sold 'that messuage known by the sign of the Royal Oak' for £100. The last mention in this series of documents is in 1701, and there is no mention of such a pub in the Land Tax Returns, so it is impossible to connect the early **Royal Oak** with its later successor (and indeed, it is thought that the early **Royal Oak** was probably in the High Street).

There is nothing further until 1846, when Richard Rogers insured the **Royal Oak** at Bromyard with the Birmingham Fire Office Company for £200 at a total premium of 13s. The special conditions in the contract stipulated 'having no Oils Gunpowder Lucifer Matches or other hazardous Goods deposited therein. Brick and Timber built and Tiled. Two Hundred Pounds'. In the 1851 census Richard Rogers was recorded as the landlord of a beershop in Sheep Street called the **Royal Oak**, while in a trade directory of 1858 he was described as a shopkeeper. The premises were located on the upper corner of the entrance to the **King's Arms** yard, in the premises now occupied by a printer's business — the upper corner was in Sheep Street, the lower corner in Cruxwell Street.

Angel Place from the High Street before its demolition in 1957

Richard Rogers may have subsequently moved premises, as in 1867 there was a publican of the same name at the **Crown and Sceptre**. In that same year the **Royal Oak** was held by George Tarbath, the father of the James Tarbath who later held the **Lion**. As well as being a grocer and provision dealer, George Tarbath was also a carrier to Worcester. The pub probably closed soon after this.

The other pub in Sheep Street was the **Apple Tree**, held in 1851 by Richard Reynolds, and this was probably short-lived also. Its location is not at present known, except that it was on the opposite side of the street to the **Royal Oak**.

Finally, there are three other pubs that have not been located, and it is possible that one of them was in Angel Place. In 1822 there was a pub somewhere in Bromyard called the **King's Head**, run by Thomas Fowles. This was not a mistake for the **King's Arms** as this appears in the same directory, and the only other reference is in the Land Tax Return for 1822/3, when 6s. was paid on the property.

A longer surviving establishment was the **Hare and Hounds**, assumed to be a pub because of its name. It is mentioned in the Land Tax Return of 1777 and up to the return for 1817 and then no more. Latterly it paid a tax of 8s. and so was a substantial building.

However, there is no reason to think that it was an earlier name for another pub.

A property that only paid 2s. in Land Tax in 1818/9 was called the **Sun**, again very suggestive of licensed premises. This is confirmed by the fact that the occupier was William Baggott, who bought the **King's Arms** in 1819. In 1824/5 James Baggott was at the **Sun**, presumably moving there after his money troubles, and then it is mentioned no more.

CHAPTER SIX

Pubs around Bromyard

WESTWARDS ALONG THE A44

Bromyard is a natural centre for its area, and the roads radiating from it were developed by the Turnpike Act of 1752 which set up the Bromyard Turnpike Trust. This had responsibility for the roads for a radius of about 4 miles from Bromyard except for the road between Bromyard to Hereford, which was already covered by the 1730 Hereford Turnpike Act.

To the west the turnpike road from Bromyard headed for Leominster — now the A44 — although the road towards Bredenbury has since been realigned and straightened. Bredenbury is the first village reached, and on the right is Bredenbury church, rebuilt on a new site and rededicated in 1877. Beyond the church, about four miles from Bromyard and on the right-hand side of the road is the **Barneby Arms**, formerly known as the **New Inn**. The **New Inn** is marked on Isaac Taylor's map of the county, first published in 1758. The *Hereford Journal* of 1 January 1794 carried an advertisement stating that the freehold estate, called the **New Inn**, which included about 30 acres and which was then in the possession of Richard Smith, was to be sold by auction at the **Falcon Inn**, Bromyard, on 30 January 1794. What happened is not clear, but on 8 November 1797 a farm called Little Wacton was advertised as being for sale by private contract:

> And also, all that other Freehold Messuage, Farm and Lands, called or known by the name of the NEW HOUSE, or NEW-INN, late in the possession of Giles Herring, adjoining the above-mentioned Farm, containing Thirty-six statute Acres (be the same more or less), of Arable, Meadow, and Pasture Land, Orcharding, and Hop-Ground.

The Dwelling-house, which is a substantial Brick Building, is situate near to the turnpike-road leading from Bromyard to Leominster, and now occupied as a Public-House, in a good run of business.

However, the position of the **New Inn** as marked on Taylor's map is slightly further along than the present establishment, and corresponds with the position of Old New Inn Farm on Bryant's map of 1835, which shows the **New Inn** on its present site. Clearly the licence had been transferred, probably in the early 19th century. By 1851 the inn was in the hands of Philip Watkins who also kept a shop. In November 1851 he was fined 7s. with 9s. 6d. expenses for having three defective weights. He was evidently a busy man, as he was described in a directory of the same year as a victualler, farmer, carpenter and joiner. How well the various businesses flourished is open to some doubt, as in 1867 he was described as a brickmaker. Shortly afterwards the inn was taken over by James Addyman, who had spent more than 20 years in the Royal Marines travelling to many places in the British Empire. In 1879 he started a grocery business in the Square in Bromyard, a business that continued in the hands of various members of the family until it was sold in 1975.

He continued at the **New Inn** for some years after starting his business in Bromyard, but in 1882, still during his tenure, it was

The New Inn at Bredenbury early in the 20th century

Anno vicesimo quinto

Georgii II. Regis.

An Act for repairing the several Roads leading from the Town of *Bromyard,* in the County of *Hereford,* to the several Places called the *Halfway Ash,* in the Parish of *Docklow, Herefordshire Lake* in the Parish of *Whitburne, Perry Bridge* in the Parish of *Stoke Blifs,* leading through the several Parishes of *Edwin, Ralph, Collington,* and the Hamlet of *Little Kyre, Sapey Wood* in the Parish of *Upper Sapey, Bishop's Froome, Wooferwood Gate,* and *Herefordshire Lake,* in the said Parish of *Bromyard,* in the Counties of *Hereford* and *Worcester.*

ᴴᴱᴿᴱᴬˢ the several Roads Preamble. hereafter particularly mentioned; that is to say, From the Town of Bromyard, in the County of Hereford, to a Place called the Halfway Ash, in the Parish of Docklow, being Four Miles, or thereabouts; and to a Place called Herefordshire Lake, in the Parish of Whitburne, being Four Miles, or thereabouts; and to a Place called Perry Bridge, in the Parish of Stoke Blifs, leading through the several Parishes of Edwin, Ralph, and Collington,

14 L 2

The Bromyard Road Repair Act

bought and turned into a coffee house, together with a butcher's shop and grocery, by several local magistrates, including W.H. Barneby of the well-known local family. In 1885 it was referred to as the 'New Inn Hotel & Grocery & Provision Co. (James Addyman, manager)', and in similar terms in 1891. By 1902 Sergeant Robert Carr was the manager. In 1940 John Martin, the proprietor, still kept the **New Inn** stores, and at that time the St. Andrew's Lodge of Oddfellows met at the **New Inn**. The name was changed to the **Barneby Arms** in about 1970, the name being taken from the well-known local family.

A short distance after the **Barneby Arms** the road passes through the parish of Grendon Bishop where in 1851, Thomas Busk, who supplemented his trade as a boot and shoemaker, and Thomas Carter were both selling cider. This was probably in the settlement called Grendon Green.

Half-a-mile further on was formerly a tollhouse and gate at Billfield, where a near tragedy took place in 1828. The *Hereford Journal* of 22 October reported:

An accident of alarming, but, happily, of no very serious nature, occurred on the Leominster to Kington mail, on Monday sen'night, when descending the steep pitch approaching the Blithfield [Billfield] turnpike, between Bromyard and Leominster, one of the horses proved refractory, and the driver (not the regular coachman, who is unwell) from no want of skill or care, was unable to clear the gate, consequently the splinter bar caught the post. The concussion was so great that the pole was wrenched out, the traces snapped, and the horses completely detached from the carriage. The coachman, and three out of the four passengers, were unseated; the former, and one of the latter (a female) only were hurt, and they, fortunately, but slightly. The guard, perceiving the danger, had got down before the shock. The horses went on the pole etc. to the next gate, where, we understand, one of them fell, and was so much lacerated that it is expected it might be destroyed.

The next gate was at Half Ash in Docklow, where the Bromyard turnpike met the turnpike from Leominster which had been built after the Leominster Turnpike Trust had been set up in 1728. Neither of the toll-houses survive. It is not really surprising that there is a pub at Docklow, although the centre is about a mile past the toll bar. This was, and still is called the **King's Head,** and in 1858 it was held by Joseph Wood, who was also a blacksmith and agricultural implement maker. By 1867 the business, including the blacksmithing, was being run by his widow, Mrs. Elizabeth Wood. In 1891 the landlord was Ernest William Smith, and in 1940 it was Mrs. Nellie Shock.

During 1950 the police received a tip-off that late night drinking took place at the **King's Head**. On the night of 18 October, two policeman were keeping watch on the inn. The door was locked and the curtains drawn so they couldn't gain access or see in, but they were able to listen to laughter, talking and 'the sound of cash and noise of bottles against glasses'. Sums of money were also being mentioned which appeared to relate to the cost of a round. When they eventually gained access, as some of those left the premises, they found the licensee, Mr. Shock, asleep in a chair in the corner of the room, with Mrs. Shock and others playing cards. She immediately awoke him and he explained that he had brought a few friends back from Leominster for a game of cards. The

The King's Head at Docklow in 2000

police immediately sought the addresses of those present to discover that none came from Leominster. Mr. Shock then explained that actually they had been playing darts at the Three Horseshoes in Leominster, followed by skittles at the Conservative Club before ending up at the **King's Head** where the drinks, he said, had been on him. The sound of cash and sums of money being talked about related to the game of cards. However, the Court found for the police and he was fined £20 with 5 guineas costs for supplying beer out of hours.

The King's Head sign

The **King's Head** changed hands in 2002 and since then the whole pub has been smartened up, the dining facilities have been extended and a full menu based on local produce is offered.

South-west of Docklow, but a long way round by road, is the hamlet of Risbury, in Humber parish. Here until recently was an old-style pub called the **Hop-pole Inn**, one of only three in Herefordshire recommended by CAMRA for their old-fashioned interiors. There is no mention of this pub in the 1867 trade directory, but by 1891 it had been opened and was being run by George Diggory, who was also a coach builder and carpenter. From the 1920s it was held by the Ryall family. After war service in the Royal Navy it was taken over by Albert Ryall, and he ran it single-handed. In 1985 CAMRA reported on the pub in the following terms:

> A truly incredible pub, built in 1657, which is half a pub and half a farmhouse. The pub itself consists of a single spartan bar which is furnished with old coach seats, and commands an excellent view of the surrounding countryside. Other features of interest, apart from the landlord himself, include only one beer on tap — no keg at all, an interesting collection of old beer glasses and pub name built into the garden wall. A 'must' if you're in the area — bring your own food.

In later years, as his health failed, Albert Ryall only opened the pub on Friday evenings, selling beer and cider to locals, and helped by his nephew. At about 1 p.m. on 13 November 2000 Albert Ryall was found dead, from a heart attack, but he had bruising consistent with an assault

The Hop Pole at Risbury in 1999

although this could not be confirmed. There was also a safe missing. At the beginning of 2003 the mystery has not been solved, despite an appeal for information made in the *Hereford Times* 12 months later. Since the tragedy happened the pub has, regrettably, been demolished.

EASTWARDS ALONG THE A44

Eastwards from Bromyard the Worcester road was turnpiked as far as Herefordshire Lake, on the edge of Whitbourne parish. Leaving Bromyard the road rises through the area called Linton, one of the townships of Bromyard, with the former workhouse, later used as a hospital and now converted to residential use, on the right hand side. Somewhere about here in 1851 one Samuel Summers was a cider retailer and cottage farmer. A little more certain is that cider was sold from Washcroft, on the right just past the old workhouse, for before the First World War it was the custom that the youngest ringer at Bromyard parish church had to collect cider from here, a walk of over a mile, to be consumed by the ringers in the belfry.

Over the brow of the hill the road drops down towards Bringsty Common, partly in Bromyard and partly in Whitbourne. To the right across the common is the **Live and Let Live**, whose amusing sign of a cat eyeing up a bird could formerly be seen on the roadside. It is rumoured that very large cats roam the common. A 4x4 vehicle left overnight on the common on the night of 14 December 2001 was found the next morning to have on the bonnet the paw prints of a very large member of the cat family.

The **Live and Let Live** is one of the oldest buildings on the common and dates from *c.*1700. Formerly thatched and colour-washed, it is now tiled with the timber framing exposed. Samuel Harris was tenant in 1842; in 1851 he was 40 years old and was described in the census as a labourer with two acres of land. He lived there with his wife and five children, and in a trade directory of the same year he was described as a cider retailer. He was still tenant when the premises were sold in 1853 being described as 'all that cottage then used as a public house in the possession of Samuel Harris'. By 1859 he was also keeping a shop, and so subsequently did his widow and son. At the beginning of the next century Edmund Morgan was the publican.

The Live and Let Live in 1910, when it still had a thatched roof

The **Live and Let Live** was one of a number of lots that were offered for sale by auction on 13 June 1927. At this time the pub was in the hands of the Holland family, but Mrs. Anne Holland died in 1930 at the age of 64 and her son, H.R. Holland, was the tenant when it was offered for sale in 1931. He stayed there until he transferred to the **Herefordshire House** at Stanford Bishop in 1955.

By direction of W. T. Barneby, Esq.

LOT 4. The Valuable FREEHOLD PROPERTY known as

THE LIVE AND LET LIVE

Bringsty Common, *being a Free Beer and Cider House, with on and off License,* about 2 miles from Suckley Station G.W.R., 3 from Bromyard and 11 from Worcester, in the occupation of Mr H. Holland at £45 per annum, Tenancy expiring 2nd February, 1932.

The House which is of the black and white style is in an excellent state of repatr and contains Tap Room; Private Bar; Back Kitchen; Beer Cellar; Hall with Cupboard; Private Room with modern grate; 3 Bedrooms; Wash House with furnace, Baking Oven and Coal House.

The Outbuildings comprise Mill House with Cider Mill; Loft over; Fowl House; Lean-to galvanised Cart Shed and 2 Pigstyes.

Capital Kitchen Garden and excellent Pasture Orchard, exceptionally well planted with choice sorts of Fruit Trees, the whole containing

2a. 0r. 6p.

more or less.

Tithe 7/8d.

Mr. Barneby will supply some Young Fruit Trees to replace dead and dying trees

---

The 1931 sale of the Live and Let Live

Between the wars, when cars were few and far between, Bringsty Common and Bromyard Downs were favourite destinations for cyclists from Birmingham, and groups of up to 40 or 50 used to cycle down on a Sunday to picnic and visit the **Live and Let Live**.

From 1955 until 1991 the pub was run by Don and Mavis Griffiths; Don also working as the postman for the Common. In 1991 he retired, the brewery having a rule that a tenant had to retire at the age of 65, and the pub was then sold. In 1996, after the new owner had tried unsuccessfully to sell the pub as a business, an application was made to turn the building into a private residence, but this was turned down. A local consortium then put together an offer to buy the

The approach view of the Live and Let Live in 1996

The Live and Let Live in 2002

premises, but this came to nothing. A further application to change the pub into a private house was withdrawn in December 2001 and an offer for the pub was accepted by the owners. However, the pub was sold again in August 2002 and in the spring of 2003 the new owners were in the process of renovating the pub and intend to reopen it as a business.

Just to the north of the **Live and Let Live** is **Holly Cottage**, which in 1851 was tenanted by Thomas Wood, described as a carpenter and beer retailer, who paid a rent of £15 per year. However, the beer retailing side of his business does not seem to have lasted long. Also in 1851 there is a record of John Watkins who was a cider retailer on Bringsty Common, but the place of his business has not yet been located.

The one-time Mason's Arms in 2002

To the south of the **Live and Let Live**, yet further across the common, was the **Mason's Arms**, the older part of which was built about 1825. In 1835 it was owned by Henry Stepells of Hereford but tenanted by Henry Perkins. It was run by James Ballard in 1902. Bill Matthews of the Batch, Whitbourne, expanded his haulage business here in 1931 and in 1936 the licensed premises was closed and the property was renamed Malvern View — the open aspect giving a clear view of the Malvern Hills. Just before it closed, a village fête and dance was held here, the Bromyard Town Band being engaged to provide the music. The tune *Sweet Adeline* being a favourite of the bandmaster, it was repeated a number of times until certain members of the band became bored, and played another tune! In one of those amazing coincidences, many years later one of the members of the band met someone who had been at that event, the only thing of which he could remember was the band which, he said, had only one tune in its repertoire, called *Sweet Adeline*!

The winding descent over the common flattens out by the left turn to Whitbourne, on the corner of which is the **Wheatsheaf Inn**. In 1695 the site of the **Wheatsheaf** was a blacksmith's shop called Sapey Bridge; the inn seems to have been built *c*.1780 by John Freeman, a local landowner, as a coaching inn on the newly turnpiked stretch of the road from London to Aberystwyth. The turnpike gate was just beyond the **Wheatsheaf**, opposite Gaines Lodge, and the house itself survived until about 20 years ago, but was demolished on the grounds of road safety. An agreement of 1787 in the parish records relates to two of the inns in Whitbourne, one of which was the **Wheatsheaf Inn**.

We whose names are under written, do hereby promise strictly to conform ourselves to the following regulations.

1st. That we will not suffer cards, dice, nor any other kind of gaming to be carried on within our respective houses.

2nd. That we will suffer no person, travellers only excepted, to continue in our houses during the winter season after 10 o'clock, nor during the summer season after 11 o'clock at night, & that we will not under any pretence whatever draw liquor for any person after those hours.

3rd. That we will draw no liquor on Sundays, but that for the necessary uses of our family, nor suffer any persons to remain loitring in our houses during the times of Divine Service.

Whitbourne   The mark x of John Vernols

16 Sept[r] 1787
Samuel Hadly in behalf of Margaret Howles

The 'regulars' gather outside the Wheatsheaf in 1910 for this photograph

As the **Wheatsheaf Inn** was the house of Mrs. Hadley in 1821, the names suggest that Margaret Howles was the predecessor of the Hadleys at the **Wheatsheaf Inn**. By 1839 Samuel Pitt was the landlord, and he was still there in 1861 at the age of 67. His widow, Sarah Jane Pitt, had succeeded him by 1867, and in 1871 the inn was held by a much younger man, John Lewis, aged 29, who was also a farmer. His successors for many years were also farmers as well as publicans. Charles Williams, who took over in about 1890, was also a carrier, and his widow Dinah carried on with the farming side of the business, but Albert Partridge, here during the First World War, was only a publican. He was the son of Joseph Partridge who was at the **King's Arms** in Bromyard.

The Wheatsheaf towards the end of the 20th century

It is said that many years ago a landlady was drowned in the Sapey brook, and that a landlord hung himself inside the building, but these may just be local legends. About four years ago the **Wheatsheaf** was renovated, a new porch was added, and the dining area extended into the single storey building at the west end. Home cooked lunches and dinners are served and, unusually, a sign reads 'Coaches Welcome'!

Turning left and rising to Meadow Green, but still part of Whitbourne, on the right-hand side is yet another pub called the **Live and Let Live**. Essentially a late-17th century timber-framed building, it has been extended over the years. It began as a beer house in the

The Live and Let Live at Whitbourne in 1914

1860s, when it was held by John Collins. Although there was no name recorded in the 1867 directory, the 1871 census shows that the name was then, as now, the **Live and Let Live**; that John Collins was aged 47, a landowner and publican, and that he had been born at Stourport. He does not seem to be have been related to the Joseph Collins who was at the **Boat Inn** (see below). John was succeeded by Thomas Collins, described in 1895 as a butcher and beer and cider retailer, but by 1902 Thomas Collins was resident in Worcester and only ran the butcher's shop at Whitbourne, and the **Live and Let Live** was being run by George Aylett. A few years later the pub was kept by Sidney Lewis, and a fine photograph of Mr. & Mrs. Lewis and their daughter Olive was taken in 1914. Sidney Lewis seems to have been succeeded by Frank Hulme (who appeared as a witness in a court case in 1922) and then by W.E. Hancox, who had a problem with his Schedule D income tax for 1928/29 and successfully appealed against his assessment. He was still there at the beginning of the Second World War. As with most country establishments that have survived, it is now much more than a drinking place, and as well as fine ales provides food in the restaurant, with provision for children in the outside play area. There is also a busy outside catering business, going under the name of the Booze and Pig Co.!

Also at Meadow Green is the house now known as The Croft, previously called **Meadow Green House** which is said to have been a cider house. Certainly there was a cider retailer called Job Clarke in Whitbourne in 1851 and 1858. Although it is not known where he lived, it may have been here.

The Ring of Bells, which may have been a pub in the 17th or 18th century

Continuing and bearing left at the bottom of the bank, the first house on the left is called the **Ring of Bells**, a not unusual name for a house near to a church, although this was not the original name for the building. This house is of medieval origin with early 17th-century work in the main block and additions later in the century. It is said to have been a hostelry, but if so it closed many, many years ago. Certainly if it was an inn it would have been very convenient for the ringers from the church! It is at least possible that the Martha ffarely who kept a tavern in Whitbourne and died in 1671, leaving assets to the value of £182 13s., was resident here. At that time the property was called Sandalls. In the 1871 census, when there were three families resident there, it was referred to as the Old Ring of Bells.

Another place that is now more remote than it would formerly have been is the site of what was the **Boat House Inn**. Boat Lane leads down from the church to the river, on the banks of which the inn stood.

Rebuilt some time in the middle of the 18th century by the Collins family, it was first a house called the Scar. There was a ford here and early in the 19th century a boat service across the river, marked on Bryant's map of 1835, was provided. Lascelles' *Directory* of 1851 shows that John Collins was a cider retailer in the parish of Whitbourne, although his premises were not named, but the 1861 census records that the **Boat House** was occupied by Joseph Collins, then aged 56 and described as a mechanic and victualler. The mention of a mechanic is not so surprising as it might seem, as his son Joseph Collins jun. was an engine driver, probably for a steam engine that drove either a steam plough or thrashing tackle. He is likely to have worked for someone local, for in 1867 Joseph Griffiths of Ford, Whitbourne, was a machine owner, so it may well have been him. In 1871 it was named the **Boat Inn**, and Joseph Collins was then described as a landowner and publican. Time clearly moved slowly in Whitbourne as he had only reached 63 years! The property was sold to Edward Bickerton Evans of Whitbourne Hall in 1876 and the house was pulled down at the beginning of the 20th century, but it had not been used as a pub for many years, probably since it was sold in 1876.

NORTH ALONG THE B4214

From Bromyard the B4214 — turnpiked for the four miles to Perry Bridge — leaves Old Road by the side of the **White Horse**. This is now Tenbury Road but was formerly called Milvern Lane, a much nicer name, and by the side of the **White Horse** it was very narrow, causing problems for vehicles turning into or out of the lane.

For the traveller there was little in the way of refreshment along the journey to Tenbury. Just outside Bromyard, on the left-hand side is the embankment of the former Bromyard to Leominster railway then the road crosses a small stream. Somewhere about here was the **Rock Tavern** at Instone Bridge, which was offered for sale by auction at the **Falcon** on 7 July 1784, when it was described as a dwelling-house, garden and piece of meadow ground. This may have been the rather pleasant red-brick-fronted house, or at least its predecessor. A little

This cottage may have been the Rock Tavern

*The one time Worcestershire Arms
in Stoke Bliss*

further along the road on the right-hand side is the **Rock**, a farm which was run by James Perkins who in 1851 was described as a farmer and cider retailer, but it seems unlikely that this was the same as the **Rock Tavern**. In 1867 John Maund was recorded as a cider retailer and shopkeeper at Wood House in Edwyn Ralph parish — on the right as one passes through. Then there was nothing until arriving at the **Worcestershire Arms** at Pie Corner in Stoke Bliss which is just over the county border and so in Worcestershire. Formerly the part of the parish of Stoke Bliss around the church was in the county of Herefordshire and consequently in the 19th century Stoke Bliss appeared in trade directories for Herefordshire. In 1897 the boundary was adjusted so that all of the parish was in Worcestershire. But the part of the parish where the **Worcestershire Arms** lies has always been in Worcestershire, but as it is so close to the boundary a mention is at least called for. In 1867 Lawrence Lynass was at the **Cross Keys Inn** at Stoke Bliss, but by 1879 the name had been changed to the **Worcestershire Arms**, still with Lynass as licensee. The name has remained the same, but its drinking history is now finished, as the pub has recently closed.

NORTH ALONG THE B4203

The B4203 from Bromyard to Stourport was turnpiked for four miles to Sapey Wood at Upper Sapey. The township of Norton lies either side of the B4203 and includes Saltmarshe, Brockhampton, and most of Bromyard Downs. At present there are two pubs within the township, but there were formerly several others. Just where the road to Stourport begins to rise to climb over the Downs is **O'Malley's**, until recently known as the **Holly Tree**. However, this was not its first name, as it seems to have started in the 1860s as a beer house called the **Saddler's Arms**, when it was held by John Wilson. Born in Hereford, in 1871 he was aged 58. Although his name appears in a directory of 1876/7, it was soon taken over by Herbert Page, and the name was then changed to the **Holly Tree**. Not long after the last war the licensee was Jack Smith, who was something of a character. If he fell out with one of his customers — a not uncommon occurrence — then he would stop tap and there would be no more drinks served that night. On one occasion some of the local lads turned up with a piglet in a box, and asked if Jack had any ham sandwiches. Of course he hadn't — they wouldn't have asked otherwise — whereupon they offered him the piglet, at which he flew into a rage with the expected result. In years gone by there was a much greater sense of local community and in October 1955 the *Bromyard News and Record* reported that the ninth annual Harvest Festival had been held at the **Holly Tree Inn**, conducted by the vicar,

The Holly Tree in the early 20th century

O'Malley's, once the Holly Tree, in 1999

the licensee being then Mr. Sidney Griffin. A collection raised £18 6s. 6d. towards an outing for the children and old age pensioners of Norton.

By the side of **O'Malley's** is Burying Lane, leading up to the maze of little roads and tracks over the Downs. The name is unusual, and locally it was said that it took its name after a mass burial that took place during the Black Death in the 14th century in a field on the right-hand side of the ascent. It would seem to be as good an explanation as any!

The Stourport road climbs up the side of the Downs, passing **Roberts Hill** on the right-hand side. This is said to have been a cider-retailing house which had a bowling alley to attract customers. In 1838 it was owned by John Mitchell, and it is possible that the Benjamin Mitchell, who was recorded as a cider retailer on the Downs in 1867, was in business here.

Almost at the top of the hill a right turn leads to the **Royal Oak,** an 18th-century building which, it has been suggested, was a droving inn. This does not appear by name in directories until the 20th century, previously appearing just under the name of the proprietor as it was a simple beer house. In 1838 the tenant was William Booton who also rented other land in Norton. In 1858 Joseph Booton, of the **Mason's Arms** at Norton, was a carrier to Worcester — outwards on Tuesdays

The Royal Oak in 1999

and Fridays, returning Wednesdays and Saturdays. This was probably the pub in Church Street, Bromyard, and not the one on Bringsty Common. Joseph Booton was a beer and cider retailer as well, and kept the **Royal Oak**. By 1871 the **Royal Oak** was in the hands of Ann Booton, his widow, then aged 51 and described as a beer-house keeper. In 1923 Charles Day was still a beer retailer, and in 1941 the licensee was Mrs. Leonora Johnson, who was previously at the **Hop Pole**, although it seems to have been run by her son. Not too many years ago the building was closed and in disrepair, vandals having got in and stripped out the plumbing. It was then bought by a local builder and repaired and reopened and has since continued to serve the area and its visitors.

Close to the **Royal Oak** were several other establishments, approached from either the top of the Downs or from Burying Lane. About a quarter-of-a-mile south-west of the **Royal Oak** was the **Bowling Green Inn** which seems to have become licensed premises in the later 19th century (in 1871 the occupier was described as a farmer of 7 acres), and it remained in licensed use until about 1920; there still being evidence within the house. Butt House was later built on the bowling green after which the pub was named. Between the **Royal Oak** and the **Bowling Green Inn** is **Fox Cottage**, thought to have been a pub at some period (although in 1871 the occupier, William Oseman, was a mason), as was **Sunnyside Cottage**, three hundred yards

The Licensing Acts, 1828 to 1904.

COUNTY OF HEREFORD.
DIVISION OF BROMYARD.

Notice is hereby given that the GENERAL ANNUAL LICENSING MEETING for the above mentioned Division will be held at the COURT HOUSE at Bromyard, on MONDAY, THE 6TH DAY OF FEBRUARY NEXT, at the hour of *Eleven* in the forenoon, for GRANTING and RENEWING LICENSES and CERTIFICATES for the following purposes, viz. :

    1.—For the sale by Retail, in Inns, of Intoxicating Liquors.

    2.—For the Sale by Retail of Beer, Cider, or Wine.

    3.—For the Sale of Spirits, Liquors, and Sweets by Retail.

    4.—And also for the transaction of any business which may be or is required to be transacted at the General Annual Licensing Meeting.

Dated this 2nd day of January, 1905.

A. W. KNOTT,
BROMYARD,
Clerk to the Licensing Justices.

Reminder of the 1905 Annual Licensing Meeting addressed to Adam Sharples at the Bowling Green Inn

Sunnyside Cottage on the Downs in 2002

south-south-east of the **Bowling Green Inn**. Inside **Sunnyside Cottage** was formerly a wall complete with a serving hatch — evidence of its former use as a licensed premises. All these are quite likely, as in 1851 Edward Moore was a beer retailer at the **Bell** on the Downs, and in 1867 Alfred Gillet of Norton was a beer retailer on the Downs. At present it is impossible to connect them with any specific properties.

On the far side of the Downs the road drops down, and then rises again. On the left-hand side on both inclines are former lodge houses to Saltmarshe Castle, the second one just past the wood yard. In the 19th century the Saltmarshe estate was inherited by Edmund Barneby from his greatuncle William Higginson, and consequently he changed his surname to Higginson. About 1840 he built Saltmarshe Castle, an elaborate pile complete with tower and battlements, on the site of the old Saltmarshe House, the extensive walled gardens and outbuildings of which incorporated earlier farm buildings. Edmund Higginson died unmarried in 1871 and the estate was left to his nephew William Barneby, succeeded in turn by his son William Theodore Barneby in 1895. He kept up the style of the Castle through the 1930s when there were eight servants within and three gardeners to keep the grounds in order. His only son Christopher was killed in Burma in 1944 and after the death of William Theodore in 1946 the estate was sold. The Castle was demolished in 1955 and the site is now a caravan park, although some of the outbuildings still remain.

Beyond the second gatehouse the road continues to rise to the area known appropriately as High Lane. To the west is the parish of Tedstone Wafre, with Harpley to the east. The county boundary runs along here, and the next establishment, the **Gate Hangs Well**, is to the east of the road and so in Worcestershire, but being so close to the boundary it must be mentioned! This pub was at the centre of the local community, and before the last war a popular flower and vegetable show was held here in the second week in September. The patron of the show was a local landowner, Dr. Evans of Harpley House, and the show secretary was Arthur Powell, a blacksmith who lived down the road towards Tedstone Delamere. The landlord of this free house was Ben Ivison, who was succeeded as licensee first by his wife and then by

The Gate Hangs Well in 2001

his daughter, who held the pub until recent years. Regretfully the show did not start again after the war. The pub, originally based on the front room, expanded, but, like many other small country pubs, has recently closed and converted to residential use.

The Baiting House in 2003

There is one inn on the road, before the county boundary is reached — the **Baiting House** at Upper Sapey. This may have had its origin in the middle of the 19th century, as in 1858 one Peregrine Perkins was recorded as a carpenter but by 1867 he was recorded as an innkeeper as well and it is almost certain that he kept this pub. The name suggests that it may have been a stop on a journey to attend to the horses, and certainly this was so many years ago. Hops were formerly an important part of the local economy in the area around Bromyard and in the 19th century, and up to the beginning of the First World War the coke ('chark') that was used to dry the hops was brought from collieries at Pensax or Mamble, often by the farmers themselves or their workmen. The last load to be hauled to Gold Hill Farm in Bosbury was in 1908, the round trip taking two days. On this particular trip the wagons were ambushed twice in High Lane and only the presence of the dog in the wagon prevented a robbery from taking place. The journey was broken at intervals to water the horses, and one stop was at the **Baiting House**. The timing was such that on the outward leg the morning 'bait' would be taken there.

In 1941 the publican was William George Prosser, a bachelor, who had kept the pub for many years. No doubt he would be surprised by the recent expansion of the pub by the addition of a large conservatory, making the pub much more attractive to passing trade as well as locals.

CHAPTER SEVEN

Bromyard to Hereford

Just out of Bromyard on the road towards Hereford, the road to Bishop's Frome and Ledbury forks off to the left and the main road bears right. The first village on the main road is Stoke Lacy where the **Plough Inn** is on the right at the top of the bank. In the middle of the 19th century the landlord was Thomas Busk, who supplemented his earnings from the pub by his work as a blacksmith. At the beginning of the 20th century the landlord, James Hodges, was also a farmer and hop grower, while in 1941 it was held by William Symonds, and was described as an 'Hotel', a relatively common pretension at that time. William was better known as the proprietor of Symonds Cider Works. It was in 1938 that Bill Symonds moved the long-established family cider business to this site, the cider-making plant being situated behind the **Plough**.

This family-run business continued in a relatively small way until it was bought out by Greenall Whitley in 1984, after which there was a dramatic expansion on the ten-acre site. Bulmers took over the business in 1988 and the old oak vats were gradually replaced. In 1990 one of these demolished the weighbridge office when it ran free during removal. After an expansion of the Hereford factory the production of the Symonds range was moved there, the Stoke Lacy works closing in January 2001, bringing to an end a tradition that dated back to 1727.

Fortunately the factory has been taken over by the small Wye Valley Brewery which moved its operations here in April 2002, leaving behind its outgrown premises behind the Barrels Inn in St. Owen's Street, Hereford. It is hoped that the move will increase production from 100 to 300 barrels of beer each week. The not-unpleasant smell of brewing can now be detected on the wind in the surrounding countryside.

The Plough at Stoke Lacy in 1999

The **Plough Inn**, had been bought in 1962 by A.L. Davis, and then was in other hands in the early 1980s before being bought by Greenall Whitley. There have been a number of managers since, and it changed hands again in 1998 and on 10 May 2002 a new licensee took over, and the restaurant trade has expanded dramatically. The **Plough Inn** may have had an earlier name, for an advertisement in the *Hereford Journal* of 17 June 1773 states that tithes were to be sold by auction 'At the dwelling house of George Lea, known by the sign of the **Three Cocks**, in Stoak Lacy, Herefordshire'.

Dropping down into Stoke Lacy, the road goes past the church and then rises as it climbs out of the village. On the right hand side is **Brick House**, said to have been formerly a cider house. By the next right turn, almost at the brow of the hill, there is a sign indicating that the **Three Horseshoes** can be found a mile-and-a-half along that road, at Little Cowarne. Starting as a small house, it has been much extended in recent years. At the time of the tithe map in 1840 it was owned by Mr. Edward Abel, a member of a family that has been at the White House in Little Cowarne since at least the middle of the 17th century. In the following year it was rented by John Turbill, who also worked as a blacksmith. By 1851 William Turbill had taken over 'The Tavern', and he was described solely as

The Three Horseshoes in Little Cowarne in 2003

a blacksmith, the beer retail side evidently being a service offered to customers, while he was making the three horseshoes into four. The establishment continued in the hands of the Turbill family for most of the rest of the century. The custom of celebrating May Day by dancing around a maypole was still carried on outside the **Three Horse Shoes** towards the end of the 19th century. James Wagstaff was publican here in 1902 and about 1905 Mr. J. Bayliss took over, followed by Mrs. Rose Bayliss, his widow, who was still there in 1941. It was bought in 1989 by Janet and Norman Whittall who were then managers at the **Plough** in Stoke Lacy, and they renovated it and moved in during 1990. The modern extensions would make the pub almost unrecognisable to the Bayliss family.

Over the road from the **Three Horseshoes** is **Tavern Acre** and it

The sign

has been suggested that there was a tavern there many years ago. It is more likely, however, that it took its name from the **Three Horseshoes**. However, in the 1850s there was definite competition, for in 1851 there was a cider house at **Three Elms** (on the right before the **Three Horseshoes**) and

115

The Three Elms at Little Cowarne in 2003

New House Farm, Little Cowarne, in 2003

opposite that was the **New Inn** at New House Farm — both lapsing as drinking establishments by 1861. Elizabeth Piner, in 1851 a widow of 52 and landlady at the **Three Elms**, made the pages of the *Hereford Times* of 15 November that year when it was recorded that she had been fined £3 with £1 0s. 3d. expenses for allowing card playing on her premises and so transgressing the tenor of her licence!

From the **Three Horseshoes** the road drops sharply and dog-legs before climbing the other side of the valley. On the left, across the brook, can be seen the White House, a fine half-timbered farmhouse where the Abel family still lives and farms. Climbing over the top and dropping again, past Pencombe Hall on the right, the road drops into Pencombe. On the left hand side, opposite the turn to the former post office (which closed in 2002), was the **Burghope Inn**. This was the residence of Benjamin Jones, recorded in 1858 as a cider retailer at 'Bury Hope' but who, by 1867, had become a farmer and beer retailer. By 1881 his son, another Benjamin, had taken over the running of the inn, although the older Benjamin Jones (then aged 73) was still in residence and presumably retired. He died in 1887 and the inn was inherited by his 34-year-old son Benjamin.

A directory of 1902 shows that the younger Benjamin Jones was also assistant overseer for the parishes of Pencombe, Stoke Lacy, Ullingswick and Bredenbury. He must have been busy as he also farmed at Pencombe Mill farm, one of the farms on the Hampton Court estate, owned by the Arkwright family, but later bought by

The Burghope Inn in 2003

Benjamin Jones. In 1923, he, in his turn, sold Pencombe Mill with 144 acres, another 44 acres, and Brook House in Pencombe to Mr. Charles Jones, who was then farming at Pencombe Mill, for £3,500. Benjamin Jones died intestate at the age of 72 in 1925, and his wife administered his estate as his personal representative. The abstract of title to the property owned by Benjamin Jones, prepared in 1926, includes the **Burghope Inn**, and in the same year this was sold by Mrs. Jones and her son Benjamin to another son, Hubert, for £750.

At the Brewster Sessions in Bromyard in 1938 the sanitary arrangements at the **Burghope** came in for criticism. The chairman of the Bench, Col. J.T. Lutley, in making remarks about unsatisfactory premises, first mentioned the **Fir Tree** at Much Cowarne and then the **Burghope**. However, the pub continued in the hands of the

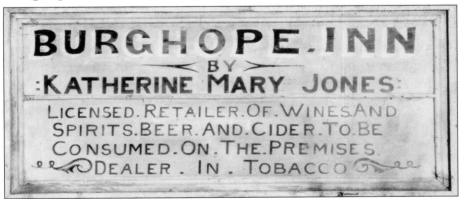

Aunty Kate's sign board at the Burghope Inn

117

Tally Ho! once the Huntsman's Tavern, in 2003

Jones family until it closed in the 1950s, the last licensee being Kate Jones, known universally in Pencombe as 'Aunty Kate'.

At the crossroads in the centre of Pencombe was a short-lived pub called the **Huntsman's Tavern**, a house on the right-hand corner, as one heads towards Hereford, which is now called Tally Ho! This was held by F. Seaborn in 1856 and by William Mapp in 1867, but when the 1881 census took place it was said to be the 'late Huntsman's Tavern'. It was sometimes referred to as the **Flying Horse**. Also belonging to the Arkwright family, when it was sold by auction in 1911 the name had been changed to Brook House. It subsequently belonged to Benjamin Jones from the **Burghope Inn**. The name Brook House has now been transferred to the modern house built just across the brook from Tally Ho!

Turning left at the crossroads, a few yards along on the right-hand side is the **Wheelwrights Arms**, a name that was adopted in the 19th century. In 1858 Charles Lawrence, a beer retailer, was recorded in Pencombe, while in 1861 the name of his establishment was given as the **Wheelwrights Arms** for the first time. A directory of 1867 states that he was not only a beer retailer, but also a carpenter, wheelwright and shopkeeper — hence the name of the pub. In 1881 he was aged 79 and lived at the **Wheelwrights Arms** with his daughter and grandson and three lodgers. But to make the picture more confusing, Frederick Bishop, described as 'formerly Publican', also lived at the **Wheelwrights Arms** with his family; presumably he looked after the pub side of the business. Charles Lawrence died in 1883 and by 1885 William Hoskins was at the **Wheelwrights Arms**. About 1889 the pub was taken over by J. Wellings, who had moved down from Shropshire, but after a few years he left to take over the Tack Farm in Ullingswick. Arthur Jenkins took over the pub in 1895, and he kept up the custom of having a maypole outside the pub. Jean Hopkinson records:

> The custom did not die out in Pencombe, for when Arthur Jenkins went to the Wheelrights Arms in 1895 he continued the practice of erecting a maypole on 29 May, Oak Apple Day. The pole stood in a barrel just inside the gate and was dressed with flowers. Red and white lilac, double and single, may and whitsun rose (guelder rose) were brought piled high in wheelbarrows. The flowers were fastened to the pole with string and sally [willow] hoops were decorated with pretty paper and hung on crosspieces. After school there were flat races for the children and an egg and spoon race for the older girls. The men had shot put, iron quoits, pillow fighting, high jump (regularly won by the late Bill Baker senior from Little Cowarns) and a tobacco race. For the last-named a table was placed halfway along the course and littered with clay pipes, loose tobacco and matches. The men ran to the table, filled pipe or pipes, lit them and then finished the race puffing away. Boots would come off to run faster but not everyone got beyond the table. There was free beer and the prizes, 6d. for the children and 2s. 6d. for the men, came from subscriptions collected in the Wheelwrights for a couple of months beforehand. Mr. Jenkins became ill in 1931 and the maypole ceased to be a regular event.

The Wheelwrights Arms about 1900.
The advertisements are all for Arnold Perrett & Co. of Hereford

The Wheelwrights in 2002

Arthur Jenkins was also a wheelwright and carpenter and indeed was the last wheelwright to work there. He died in 1931 at the age of 69 and his gravestone lies to the north of the church. However, although he was still at the **Wheelwrights Arms** in 1926, by 1929 William Poyner had taken over and so Arthur Jenkins had presumably retired. About this time the ownership of the pub changed from that of Arnold Perrett & Co. to the Cheltenham Original Brewery.

In recent years an eccentric landlord who barred almost (if not all) local organisations from the **Wheelwrights Arms** nearly caused its closure, but there has been a great

The dog-Latin inscription in the porch reads:
EDERE BIBERE ET HILARUS ESSE
NOSTER DOMI
which could be translated as:
'In my house eat, drink and be merry'

change in the last few years under the present owners. A hint of this is given in the new oak porch on which there is a greeting in Latin. The plain 19th-century brick exterior has been rendered over and there are modern windows, but step inside and you are taken back to a much earlier time, with timber-framed walls and wooden beams. The fame of the pub has spread much further than its immediate vicinity, and a visit on the first Tuesday in the month will discover a 'jamming' session, with visitors from as far as Birmingham, giving poetry readings and playing live music.

Returning in the direction of the main road to Hereford, about a mile past the **Three Horseshoes** there is a right turn signposted for Ullingswick. Down here is the **Three Crowns** which is almost on the eastern boundary of the parish of Ullingswick. The area around the present pub is now called Bleak Acre, but was formerly Blessed, Blest or Blete Acre. This latter name was also applied to the house next door (now Bleak House) in an advertisement of 2 June 1847, where it was stated that it was newly erected. In the 1851 census the three householders recorded in 'Blest Acer' were all labourers, and there was no publican mentioned. While there was no publican recorded in the 1861 census, by 1867 John Owen, farmer, beer retailer, and assistant overseer, was at Blestacre. The tithe reapportionment map of 1870 shows that he occupied the present premises, although no name was given to these. His name appears until 1879 but by 1890 Charles Taysom had taken over. By this time the premises were called the

Three Crowns, being marked as such on a map of the Ullingswick Estate that was sold by the Church Commissioners in 1887. In 1922 the licensee was George Ernest Worwood, and the licence stayed with members of his

The Three Crowns at Ullingswick in 2003

family until about 20 years ago. A hop-picker, who was working for the Baskerville brothers at The Farm, Moreton Jefferies, in 1939, later remembered '…and about two fields away there was a little pub called the Three Crowns. We used to fetch fresh crusty bread from there, also Smith's crisps at 1d. per packet'.

Dora Aitken, who was evacuated to Ullingswick during the last war and who stayed at Upper Court, remembered that there was a settle by the fire, much used by the locals, and as Mrs. Worwood used a range by the fire to cook, when she prepared the Sunday dinner she had to pass the saucepans along the locals to put on the range. Mrs. Aitken's husband used to visit Ullingswick at weekends, and on one occasion was walking past the **Three Crowns** on his way to Upper Court, when he met Mrs. Worwood on the roadside, and on his expressing his need for liquid refreshment she produced a jug of cider. Thereafter she was waiting for him with a jug of cider when he came past at his regular time at the weekends.

One of the problems with hop-pickers was that they tended to move between pubs, and took the glasses with them. To overcome this problem and to identify her property, Mrs. Worwood scratched the name of the pub on the bottom of her glasses, and some of these glasses survive to this day.

In recent years the premises have been renovated and extended by the various owners since the Worwood family held the licence and the pub now has a very good reputation for the quality of its food — but no crisps at 1d. per packet! Indeed, in the *Hereford Times* of 30 May 2002 it was announced that the restaurant at the **Three Crowns** had been named as the best restaurant in the region in the first Heart of England Tourist Board, Food & Drink Excellence Awards.

From the **Three Crowns** the road drops down through the scattered village of Ullingswick, past the present main centre of bungalow development and then down to the main road. A couple of hundred yards before arriving at the main road, on the left hand side, is the site of a short-lived beer house and shop called **Half Way House**. In 1862 this was run by Mrs. Mary Bevan, the wife of a drainer. On 20 October in that year the pub was central to a murder that was perpetrated in Ullingswick. At about 9.30 on the evening of that day Mrs. Skerrett, a widow who lived in Ullingswick, sent her 16-year-old servant Mary

Corbet to buy some candles from the shop. In the beer house was William Hope, a local bad hat, who had previously served a term of transportation. He inveigled Mary Corbet into drinking some beer, but she was so upset that she forgot her errand and had to return later for the candles. After she left for the shop for the second time, Hope followed her, and the evidence given at his trial proved that he attacked and strangled her further along the roadside. The spot where her body was found is still pointed out by old residents of Ullingswick. Hope was found guilty of the crime and was hanged in public above the gate of Hereford Prison on 15 April 1863 in front of a great many spectators, the last public hanging in Hereford. Two broadsheets were published to mark the occasion, one having a woodcut representing **Half Way House**.

The pub does not seem to have lasted long after this but the building itself survived in a semi-derelict state to within the last 20 years. Despite the appalling conditions — no electricity, water or drainage — it was inhabited by a local character called Bunny Godsall, noted for his antipathy to work. There was no woodwork in the house because Bunny had broken down the floors and doors and used the wood

Woodcuts of the 1862 murder.
Left: William Hope outside the Half Way House
Right: The unfortunate Mary Corbet

on his fire. He used to cycle to Hereford every day and spend time and what little money he had in the betting shops. After his bicycle was stolen he walked to Hereford, but still kept his cycling clips on his trousers in case he found his bike. Eventually he was taken into care and it was said locally that the bath that he received — the first for many years — was a contributory cause of his death. As soon as the cottage became vacant it was demolished.

At the crossroads the minor road from Ullingswick to Preston Wynne meets the main Leominster to Ledbury road. This particular stretch of main road was built as a turnpike road in the early 19th century and was to the east of 'Bebbury' Field, one of the old common fields of this part of Ullingswick. Not very far along the main road in the direction of Leominster was an alehouse called the **Prince of Wales Inn**, although it was known locally as the **Ramping Cat**. This was no doubt a waggish allusion to the heraldic 'Lion Rampant' (a lion standing on its hind-legs with its fore-paws in the air). The inn, which had not been built when the tithe map was surveyed in 1839, still stands by the side of the main road but is now called Westoe.

In 1851 the public house was held by Thomas Pugh, who was described as a publican and stone mason. At the Bromyard Petty Sessions in June 1852 there was a case about a brawl at the **Prince of Wales** beer house in Ullingswick, which was dismissed. Thomas Pugh died on 30 October in the same year 'in the 69th year of his age, much respected by all who knew him' as the *Hereford Journal* recorded. In 1861 the **Prince of Wales Inn** was held by Mary Pugh, Thomas Pugh's widow, who was described as a beer house keeper. It was still open in 1870 but must have closed soon after.

Once the Prince of Wales at Ullingswick

A few hundred yards north of the **Prince of Wales Inn** on the main Leominster road is the hamlet of Cornett, and here at Cornett Bridge in Bodenham parish in 1851 one William Holt makes a brief appearance as a cider retailer. It may be that he was at the place that was advertised on 3 May 1820 to be sold by auction at the **White Horse Inn,** Bromyard on 15 May 1820, the sale including 'All that MESSUAGE or TENEMENT, well calculated either for a Shop or Public-house ... situate at Cornett, in the Parish of Bodenham...'.

The best known and latest surviving of four closed establishments in the immediate vicinity of the crossroads was the **Crozens**, along the Preston Wynne road. The position of the inn was more significant in years gone by, for this is where the old road which followed the western boundary of Bebbery Field crossed the Preston Wynne road. Over the years the name of the pub was spelled in various ways and it was usually described as being at Felton, but strictly it was in the township of Whitechurch Maund in the parish of Bodenham. In the 1851 census there was no mention of a public house in the hamlet of the Crozen, nor indeed in the 1861 census, but the 1870 Ullingswick tithe reapportionment map marks it as the **Three Crosses**. In 1876-7 Walter Prosser, shopkeeper and beer retailer, held the licence of the establishment called the **Crosen**. In 1881 he was aged 74 and lived there with his wife, son Walter, son's wife and three children. By 1890 Walter Prosser junior had taken over and he and then his widow held the licence until the 1920s. By 1926 were followed by John Walby who was there for a number of years. In 1937 the pub was sold by Arnold Perrett's to the Cheltenham Original Brewery.

The Crozens Inn in the 1930s

125

*The 1933 Felton football team, based at the Crozens,
outside an unidentified pub*

A case of late night drinking at the **Crozen Arms** was reported in the *Leominster News* in 1945. When members of the Bromyard police called at the pub at 10.55 p.m. they found eight people still on the premises, two of whom had drinks in front of them. The landlord said that they had been served before 10 p.m. and that, until the police had arrived, he had not been aware that they were still present. After he had served them, he said, he had gone to look at a sick cow with Mr. Morgan, a farmer off whom he had bought the cow the previous day. It appeared the cow had 'gargett', so the two had drenched her before Mr. Morgan had honourably offered to take her home and refund the purchase price. They were still at the back of the inn discussing this when the police arrived. In the bar, only two of the men still had beer in their glasses, all the rest were empty. The two, who were charged with after hours drinking, said that they were discussing the allied break-through on the Rhine and were concerned for members of their family, one had two sons in the army, the other two brothers. Their concern and discussion had made them unawares that they were still drinking. Capt. Evans of the Bench, on agreeing to the two men being fined, added that he didn't consider that any member of the Bench was prepared to consider that good war news justified a breach of the law.

The Crozens in 1998, shortly before it closed

Rural businesses such as this have suffered in recent times, and in 1998 the owners, Mr. & Mrs. Sands, applied to turn the pub into a private residence. They had bought the property in 1990 for £180,000 and over the next four years spent a further £47,000 on it. In April 1998 it was valued for sale as a business at only £145,000! The application was approved by the planning authority and the premises became a private house.

Also in the township of Whitechurch Maund was a cider house. Lascelles' *Directory* of 1851 lists Hannah Ovens as a cider retailer and shopkeeper. By the time Littlebury's *Directory* was published in 1867 it was occupied by Richard Pritchard 'beer retailer and shopkeeper'. In 1881 he was stated to have lived at 'White Church Maund Cider Shop' and to be a fruit and cider dealer. Living with him were his wife and five children, two of whom were 13-year-old twins, sadly stated to be imbeciles. In 1890 the cider house at Upper Maund was named as **Half-way House** and Pritchard's name appeared in directories until 1900. For most of the first half of the 20th century the cider house was run by the Minton family but it seems to have been closed at about the time of the Second World War, although the half-timbered house is still there. Access from the Crozens to Upper Maund was over the fields; to get there by road it was necessary to carry along the main road to

Maund Bryan before turning off to the left and bearing left again over Maund Common.

From the Ullingswick crossroads the main road to the south leads towards Burley Gate. A short distance along on the left hand side is Marsh Farm, which makes a brief appearance in 1870 as a public house called the **New Inn**, owned and occupied by John Evans, and then is mentioned no more. On the right hand side after about a mile or so is a house called Hollington House, and this may have been the house and three and a half acres of land that was advertised as being to let in the *Hereford Journal* of 16 March 1836 as being '... well situate for a Public-House, being on the New road-side from Leominster to Ledbury'. On the tithe map of 1839 Hollington House was recorded as yet another public house called **Halfway House**, owned by Nathaniel Derry and

Once the Half-way House at Whitechurch Maund

Marsh Farm, Ullingswick in 2003. For a short time this was the New Inn

Hollington House was yet another pub called the Half-way House in the mid-19th century

tenanted by George Kedward. In this case the name was probably derived from a milestone which was formerly nearby, said to be halfway between Ledbury and Leominster. In 1851 the pub was held by Francis Derry, a publican and grocer who was described in 1858 as a shopkeeper and cider retailer, and in 1861 as a beer-shop keeper. Francis Derry would actually seem to have been of a slightly higher social status as, on the death of his wife in 1855, he was described as 'Mr.' Francis Derry. The pub probably closed soon after 1861.

At Burley Gate the A417, the Leominster to Gloucester road, crosses the A435, the Hereford to Bromyard road. A crossroads is a usual place for an inn, but the inn at Burley Gate was an exception, being a short distance along the road towards Bromyard. On 12 August 1795 an advertisement in the *Hereford Journal* stated that a tenement in Ullingswick as well as various pieces of land would be sold by auction 'At the Public-House at Birley-Gate, in the parish of Ocle-Pitchard', implying that there was only one public house here at that time.

An advertisement that appeared in the *Hereford Journal* of 9 June 1802 stated that a dwelling house at Ullingswick would be sold by auction at the **Plough Inn**, Burley Gate, while another of 11 January 1815 gave details of an auction of coppice wood on the Lower Hope Estate at Felton that would take place on 24 January at the **Jolly Crispin** at Burley Gate 'in the parish of Ocle Pitchard'. A crispin is another name for a shoemaker, and so beer selling may have been a sideline for the local shoemaker. Another advertisement in 1819 stated that certain land in Ullingswick would be auctioned at the **Mason's Arms Inn** at Burley Gate on 11 February. An advertisement in the issue of 26 October 1831 asked for information on 'a good HEREFORDSHIRE COW in CALF, with a white face, and white about her neck and behind her shoulders, with an iron knob on one horn' that was missing from the **Mason's Arms** at 'Birley' Gate. However, between these two latter advertisements, an auction of land at Ullingswick on 6 September 1827 was advertised to take place at **Burley Gate Inn**. The **Mason's Arms** was certainly another name for the **Burley Gate Inn** and the others may be as well.

The 1851 census states that 68-year-old James Hodges was the head of household at the **Mason's Arms Inn** at Burley Gate and that he was a mason by trade: the alternative name for the inn thus derived from his trade. James Hodges died within a few years, and it was decided to sell the pub. The event was advertised by a poster, which was copied in the *Hereford Times* of 23 January 1858 with the addition:

On THURSDAY, the 18th of FEBRUARY, will be sold, on the above premises, commencing at 11 o'clock, a famous dark-brown Mare, 7 years old, in foal, and a powerful Cart Gelding, 9 prime Ewes in yean, and 3 Yearlings, Rick of Wheat, ditto of Hay (to go off), light Spring Cart, light narrow-wheel ditto, upwards of 30 hogsheads of prime Cider and Perry with the Casks; Household Furniture, Brewing and other requisites, which are fully described in handbills to be had on the premises.

Cassey's *Directory* of 1858 gives the name of Eleanor Hodges as holding the **Burley Gate Inn** but she had died shortly after her husband. Thomas Ovens, landlord in the 1890s, was a retired superintendent of police from Bromyard, where he had served from 1875 until 1891. He must have been an energetic person as he also farmed at the Bach Farm in Much Cowarne. His successor, Walter Williams, was also a retired policeman, and he bought the inn after his marriage to Mrs. Mary Morgan, a widow whose first husband had farmed just outside Hereford. Walter Williams died in 1911 and his widow continued to run the pub. Her third marriage was to Isaac Davies, who travelled the area with Shire horses, and used the **Burley Gate Inn** as a base.

Just after the First World War there were enough youngsters in the immediate area to form a football team, called the Robins from their red shirts, and this team continued for several years. The pitch was behind the pub and a corrugated iron building on the east side of the pub, known as No. 7, was used as a changing room. Facilities were primitive, and after a game the youngsters had to strip off outside and wash under a cold water pump, the last youngster arriving at the pump getting the job of operating the handle.

At hop-picking time the pickers were not allowed inside the pub (the door was kept locked and the regulars had to knock to be let in) and the hop-pickers had to drink their beer in No. 7. The hop-pickers at nearby Cowarne Court were usually Welsh, and it was not unknown

MASON'S ARMS, BURLEY GATE

FIRST-RATE ROAD-SIDE

PUBLIC HOUSE

AND

LAND.

OAKLEY & SON

WILL SELL BY AUCTION,

ON THE PREMISES,

ON WEDNESDAY, 17th FEBRUARY, 1858,

At 3 o'Clock in the Afternoon, subject to Conditions of Sale, by direction of the Executor acting under the Will of the late Mr. JAMES HODGES,

ALL THAT HIGHLY DESIRABLE

FREEHOLD

LONG ESTABLISHED AND WELL-FREQUENTED

INN,

Substantially built, in good repair, and replete with every convenience for carrying on an extensive and lucrative Retail Business, suitable Outbuildings, Cider Mill, &c., and about TWO ACRES, (more or less) of exceedingly Rich and productive GARDEN and ORCHARD LAND, thereto adjoining, and known by the Name of

THE MASON'S ARMS,

SITUATE AT BURLEY GATE, IN THE PARISH OF OCLE PITCHARD,

Midway between **Bromyard & Hereford, and adjoining the Turnpike Road,**

For many Years in the occupation of the late Proprietor, Mr. JAMES HODGES, and now of his Representatives.

To View, and for further particulars, apply to the Executor, Mr. E. HODGES, on the Premises ; or the Auctioneers, Bromyard.

HENRY E. OAKLEY, PRINTER, BOOKSELLER, AND STATIONER, BROMYARD.

The 1858 sale of the Mason's Arms at Burley Gate

*Two very different views of the Burley Gate Inn at the beginning of
the 20th century. Walter Williams is holding the tray of drinks*

for trouble to flare up outside the pub between these and other pickers from the Black Country, but the arrival of the local policeman usually defused the situation.

In the early 1920s Florence (Florrie) Badham was a barmaid at the **Burley Gate Inn**. She kept a notebook and this shows that from October 1921 she was paid £1 13s. 4d. per month, out of which she had to pay 1s. 4d. for a stamp (presumably some sort of national insurance), which went up to 2s. in January 1926. Her notebook finishes in June 1927.

After the death of Mrs. Davies, her husband continued to run the pub until his death just before the Second World War, and it was then sold and subsequently belonged to the brewery. The inn closed about 10 years ago and is now a private house, a second house having been built in the pub car park.

There may have been another licensed establishment at Burley

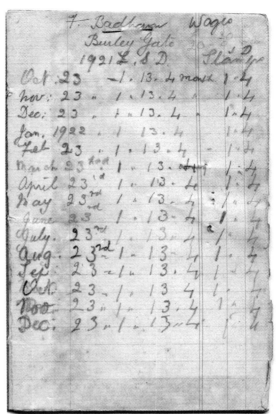

A page out of Florrie Badham's notebook recording her wages in 1921 &1922

The Burley Gate in 1999, shortly after it closed as an inn

Gate. A few yards along the Much Cowarne road, just over the parish boundary, is a black-and-white cottage, now called Hilton but formerly called Griffiths Farm. When this was repaired and renovated some years ago, a serving hatch was found between two rooms, implying that it may have been used as a beer or cider house.

Heading towards Hereford along the A465, soon after the turn for Preston Wynne there is an exotic gatehouse on the right hand side, and by the side of it a drive leading up onto an eminence, which was called Summer House Hill in the middle of the 19th century. On top of this a mansion called Thinghill or Withington Tower was built in 1871 for Henry Higgins, a northern industrialist. The style of the house was described as a mixture of Scots Baronial and early French, and a directory of 1902 states that it was 'in the castellated style, and is a conspicuous object for many miles. It commands a magnificent view of an immense range of fruitful country'. The Higgins family was here for less than 30 years and the property then passed through several hands before being demolished in 1929.

A quarter of a mile or so past the gatehouse the road enters the part of Withington known, from its low-lying nature, as Withington Marsh. On the right hand side, by the disused petrol station, is a former pub called the **Thinghill Arms**, which seems to have started as a pub called the **New Cross Keys Inn**. In 1851 Samuel Pumphrey, a native of Tewkesbury, was recorded as a coal dealer and labourer living in Withington Marsh, and by 1858 his premises were advertised as the **New Cross Keys Inn**, although the 1861 census shows that he was also still a coal merchant. By 1867 Mrs. Mary Pumphrey, his widow, was running the business, and she was also a coal merchant and

Once the Thinghill Arms, and earlier the New Cross Keys, in 2003

134

shopkeeper. In 1871 John Pumphrey, the son, was at the **New Cross Keys Inn**, and at about this time the present building is said to have been built by Henry Higgins of Thinghill. Although in 1881 the name was still the same, by the time the 1886/7 25-inch OS map was published the name had been changed to the **Thinghill Arms**. However, it did not last long after this, for although it was still called the **Thinghill Arms** in 1902, it was then occupied by Henry Mason described as a market gardener and plant grower and not a publican.

A few yards past the **Thinghill Arms** the road crosses the line of the old Goucester/Hereford canal; the buildings on the left hand side were associated with the canal. One of the last boats to use the canal was called the *Thomas* and when the 1881 census was taken, there was a narrow boat of this name lying here, crewed by the Bellinger family from Gloucester, captain Benjamin, his wife Sara and their 15-year-old son Charles.

A short distance along the main road towards Hereford, a right turn leads towards Bodenham. Along this road, after crossing the stream, there is a very noticeable rise where the road crosses over the former canal. By the side of the bridge is a house that was formerly the **Bridge Inn**. It may have been here that John Racster lived, recorded in 1867 as a beer retailer, shopkeeper and warehouseman. The 1881 census gives Thomas Pritchard, who also worked as a carpenter, as the innkeeper at the **Bridge**; aged 46, he and his 44 year old wife, Emma, had six children. He was a tenant in the beerhouse and had also worked as a wharfinger on the canal. The inn was sold in 1887 to Joseph Bailey of the Swan Inn, Aylestone Hill, Hereford for £300. It seems that Bailey wanted the Pritchards to move and described them as 'undesireables'. In the Deeds the property is described as:

All that messuage or tenement and Inn called 'The Bridge Inn' with the yard garden and buildings thereto adjoining and belonging containing by estimation 25p[erches] or thereabouts adjoining the road leading from Bodenham to the Highway to Bromyard and bounded on the South West by the said road and on the North by the towing path of the Hereford and Gloucester canal ...

There was also a small piece of land on the other side of the canal belonging to the inn. The Ledbury to Gloucester section of the canal had closed in June 1881, but a little local traffic may have continued

The Bridge Inn in 2003

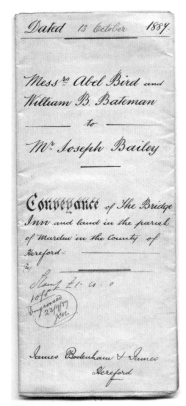

Sale of the Bridge Inn in 1887

for a while on the Ledbury to Hereford section. In 1902 the inn was run by Mrs. Ann Walker, a beer retailer and shopkeeper, while in 1937 the landlord was William Jancey. It was licensed until at least 1964 and closed soon afterwards, but the wrought-iron bracket for the inn sign still hangs from the building.

Carrying along this road — called Wyatt Road — towards Marden, brings the traveller close to the site of a long-lost pub called the **Frenchman's Inn**, a record of which has been preserved in the local oral tradition and nowhere else. About half a mile after the **Bridge Inn**, the site is a quarter of a mile across the fields to the right, just to the north of a small pond. It can be identified from odd pieces of stone lying about in the field, and is just within the boundary of the parish of Preston Wynne. Such a remote situation argues for a very early foundation, before the present road layout was finally fossilised, and it has been suggested that the Frenchman to whom it refers was a Norman.

On the left-hand side of the main road, after the turn to Marden, is the **Old Cross Keys**. Built of large blocks of local stone, this locals' pub has an unspoilt interior with boarded ceiling and real fires. The roadside sign proudly proclaims 'Circa 1787' and

The Cross Keys in 1999

although this date is just the sign-writer's fancy, there may well be more than a grain of truth in it. There was a pub in the area in the 18th century, for there was an advertisement in the *Hereford Journal* of 24 January 1798 which stated that a tenement was to be sold by auction 'at the sign of the Compass, on Withington Marsh…'. An advertisement in September 1799 refers to it as the **Three Compasses**, 'Withington's-Marsh' and it seems most likely that this was an early name for the **Cross Keys Inn**. Certainly it was called the **Cross Keys** by 1820 for there is an advertisement in the *Hereford Journal* of 29 March 1820 for timber that was to be sold by auction at the **Cross Keys**. In 1851

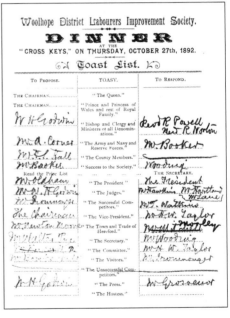

The formality of the Dinner for the Labourers Improvement Society held at the Cross Keys in 1892 is well shown by this Toast List

Sale of Timber at the Cross Keys in 1862

it was no doubt the unnamed public house that was recorded in the census — there was only one in the Marsh at that time — with William Jones the licensed victualler. He lived there with his wife, four children, and two servants. By 1858 it had been taken over by William Daller and it was called the **Old Cross Keys** to distinguish it from its rival up the road. Jane Daller, his widow, was in charge in 1861 when it was stated to be a lodging house as well as an inn, and she was described as a retailer of drink and provisions. Within a few years she had been succeeded by William Nicoll, a Scotsman, who also farmed 6 acres.

One of his lodgers in 1871 was Charles Barber, a member of a well-known local family of pump makers. Making wooden pumps to get water out of a well was a very skilled business and at one time their services were in much demand, and there were at least four generations of the family who made pumps. The pub was still called the **Old Cross Keys** in 1902, when William Farmer was there, and in 1941 when it was run by the splendidly named Albert Pontifax Price. Subsequently it was simply called the **Cross Keys**, but has recently reverted to its previous title.

From Cross Keys, Withington, the road passes through Eau (pronounced 'Ee') Withingon, and then joins the main Hereford to Worcester road near Lugg Bridge.

CHAPTER EIGHT

Bromyard to Ledbury

ALONG THE B4214

Ledbury lies more or less to the south of Bromyard, there being a choice of two roads leading from one to the other. To the west is the B4214, initially turnpiked for the three miles to Bishop's Frome. Leaving Bromyard along the main Hereford road, the B4214 swings off to the left just outside the built-up area, about a quarter-of-a-mile past the Top Garage. The first place along the B4214 is Munderfield Row, little more than a few scattered houses, and then the small settlement of Munderfield Stocks where there was formerly a pub called the **New Inn**. A poster advertising the sale by auction of three cottages at Ullingswick indicated that the sale was to take place at the **New Inn**, Munderfield Stocks, on 11 September 1850. But the name seems to have either changed or lapsed very soon, and is not found again until a mention in the 1871 census of a New Inn cottage occupied by an agricultural labourer. In the 1851 census the only person retailing alcoholic drink was Peter Pitt, who was running a cider house called the **Holly Bush**, where he also had a shop and farmed 7 acres. This identifies his holding as the **Holly Bush Inn**, on the south side of Munderfield Stocks, which closed within the last 20 years and is now called Hollybush House. He was succeeded in the 1870s by one Thomas Dennis, cider retailer and shopkeeper, whose name appears in a directory of 1879. Directories in the 19th century did not distinguish between the two Munderfields.

In 1932 the **Holly Bush Inn** was described by the Royal Commission for Historical Monuments as being of 17th-century date, with the lower walls of rubble and having a thatched roof; it had modern extensions on the east and west sides, and photographs show that this was a picturesque building. Edward Pontifex Price held the licence in 1941. The building was destroyed by fire in 1945 and has since been rebuilt. Problems continued and on 12 January 1956 the *Bromyard News and Record* recorded yet another fire at the **Holly Bush**, which was fortunately brought under control. At that time it was reported that the **Holly Bush** had burnt down twice in the recent past, and that more recently the outbuildings had also suffered.

Just past the **Holly Bush Inn**, but on the opposite side of the road, is the drive to Instone Court, where formerly hops were grown. Mention of the **Holly Bush Inn** is made in *A Pocketful of Hops*, published in 1988, where it is explained that tramps working as hop pickers at Instone Court would leave small sums of money with the landlord of the **Holly Bush** for future use. There is also the amusing story of the negotiations about the hop-pickers' pay:

> While at Instone Court there used to be a ritual confrontation with Sidney Parker which would start noisily but usually end with jokes and laughing and a visit to 'The Tiddly', the Holly Bush: drinks all round on the 'Gaffer' and, weather permitting, the pickers would be back at work the next day.

The Chase Inn and the Green Dragon in Bishop's Frome
at the beginning of the 20th century

Every pub has its regulars, and in the 1950s one at the **Holly Bush** was Bert Bridgewater from Stoke Lacy. He was well known for his prize-winning elderberry wine, and he often spent his early evening sampling his own brew and then going to the **Holly Bush** to finish off a convivial evening — with the inevitable result from mixing his drinks!

Holly Bush House is in a prominent position, facing south down the steep hill towards Bishop's Frome — the next place along the road, where there have been two licensed establishments for many years. The first that comes to view, on the right-hand side, is the **Chase Inn,** held by James Hill, who was unmarried in 1861 and widowed by 1871! He was probably the first landlord as the present building dates from *c.*1860 and there is no mention of a pub of this name in the 1851 census. Subsequently the inn was run by the redoubtable William Farmer Pudge. He was born at New House, Bishop's Frome, in 1851 and gained experience at a butcher's shop at New

---

To Brewers, Licensed Victuallers and others.

PARTICULARS

OF

The Valuable Freehold Property

COMPRISING THE

Well-known and Old-Established COUNTRY INN

Occupying a most Prominent Position

in the centre of the Village of Bishops Froome, and a very large Hop Growing and Agricultural District at the juncture of 3 main Roads from Hereford, Bromyard and Ledbury, known as

"THE CHASE"

WITH EXCELLENT ACCOMMODATION

which comprises :

IN THE BASEMENT.—Good Beer and Wine Cellars with a convenient Rolling way from the Road.

ON THE GROUND FLOOR.—Front Sitting or Private Room, a well fitted Bar with Oak Counter and Range of Shelves, a large and lofty Tap Room with seating round, 18ft. x 18ft., Second Tap Room, Dining Room, Kitchen with Modern Range, Cupboards and Sink, Pantry, etc.

ON THE FIRST FLOOR.—4 Best Bedrooms, and an

EXCELLENT CLUB ROOM

33ft. x 18ft. with Ante-Room adjoining, and an Iron Outside Staircase from the Yard.

ON THE TOP FLOOR.—2 Bedrooms.

THE OUTBUILDINGS AND STABLING

are approached by a separate Gateway and include :

2 two-stall Stables, 3 Trap Houses, Long Stable, Lofts, Coal House, Wash-house with Furnace, Bake House with Oven, W.C's, etc.

In addition there is a

BUTCHER'S SHOP

and a

GROCERY AND GENERAL STORE

The Property is in a good state of repair, the Inn being Brick-built with a Slate Roof and the majority of the Outbuildings either of similar construction or Brick and Stone with tiled roof.

Considerable improvements were made to the Property only a few years ago, when additions were made which include the Large Tap Room, Club Room and Kitchen.

VACANT POSSESSION

will be given on completion or sooner by arrangement.

The Property is in the occupation of Mr. T. Foley, who claims certain Fixtures, a list of which will be produced at the Sale, or may be obtained on application to the Auctioneers.

The Fixtures together with the Trade Furniture, Fittings and Stock-in-Trade shall be taken to by the Purchaser in the usual way.

THE CHASE is a NOTED FREE HOUSE Licensed for Beer, Porter, Cider and Wines, about 5 miles from Bromyard, 8 from Ledbury, 12 from Hereford and 13 from Worcester. In addition to an extensive Calling and Local Trade a highly remunerative Business is done throughout the Hop and Fruit Season ; the Tenant has carried on a very profitable Trade at the Grocery and General Stores and the Butcher's Shop has been sub-let.

The 1922 sale of the Chase

An accident outside the Chase Inn in the 1950s

House so it is not surprising that he ran the butcher's shop behind the pub. However, he decided to concentrate on growing hops, and in the 1880s and 1890s bought several properties for this purpose, his brother Charles Edward Pudge taking over the **Chase Inn** and butcher's shop. When the pub was offered for sale by auction on 26 July 1922 it was described as 'A well-built Country Inn, Licensed for Beer, Cider and Wines …'. Vacant possession was offered on completion, although the outgoing tenant, Mr. T. Foley, claimed certain fixtures. William Farmer

The Chase in 1999

Pudge became a celebrated grower of hops and between the wars was said to be the largest private grower of hops in England. In 1926 he built a new complex of hop-drying kilns behind the **Chase Inn** — the largest in England. His business needed many hop pickers in the season, some of whom were of gypsy families. Their dealings are described in *A Pocketful of Hops*:

> They always had a number of horses and ponies with them, and on Sundays horse dealing would go on outside the Chase Inn, the men running up and down the road to show off the good points of their animals. Wads of money were seen to change hands, always going to the head of the family.

William Farmer Pudge died in 1938, and his hop business was wound up about 1962. The drying complex became a warehouse which has since been demolished to make way for houses.

Just round the corner from the **Chase Inn** is the **Green Dragon Inn** — there has been an inn of that name in the village for at least 200 years. An advertisement appeared in the *Hereford Journal* of 10 March 1790 for property to be sold by auction 'at the dwelling house of Mr. Robert Veale, known by the sign of the Green Dragon, in the Village of Bishop's Froome ...'. Later advertisements show that the name was correctly Robert Vale, and he was still there well into the 19th century. The Land Tax Returns record that Robert Vale paid an

The Green Dragon in 1999

143

The splendid Green Dragon sign

annual tax of 4s. on this property. In 1812 the name of Philip Dutson appears for the first time, and the Returns from that year show that he paid a tax of 2s. on a property named as the **Green Dragon**. As Robert Vale continues to appear in the Returns, this means that Vale had closed his public house and that Philip Dutson had opened another with the same name. In 1851 it was held by Jane Dutson, his widow then aged 73 who had been born at Putley, but in 1861 it was held by her 60-year-old son, William Dutson, born in Ashperton, who also worked as a blacksmith. The **Green Dragon** continued to be in the hands of later members of the Dutson family until about 1970. The present amusing sign for the pub was painted in 1980 by local artist Jamie Davidson, who then worked for Hereford City Museum and Art Gallery. Each side is different, one being set in summer and the other in winter, and each shows a benevolent dragon and a farmer quaffing a pint of ale. Peering out of the foliage on the other side of the sign is a red parrot, a reference to the name the **Red Parrot** used by some of the locals.

The **Green Dragon** is marked on the tithe map of 1844, but not the **Chase Inn**, as it had not then been built. However, there was another establishment called the **Anchor Inn** marked on the tithe map on the opposite side of the road leading to Burley Gate. Nothing else is known of this pub and it must have been superseded by the **Chase Inn**. The present building on the site is dated 1850 and so the former pub has been rebuilt.

The road by the side of the **Green Dragon** leads westwards towards Burley Gate. Two miles along this road is Panks Bridge, just in Much Cowarne parish. Here, at Panks Bridge Cottage, just before the First World War, was a short-lived cider house called the **Traveller's Rest**.

About a half-a-mile south of Bishop's Frome a left turn leads tortuously to the **Major's Arms** at Halmond's Frome, only about a mile off the B4214, but seeming much further up a steep incline called Snail's Bank. This inn seems to have had its origins in the middle of the 19th century, and in 1871 it was run by James Jennings, then aged 60. Within a few years it had passed into the hands of the Went family and in 1879 the licensee was Mrs. Jane Went, described as a beer retailer & carrier at 'Hailmond's' Frome. Within a few years Charles Went had taken over the business. This pub was for sale by auction on 29 October 1890 including over 3 acres of land. Charles Went was then paying rent of £20 per annum. It seems to have been at this time that the pub came into the ownership of the Hereford Imperial Brewery. He was succeeded in 1906 by Albert Edward Herbert, who was not only a beer retailer but also the rating officer and clerk to the Parish Council. The **Major's Arms** is referred to twice in *Herefordshire within Living Memory*, published by the Herefordshire Federation of Women's Institutes in 1993. One writer said:

A VALUABLE FREEHOLD PUBLIC-HOUSE & LAND,

KNOWN AS

"THE MAJOR'S ARMS,"

Situate at Halmond's Froome, in the Parish of Bishop's Froome, containing

3a. 2r. 14p.

The DWELLING HOUSE is Timber and Brick-built and Slated, and contains Parlour, Kitchen, Shop, Two Bed Rooms, and Underground Cellar.

The Outbuildings are : Cider Mill, with Loft over, Stable, Wainhouse, and Pigs' Cot, and the following Enclosures :—

No. on Plan.	Name.	State.	A.	R.	P.
794	House, Garden, and Orchard	Orchard and Garden	0	2	5
793	Hop Yard	Pasture	1	1	18
786	Orchard	Pasture Orchard	1	2	36
		TOTAL ACREAGE	3	2	14

Let to Mr. Charles Went, at £20 per annum, tenant paying all outgoings. The apportioned Tithe Rent Charge is 17s. 2d. Land Tax, 7s. 9d.

This Lot is bounded by Lands belonging to Mrs. Adney, Mrs. Chambers, Mr. Meredith, Mr. Walter Lloyd, and Road leading to Froomes Hill.

The 1890 sale of the Major's Arms

THE "MAJOR'S ARMS" BEER HOUSE,

Halmond's Frome, Bishop's Frome.

A Stone and Slated House.

Containing General Shop, Parlour, Tap Room, Beer Cellar and Two Bed Rooms. Cider Mill House with Loft, Cart-shed, Piggery, Stable and Garden ; also

Two ORCHARDS and a MEADOW, in all about 3a. 2r. 14p.

Let to Mr. Charles Went at a Rent of **£20 per Annum.**

FREEHOLD.

The Major's Arms was included in the 1898 sale of the Imperial Brewery

My grandfather A.E. (Bert) Herbert was licensee of the Major's Arms at Bishop's Frome from 1906 to his death in 1947 and he used to make and sell his own cider and perry for a penny ha'penny a pint. He used to boast that his perry was so strong that no one could drink more than three pints of it. Many tried and some succeeded but Bert would say, 'Ah, but you haven't walked home yet!' As they went outside, the fresh air hit them and they went down as if pole-axed. The comment would then be made, 'See, Herbert's dog has bitten you'.

Another story refers to the terrible winter of 1941:

The winter of 1941 is remembered in Bishop's Frome for its icy conditions. There was freezing rain for three days. People sitting in the Major's Arms at the time, on one of the steep hills called Snail's Bank, remember how they could hear trees falling one after another as the ice built up. The only way they could use the road was on all fours with socks over their boots.

The combined effect of Bert Herbert's perry and the icy roads is almost beyond imagination!

The **Major's Arms** has now joined the electronic age, and boasts its own website, where browsers can be rewarded with a beautiful photograph of the setting sun taken from the terrace at the rear of the pub. Not only this, but it is also the home of the competition for the Halmond's Frome International Ferret Racing Cup, which takes place each August. Normally there are six races, followed by a semi final and final. Bets can be placed on the result and the proceeds, together with those from an auction of promises, go towards local charities. In 2001 nearly £3,000 was raised in this way.

The Major's Arms inn sign

Also in Halmond's Frome was a public house called the **Swill**! This was where a James Hill carried on a business as a grocer and beer retailer from before 1858. After his death the business was carried on by his widow Hannah, described in 1871 as an inn- and shop-keeper, but who was recorded in a directory of 1879 as a cider retailer in 'Hailmond's' Frome. By 1885 George Hill had taken over, and the 1891 census shows that Henry Hill, farmer and grocer, was at the Swill, so the beer retailing side had lapsed by that time. The building is now called Crumble Cottage.

Carrying on southwards on the B4214, the road crosses the main A4103 Hereford to Worcester road at the bottom of Frome's Hill. The junction is now staggered for safety reasons, whereas formerly it was an ordinary crossroads. Another mile, and the hamlet of Castle Frome lies to the east of the road. There is no inn here, but the church is worth a detour. Essentially it dates from the 12th century, and it has a most wonderful carved font of the same period. Such is its fame that in 1983 it was loaned for an exhibition of Romanesque Art that was organised at the Heyward Gallery in London. To the east of the church are the remains of the earthworks of a motte and bailey castle, from which the hamlet took its name.

The road to Ledbury meanders southwards, and after about a mile -and-a-half at Stanley Hill, just in the parish of Bosbury, there is a disused Wesleyan chapel on the left. For many years in the 19th century Philip Clissett, the well-known chairmaker, was a steward of this chapel. A simple craftsman, he has gained a well-earned reputation for the quality of his work. He was born at Birtsmorton in 1817, moved to Bosbury in about 1838 and then settled at Stanley Hill when he was 25 and lived here until his death in 1913 at the age of 96. First he made simple chairs of various types, making perhaps six in a week. These would fetch between 2s. 6d. and 4s. 6d. each and he would often take a load on his donkey cart and travel to Hereford and elsewhere to sell them. Later he made spindle-backed chairs, often with a rush seat. Such chairs, frequently marked with his initials, now fetch considerable sums at auction, perhaps as much for a single chair as he earned in a year. About 1880 he met a London architect called Maclaren who was so interested in his work that he designed a number of chairs. Clissett followed these patterns for rush-seated ladder-back and slat-back chairs and these were sold all over England for 18s. 6d. each. His last work was a special commission for two chairs which he executed when he was over 90.

The Oak at Staplow in 1999

After another mile-and-a-half the road from Bosbury joins from the left. At Staplow, a mile further on but still in Bosbury parish, is the **Oak Inn**. This began as a cider house in the hands of the Harding family. In 1851 Richard Harding was in charge, in 1858 Hannah Harding was the licensee, while in 1867 Richard Harding had taken over as beer retailer. However, the 1871 census shows that Hannah was still in control at the **Oak** despite being 84 years old. Within a few years William Townsend, who was also a blacksmith, had taken over, but William Henry Jones, in charge in 1902, was only a beer retailer. By 1910 Thomas Bishop was renting the **Oak Inn**, together with about 3 acres, from the local brewery of Lane Bros. & Bastow of Ledbury. In 1985 CAMRA stated that it was a '17th century locals' pub, said to built around an old oak tree'.

Off to the left half-way between Staplow and Ledbury is the village of Wellington Heath, which in the 19th century had a reputation for drunken behaviour. It was referred to as 'Hell on Earth' and in the middle of the century there were two beer or cider houses in the settlement. In 1851 the **Swallow** was held by innkeeper James Lane, aged 65 who lived there with his wife, four sons, three daughters and one lodger. In 1858 James Lane was described simply as a farmer at **Swallow**, but the cider selling business is said to have carried on until the 1870s (although not recorded as such in the census). In 1873 the Hope End Estate, on the east side of the parish, was bought by Charles Archibald Hewitt, a man of strong temperance principles. The **Swallow** was on the estate, and so was closed and converted to the estate laundry.

The second inn in Wellington Heath was described in the 1851 census as the **New House**, kept by William Gardiner, then aged 43, together with his wife Elizabeth, two sons and one daughter. Although in the census he was described as an innkeeper, in 1858 he was described as a farmer at **Rose Cottage** — the 'New House' had evidently been given a name. The business was eventually taken over by his widow Mrs. Elizabeth Gardiner who, in 1867, was described as a beer retailer and shopkeeper. She is last recorded in the 1880s and it seems to have been her successor, Thomas Allen, who changed the name to the **Farmers Arms** which first appears in a directory of 1891. He had strong opposition, as in the 1890s there was an active branch of the Church of England Temperance Society at Hope End with some 85 members. But while behaviour in the village no doubt improved, there was evidently enough support to keep the pub open. In 1902 it was held by William Palmer, innkeeper, farmer and cider merchant, a native of Bosbury and then aged about 61. A later landlady was Mrs. Emily Roberts, of whom local resident Peter Garnet says:

> In the 1930s, Mrs. Roberts, the owner, kept hens and made her own butter. Customers were mostly men, although a few women were allowed in the kitchen. The footballers used to water her plants with beer. At closing time she threw a bucket of water on the fire!

She was still there at the beginning of the Second World War, and after the war the **Farmers Arms** became the base for the local football team.

In 1985 CAMRA reported approvingly 'Once a cottage, then a cider house, the Farmer's Arms is now a pleasant, secluded, country pub'. In the late 1980s and 1990s the **Farmers Arms** was the base for the Monkey Island Group, run by a number of patrons and supported by Paul Ford, the then publican. It declared U.D.I. and had its own flag and passports, and ran several tongue-in-cheek activities, including an annual Fun Day, which all raised money both for the village and for charities.

The Farmers Arms in 2001

ALONG THE B4220

The alternative route from Bromyard to Ledbury is further to the east of the B4214. Taking the A44 eastwards and climbing up the Downs past the old workhouse, the B4220 is signposted to the right. After a mile or so there is a fork in the road, the main road bearing right while the minor road to Linley Green carries straight on. Surprisingly, this minor road was formerly part of the turnpike system, and was covered by the Bromyard Trust as far as Herefordshire Lake. Just past the junction on the main road is the drive to Southington Farm where, in 1851, Samuel Lloyd was a farmer and cider retailer. The farmhouse was rebuilt about 1860 and moved up the social scale, being described as a gentleman's residence and no longer a place where a cider retailer would live.

Linley Green is within the township of Linton, and in the middle of the 19th century there were about ten houses around the road junction. One of the houses near the junction is called Ramblers, which in 1842 was a house, shop and garden, with four acres. In 1851 John Wall was a cider retailer at the **Bee Hive** in Linley Green, and it is thought that he occupied this property. By 1867 his widow, Mrs. Ann Wall, had taken over, and in Littlebury's *Directory* of 1876 the premises was called **Herefordshire House**. It is marked as such on the 1887 1:2500 Ordnance Survey map. The business continued for some years after this, but at the Brewster Sessions of 1905 the local Superintendent of Police objected to the renewal of the licence and it must have then closed.

On past the junction in Linley is Yearsett, which was the terminus of the Worcester, Bromyard and Leominster Railway Company before the completion of the line as far as Bromyard in 1877. A short way along the road towards Yearsett is **Cider House Farm**. The present house was built soon after 1800 and as it was later tenanted by John Hawkins, innkeeper of the **Hop Pole** in Bromyard, it is thought to have been a cider-retailing establishment. It was occupied by Richard Dovey, the farm bailiff. How long it was a cider house is not known, but it was probably not for very many years. After Yearsett, the road crosses over the county boundary into Worcestershire.

Surprisingly enough, at the same time as Ann Wall carried on her business in Linley Green there was another pub called the **Herefordshire House** not very far away on the main B4220 at Stanford Bishop, one of two drinking establishments in that parish. This part of Stanford Bishop parish is called Wofferwood Common, and sometimes Woodford Common in earlier times, and 'Wooferwood' Gate was the furthest point of the Bromyard Turnpike Trust in this direction. The Common, which was 212 acres in extent, was enclosed in 1862. The **Herefordshire House** is first mentioned in the 1851 census when it was a cider house run by Ann Boxhall and her husband William. It was already called **Herefordshire House** at that time, but its earlier name was Heath House. By 1867 John Bruton was in charge and he was succeeded by Thomas Bishop, beer and cider retailer. At the time of the 1881 census Thomas Page, aged 46, was running the business and when he died in 1893 he was described as a

Caleb Jones and his family outside the Herefordshire House at Stanford Bishop in the 1920s

haulier and beerhouse keeper. His widow Mary Jane made her will in 1899 and **Herefordshire House** was taken over by their son, Major Berriman Page. He was christened 'Major', his name not being a rank in the army. From 1913 and up to the Second World War the pub was run by Caleb Jones. An exchange of correspondence concerning his income tax in 1929 gives an impression of the volume of sales at a small country pub. In the 1950s the licence was taken over by H.R. Holland who came from the **Live and Let Live** on Bringsty Common. After he relinquished the

> 10th October, 1929.
>
> Dear Sir,
>
> C. R. Jones. Herefordshire
> House, Stanford Bishop. 6614.
>
> ————————————————
>
> Mr. Jones informs me that he has not kept accounts in respect of his business but he states that his sales would not exceed a hogshead and 3 dozens of bottled goods per week.
> His profit per hogshead including discount is £3 and 2/- per dozen on bottled goods.
> If you accept these figures the assessment of £250 is obviously excessive.
>
> The house is tied to Messrs. Lewis Clarke & Co. of Worcester.
>
> Yours faithfully,
>
> H. M. Inspector of Taxes,
> Lloyds Bank Chambers,
> HEREFORD.

A plea to the Tax Officer.
Mr. Jones' income was eventually
assessed at £120 for the whole year

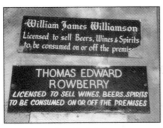

(right) The Herefordshire House has changed considerably since the 1920s

licence in the 1960s he was succeeded by William James Williamson, and then by Thomas Edward Rowberry. The latter was the son-in-law of H.R. Holland, and had hoped to take over the licence from him, but the brewery thought otherwise and he had to wait until William Williamson had had a spell as licensee. The **Herefordshire House** has continued as licensed premises until the present day.

The other beer house in Stanford Bishop was about half-a-mile down the road that leads off directly opposite the **Herefordshire House**. In 1861 Henry Allkins was a butcher and victualler at White House, later called **White Hall**. The 1881 census shows that Thomas Bowen, wheelwright and innkeeper, had taken it over, and he is described in directories in 1885 and 1891 as a beer retailer and farmer. The **White Hall** seems to have closed as an inn soon after this, but the house still retains its name.

In the mid-19th century there were two other small drinking places in Stanford Bishop. In 1851 Ann Smith, a 48-year-old widow, was a cider retailer at Slate Cottage, then in 1861 Elizabeth Williams, a 35-year-old

The White Hall in retirement

The Cliffe Arms at Mathon in 2002

widow at Eath Cottage (the name is indistinct) was delightfully described as an 'Hostess of Ale &c. Cider House'.

From Stanford Bishop the B4220 carries on through a sparsely populated area — with a consequent dearth of pubs — down to join the A4103 at Ridgeway Cross. A left turn here, a drop down a sharp hill, and then a right turn and the road becomes the B4220 again. This is in the parish of Cradley, whose various licensed establishments are described in the next chapter.

Soon after Cradley a turn to the left leads to Mathon, formerly in Worcestershire but transferred to Herefordshire in 1897. Bentley's *Directory of Worcestershire* of *c.*1841 records two pubs there, the **Cliffe Arms Inn**, and the **Fox and Hounds**. The **Cliffe Arms Inn**, right in the centre of the village, was run by Thomas Ravenhill, who was described as a victualler, and there have been a succession of landlords since. In 1941 Leslie Hatch, the landlord, still brewed his own beer and up until the 1960s his widow, Mrs. Hatch, was the well-respected landlady. After a brief interlude as the **Trundle Inn,** the name reverted to the **Cliffe Arms**. The barn to the rear has been converted to a restaurant and the beer merits a mention in the *Good Beer Guide 2002*.

At the **Fox and Hounds** the landlord in 1841 was J. Yapp, also described as a victualler, but it is uncertain how long the pub lasted. By 1871 — and probably before — there was a pub in the parish, called the **Bell**, but this was probably just a name change. It was held by James

Parsons, aged 35, described as a beer house keeper. This was located a mile or more through the village on the more southerly of the two roads to West Malvern. It was still open in 1941, but did not survive through the second half of the 20th century and is now private house, although it has very much the feel of a former licensed establishment.

At one time the Bell at Mathon

The 1871 census also recorded a pub called the **Oak**, run by William Hobbs, but this seems to have lasted only a short time.

Returning to the B4220, it is not far to the next former drinking establishment.

The Old Country Inn at Bosbury in 2002

The parish of Bosbury is very extensive and there was formerly a pub at the small hamlet of Old Country, fully two miles before the village itself is reached. It was on the left-hand side just before a nasty double bend in the road. In Lascelles' *Directory* of 1851 Kenelm Orgee appears as a beer retailer, recorded in another directory in 1858 as 'Kenlin' Orgee. By 1867 he had added farming to his occupation, but by 1891 he had been succeeded by Mrs. Augusta Orgee. When the 1910 Land Valuation was carried out, the **Old Country Inn** was being rented by William Bishop, but the owner was Alfred Orgee of The Green, Bosbury. As well as the inn, Bishop rented some 10 acres of surrounding land.

Mrs. Ada Lord was in charge in 1941, and it was still open in 1964. In that year H.P. Bulmer and Co. Ltd. issued a list of inns of Herefordshire (but inns only appeared in the list if they sold Bulmer's products!). The **Old Country** appeared as selling Bulmer's bottled products. Even so, it closed within a few years.

For such a small hamlet it is surprising that there was another short-lived beer house in Old Country, held in 1879 by Joseph Holder. The 1881 census doesn't give it a name, recording that is was just a public house with 79-year-old Joseph 'Older' as publican.

From Old Country the road meanders on its way to Bosbury, past the splendid Bosbury House behind its tall brick wall. On the outskirts of Bosbury a side road to the right leads down to Dowding's Brook, just over which was a beer house called, not surprisingly, the **Brook Inn**. In 1891 James Matthews was a beer retailer at the **Brook**, and the 1910 Land Valuations shows that it was tenanted, as it was then owned by the Royal Well Brewery Co. of Malvern. The **Brook Inn** was run in 1941 by Harry Colley, but it did not last much longer after this and reverted to a simple cottage, the front of which has been rebuilt in red brick in modern times.

On entering the main settlement of Bosbury, on the right-hand side is a building referred to in the 1997 *Transactions* of the Woolhope Naturalists' Field Club as the Dog. This is a three-bay house with a cross-wing, built initially in the 16th century and altered *c*.1600 and later. The name is suggestive of a pub, but an earlier name was Dog Farm — it has never been licensed premises. Indeed, in 1871 the Dog was the residence of Edwin Peacock, a certificated schoolmaster.

A little further along, on the left, is the **Bell** which has been an inn for more than 200 years. The *Hereford Journal* of 18 April 1776 carried an advertisement for a meeting to take place at the **Bell Inn**, Bosbury, to consult about flooding in the parish of Bosbury, while on 4 May 1791 some property was advertised to be sold by auction 'at Mr. Loggin's, the Bell Inn, in Bosbury …'. This was Samuel Loggen — the name is spelled in various ways. Thus another advertisement in the *Hereford Journal* of 11 December 1793 stated that some property to be sold at 'Mr. Leggan's, Innholder, Bosbury'.

It was during Samuel Loggen's time that an Amicable Society was established, meeting at the **Bell Inn**, the rules of which are dated

The Bell at Bosbury about 1900

7 October 1794. After his death his will, which had been made some years before, was proved on 9 January 1810. In it he was described as a victualler, and he left his copyhold estate and all his goods and chattels including his stock in trade, to his niece Mary Mutlow, subject to a payment of £10 to his sister-in-law Jane Loggen of Castle Frome, a similar payment to his niece Elizabeth Loggen, also of Castle Frome, and a payment of 1s. 6d. a week to Eleanor Loggen who was then residing in his dwelling house in Bosbury, and to allow her a room there for the rest of her life. The relationship between Samuel and Eleanor Loggen is not stated, but if she was his widow it seems an ungenerous provision for her.

The **Bell Inn** was sold by auction on the premises on 13 April 1812, and it was described in the *Hereford Journal* as:

THAT well-accustomed PUBLIC-HOUSE, called the BELL INN, in the Village of Bosbury aforesaid, together with the Land and Outbuilding; comprising a small Orchard, planted with the choicest Fruit Trees in full bearing, a large and fertile Garden, a large and good Malt-house and Malt Kiln, with a Brew-house and Cellar underneath, and an excellent Stable for Eight Horses.

Also a House or Tenement adjoining the above, with a good Shop, subject to the Life-Interest of a Woman about Seventy years of age.

The Bell in 2001

The aforesaid Public-House and Tenement adjoining are Copyhold of Inheritance, under the Lord Bishop of Hereford, little inferior to Freehold. The Inn is now in the Possession of Mr. Richard Panting, who had had Notice to quit the same at Michaelmas next.

The above Premises would, exclusive of the Public-house, be very convenient for a Maltster, Butcher, or Baker. — The Purchaser will be expected to come into Copy at the next Court, which will be holden in May, 1812.

Presumably the life interest referred to was that of 70-year-old Elizabeth Loggen.

The landlords often had other business interests, and in 1851 John Baskerville was described as a victualler and shopkeeper, and also ran the village post office. John Lewis, licensee in 1858, was also a shopkeeper, while in 1867 Henry Caundel was a horse breaker. At the beginning of the 20th century the pub was owned by the Ledbury brewery of Lane Bros. & Bastow and was tenanted by Ernest Evans. Like the Dog, the **Bell Inn** was probably built in the 16th century, but was later altered and extended to the west and south. Sections of the original barge boards with running tracery survive on the gable on the north front. Photographs taken early in the 20th century show that the front of the premises was then covered with plaster (see p.157), but this has since been stripped off and the timbering revealed.

The most noticeable feature of the village street is the detached tower of the parish church, one of a number in Herefordshire, just past the **Bell Inn** and on the opposite side of the road. There are other detached stone towers at Garway and Ledbury, while the lower part of the tower at Holmer is also stone but with a timber belfry. The tower at Richard's Castle is also thought to have been surmounted by a timber spire which was later burnt. Towers at Kington and Weobley were probably detached when they were first built. Most notable are the timber towers at Pembridge and Yarpole, which date originally from the first half of the 13th century, and this is when the tower at Bosbury is thought to have been built. It was originally surmounted by a wooden spire, but the condition of this was such that in 1812 the Vestry decided to demolish the spire and re-finish the top of the tower. This was not done immediately, however, as in June 1815 the parish authorities advertised in the *Hereford Journal* for a contractor to undertake this work.

In 1888 a bell-ringer called William Fussell was appointed as an instructor to the Hereford Diocesan Guild of Bell Ringers, and he held the post for a number of years. He kept a diary for his early years in this post, and this shows that he visited Bosbury on 26 January 1889, having walked there from Bromyard. In his diary he recorded:

> While at Bosbury I calld on Wm Jennings (age 83 next March) who was a ringer about 60 years ago when the local men only rang rounds but afterwards managed the 30s. A stone jar wh. they used for refreshments held 16 quarts & was emptied during a night's ringing. He remembered the old wooden spire, 2 yds out of the upright —pulled down for safety — it leaned toward the Bell.

In such a position, it is not surprising that the **Bell** was the pub used by the ringers!

Lascelles' *Directory* of 1851 mentions a William Jenks, a beer retailer in Bosbury, whose establishment was called the **Bells**. This

Interior of the Crown Inn about 1912

was not the same as the **Bell**, and may have been an earlier name for a beer house called the **New Inn**, first mentioned in 1858 when John Shaw was in charge. This seems to have been on the same side of the road as the **Bell**, but further along. In 1881 he was aged 63 and described as a publican, although a directory of 1879 shows that he did some farming as well. The 1910 Land Valuation shows that the **New Inn** was owned at that time by Salt & Co., Brewers, of Burton-on-Trent. It did not survive for many years after this.

At the west end of the main street, on the south side, is the former **Crown Inn**. The glory of the house is a panelled room, the pilasters of the overmantel bearing the date 1571 and the initials RH and MH for Richard and Martha Harford. Richard Harford died in 1578 and recessed in the north wall of the chancel of the church is a most splendid monument to his memory. On the south wall is another monument, erected by Richard Harford in 1573 in memory of his father John, and this was carved by John Guldon of Hereford. Guldon (the name has a variety of spellings) almost certainly carved Richard's monument as well.

About 1890 the **Crown** was visited by H. Thornhill Timmins, who described it thus:

Once the Crown at Bosbury

Quite at the far end, scarce visible in our sketch, stands the wayside inn, containing, in a fine old wainscoted hall known as the Crown Room, some traces of the ancient mansion of the Harford family, whose monuments we have already discovered in the church. This fine apartment is of considerable size, with wide stone-mullioned window. The fireplace is surrounded with old blue Dutch tiles, and over it, in handsomely-carved panels, appear the arms of the families of Wrottesley, Scrope and Fox, and the date 1571. A frieze of delicate carving runs around, and at the crossing of the massive beams in the ceiling, three bosses show respectively the bearings of Bishop Skipp, the arms of Scrope, and of Powlett first Marquis of Westminster, having the garter and coronet.

The house must have slipped in the social scale, for by the end of the 18th century it had become the **Crown Inn** — in the *Hereford Journal* of 15 August 1798 there is an advertisement for an auction to take place at the 'Crown-inn in the village of Bosbury'. As with the **Bell Inn**, a Friendly Society was established there, the rules being dated 14 July 1795.

Advertisements for the inn appear regularly in trade directories and for many years in the second half of the 19th century James Herbert Brazier was here. In 1941, when Frank Rawson was proprietor, it was advertised as 'Ye Old Crown Hotel'. Subsequently closed and converted to a private residence, it still retains evidence of its former use in the form of a brewery plaque let into the wall. The house has clearly climbed the social scale again as when it was offered for sale in the summer of 2001 the asking price was £450,000!

In the 19th century there were several beer retailers in the parish of Bosbury who are so far unlocated including George Jones (1867) and James Pugh (1891 & 1902). After Bosbury, the B4220 swings left at the junction with the B4214, on its way to Ledbury.

CHAPTER NINE

The Worcester Road

The road from Hereford to Worcester leaves Hereford over Aylestone Hill, and then swings to the right over the Lugg Flats. Here it follows the line of the main east-west Roman road from Kenchester, which passes over Lugg Bridge. On the right is the former Lugg Bridge Mills, dismantled in 1925 and now converted into dwellings. The A465 Bromyard road leaves on the left, and the main road gradually bears to the left, diverging from the line of the old Roman road. A mile or so further on is the turning for Withington village with the settlement around Whitestone — marked by an 18th-century milestone — on the main road. Surprisingly, there are no inns in the main part of this village, but John Philips, the poet and author of the poem entitled

The Whitestone

Cyder, spent much time at Withington Court.

At Whitestone, turning right along the road towards Bartestree, there was formerly a beer house on the right-hand side just before the railway bridge. It was called the **Railway Inn**, not surprising in view of its position, but was only operational for a short time. It was just within the parish of Withington and the first mention is in a directory of 1867. In the 1871 census William Cole, a native of Weston Beggard, was the beerhouse keeper, and its position is confirmed because the next property was the signal box at Withington Station. The railway between Hereford and Worcester was opened in 1861, but the number of railway personnel recorded in the census of that year still resident in Withington indicates that the work was not completed at that time. The **Railway Inn** must have been opened purely to service the increased population, but there was an immediate threat to the pub for it was in 1861 that William Godwin opened a tile works adjacent to Withington station, on the other side of the road from the **Railway Inn**. This tile works was designed both to take advantage of the new railway and because there was a suitable bed of clay which could be used to make their decorative floor and wall tiles. The factory was in production by 1863 and was at the peak of its success in the 1870s. It is said that William Godwin bought the **Railway Inn** and closed it down to prevent the workmen drinking away their wages. Certainly it had closed by 1881 and it then became known as Railway House.

Returning to the main road and turning eastwards, after a short distance is Weston Corner, where there was a competitor to the **Railway Inn**. This was a beerhouse that was first mentioned in 1861 — again the date seems significant — run by William Bayliss, a farmer and haulier. In 1871 his establishment was named as the **Weston Corner Inn**, and he was described simply as a beer retailer, evidently having retired from his more strenuous activities. At that time he was 80 years old, so it is not surprising that neither he nor his beer house were recorded in the 1881 census — it must have closed by that time. The inn was probably at what is now called Weston Corner Farm.

The next village along the main road is Shucknall, which is in the parish of Weston Beggard. Where the road enters the settlement on a left-hand bend known as Crown Corner, another road joins at an acute angle from the right. In the junction is a building that was formerly a pub called the **Crown Inn**, built by James Hollings at the beginning of the 19th century. Its position is marked on Bryant's map of 1835, but an earlier mention is in the *Hereford Journal* of 30 August 1820, when it was advertised as being to let. After the death of James Hollings it became the property of his daughter Margaret, and when she decided to marry Mr. Richard Cropper Williams in 1838 she transferred the ownership to him for at that time married women could not hold property in their own right. It was then in the occupation of Thomas Corbett.

When the **Crown Inn** was sold to Thomas Davies in 1863 it was stated that it was still in the occupation of Thomas Corbett, but this was incorrect for in 1851 Charles Redding, victualler, plumber, glazier and painter, was at the **Crown**, and

Once the Crown at Shucknall, in 2002

by 1856 he had been succeeded by John Leake. Either a former deed had been copied verbatim, or Thomas Corbett was subletting the property.

Be that as it may, John Leake was still there in 1867 when a riot took place. In the autumn of that year there were a number of Irish hop-pickers on local farms, who met at the **Crown Inn** to drink and talk, no doubt of the troubles — the potato famine and the suppression of the Young Ireland insurrection. One night things got out of hand, quarrelling began, and at about 9 o'clock John Leake called on John Baylis, the parish constable, for assistance. Clearly the arrival of this figure of authority was a flash-point, and he was set upon with cries of 'We are Fenians', kicked, his hair pulled out in tufts, and a woman pulled his neckerchief so tight that he almost choked. His head was belaboured with mugs and he was hit with an iron spittoon. His repeated cries of 'murder' were eventually heeded by a local labourer called Peter Batchelor and a stranger with a wooden leg, and he was dragged along the floor to the sanctuary of the kitchen. Spittoons were hurled, windows were smashed and there were threats to burn down the pub. The mob only dispersed when Thomas Leake, the landlord's son, fired a gun over the rioters' heads from an upstairs window. Only a few of the troublemakers were later caught. John Baylis was badly injured but survived after John Henry Wood, a surgeon from Tarrington, removed pieces of bone protruding from his skull. His ordeal was recognised by the parishioners, who held a collection to provide him with comforts. It is something of an anti-climax to record that by 1876 James Shaw had taken over from James Leake and that the **Crown Inn** probably closed soon after this.

There was another short-lived pub in Weston Beggard, run by Thomas Corbett of the **Crown**. In 1851 Corbett was recorded as a cottage farmer and cider merchant at Churchetts, in Weston Beggard. On 4 October 1856 a petition for bankruptcy was issued against Thomas Corbett:

> formerly at the Crown Inn, Weston Beggard, licensed inn keeper, victualler, cider dealer, and farmer at Newtown and Monk Hyde, Yarkhill, and at the same time farming the Lugg meadows in Tupsley, thence residing at Church House, afterwards and at present called the Bannutt Tree Beer and Cider House, Weston Beggard.

He appears as a beer retailer in a 1856 directory, but must have overcome his financial difficulties for in 1858 he was again recorded as a farmer and beer retailer. His name then disappears from the record — and so does the **Bannutt Tree**.

After skirting Shucknall Hill, the road drops down to a level stretch, where the Gloucester to Hereford canal formerly passed underneath the main road. A section of the canal including a magnificent skew bridge, which has been restored by the Hereford and Gloucester Canal Trust, is on the right towards Monkhide. The depth of the restored section compared to the unrestored section beyond emphasises not only how much work was done by the 'navvies' who dug the canal, but also how much labour it will take to restore the whole canal. Enough to drive the present day 'navigators' to drink!

A gradual climb brings the thirsty traveller to Newtown Cross, where the Worcester road crosses the A417 Leominster to Gloucester road. There is, of course, a hostelry called the **Newtown Inn**, formerly called the **New Inn**, which displays a splendid three-dimensional sign featuring a finger post. This inn was the base for one of the earliest buses in Herefordshire which was actually garaged at the **New Inn**. From 30 March 1920 services ran from Newtown to Bromyard, Hereford, Ledbury and Leominster on their various market days. Mr. Nullis, the driver, cycled out from Hereford and was paid 10¾d. per hour. In April 1920 the service was taken over by the newly formed Hereford Transport Ltd. The son of the landlord, Frederick Bunn, was trained as a driver — no problem with a PSV licence in those days —

177. YARKHILL.—THE NEW INN.

ALL THAT messuage or Inn formerly known as The New Town Inn but now known as The New Inn situate at Newtown in the Parish of Yarkhill in the County of Hereford with the yard garden stables and all other outbuildings and appurtenances thereunto belonging AND ALSO ALL THOSE two pieces or parcels of orchard land adjoining the said Inn on one of which the said Inn stands particulars whereof are set out in the Schedule hereunder written.

The SCHEDULE referred to:—

No. on Tithe Map.	Name.	Quality.	Quantity		
			A.	R.	P.
328	Orchard	Grass orchard	1	0	29
329	New Inn, shop and garden			1	36
			A.1	2	25

Sale of the Newtown Inn to the Cheltenham Original Brewery in 1937

and when the service was on a satisfactory footing he took over and Mr. Nullis moved to Dilwyn where he repeated his successful service.

This was one of the pubs that was owned by Arnold Perrett & Co. Ltd. and was transferred to the Cheltenham Original Brewery in 1937. At that time it was still called the **New Inn**, but some time later, after

The Newtown Inn in 2001

The Newtown Inn sign

another change of hands, it was sold by the Stroud Brewery to the West Country Brewery as the **Newtown Inn**. In 1985 it was described by CAMRA as a 'Friendly country pub which, in Victorian times, was used as an auction room. Once called the "New Inn", the Newtown Inn consists of two bars and a restaurant'. It changed hands in 2002 and as the new owner is a chef the restaurant is likely to figure prominently in the future.

The **Newtown Inn** is in Yarkhill parish and adjoining it is Stretton Grandison parish, where, in 1858, there is an isolated mention of a **Bridge Inn**, held by Thomas Cleaton, described as a victualler, but its location is uncertain. South from Newtown Cross along the A417, at Filling Bridge the road crosses over into the parish of Stretton Grandison from Yarkhill, but there is nothing to suggest that the house there was the **Bridge Inn**. Again, along the A4103 towards Worcester, the settlement of Lower Eggleton is also in Stretton Grandison, and it may be that the **Bridge Inn** was here, as the road crosses the Lodon Brook at this point.

However, there is no doubt about the next two drinking establishments a mile or so along the main road towards Worcester, before it ascends Frome's Hill. The first one, on the right-hand side, is the **Fir Tree Inn**, in the area known as Callow Marsh. Callow Marsh is in the parish of Much Cowarne, and this beer house was already in existence when the tithe map was drawn up about the year 1840. In 1851 Mrs. Jemima Price was a publican in 'Collow marsh' — the census does not state where she lived, but it is given as the **Fir Tree** in a directory of the same year. She had been born in Bishop's Frome, the next parish, and was then aged 50. Later in the 1850s the inn was taken over by George Burgoyne, whose name was given as 'Burgwin' in the 1861 census. He was then aged 41 and supplemented his income by his

*The Fir Tree in 2001. The main Hereford to Worcester road
runs along the side of the inn*

work as a tailor. A directory of 1867 states that Thomas Philpotts was a beer retailer at Callow Marsh, but the 1871 census gives the name of the occupier as William Philpotts, who was described as a beer-house keeper. When his widow Elizabeth took over a few years later she also ran a shop and in 1902 Charles Philpotts, another member of the family, was described as a grocer and farmer, presumably letting his wife run the **Fir Tree Inn**.

By 1917 James Bouston was described as a beer retailer of Callow Marsh, and so had taken over the business. In the 1930s there was a problem with the sanitation. At the Brewster Sessions held in Bromyard on 1 February 1938 Superintendent J. Edge first made a report, then the chairman of the Bench, Col. J.T. Lutley, in a discussion about sanitation, was reported as saying that:

> He had consulted his Brother Magistrates and they considered that he should mention the two worst cases. The one was the Fir Tree, Much Cowarne. He had occasion to make remarks about this house last year. He thought the Fir Tree was worse than anything he saw last year for filth…

The problem must have been resolved for the inn remained open throughout the Second World War. At this time it had a reputation as a place where the travelling folk met and there are stories of many bare-fisted fights taking place here.

The *Bromyard News and Record* of 3 December 1953 reported that the **Fir Tree Inn** had been bought by Mr. Price for £4,000. He was there for many years, running a successful outside catering business that supplied food at many functions. In 1985 CAMRA described it as a 'Lively two bar country pub, whose landlord has been here for fifty years'. In recent years it has expanded from a simple pub and now has a large restaurant. It also offers coarse fishing on its own lake, as well as caravan holidays in its own static caravans.

A little further along the road at Five Bridges, and now set well back because the road has been straightened, is the **Five Bridges Inn**, a 17th-century building faced in brick. Over the years several other businesses have been based on the premises. An advertisement in the *Hereford Journal* of 8 May 1799 stated that certain premises were to be sold by auction 'At the Dwelling-house of Mr. Thomas Godfrey, called the Five Bridges Inn, in the parish of Much Cowarne, on Thursday, the Twenty-third day of May instant …'. It was later renamed and was advertised for sale in the *Hereford Journal* on 18 August 1820 as 'A well-accustomed Public-House called The Lion …'. With **The Lion** went 25 acres, and the auction was to take place at Five Bridges.

Locals and the village policeman outside the Five Bridges in 1907

There was some confusion for the *c.*1840 tithe map does not show the building as a public house, whilst James Wagstaff, the occupier in 1851, is described simply as a blacksmith, evidently using the blacksmith's shop that was across the road. More confusion as Lascelles' *Directory* of 1851 states that he was a victualler and blacksmith at the **Red Lion**, but another directory of 1856 gives the name as the **Five Bridges Inn**. By 1861 it had been taken over by his 27-year-old son William, who kept the smith's shop as well as being an innkeeper. The sale of beer to waiting customers by the Wagstaffs no doubt was a welcome supplement to the income from the smithy. By 1867 Francis Hill was the licensee of the **Five Bridges Inn**, but in the 1871 census he was said to be a licensed victualler at 'Five Bridges (Lion Inn)'. It was still called the **Lion Public House** when John Pitt ran his carrier's business from it in 1891, but by 1902 his widow, Mrs. Frances Pitt, called it the **Five Bridges Inn** where she also had a grocer's business. This was not the end of the name changes for in 1913 Mrs. Elizabeth Wall was recorded as being at the **Lion Public House** at Five Bridges, followed the next year by William Abbott when it was once again called the **Five Bridges Inn**. The last mention of the **Lion Public House** was in a 1917 directory and after this it seems to have stabilized as the **Five Bridges**! In 1941 the landlord, S.R. Hyett, was one of the few in the area who brewed his own beer.

The straightening of the main road in the early 1960s has left the **Five Bridges** facing away from the new main road. However, access to the car park is from the new road and the modern extensions conceal

The Five Bridges in 2001

No. 30.

THE "WHEATSHEAF" INN PUBLIC HOUSE,

Frome's Mill, Bishop's Frome,

Brick-built Premises, situate on the Main Road from Hereford to Worcester.

Containing Bar, Bar Parlour with partition, Tap Room, Larder, Cellar in Basement, Back Kitchen, Cider House, Spirit Room, Four Bed Rooms and Store Room.   Small Yard with pump of water, Three-stall Stable with Loft over, W.C., another Stable for Eight horses, Barn and large Garden.

Also an ORCHARD and TWO MEADOWS, in all about 7a. 2r. 24p.

The whole let to Mr. W. H. Hopkinson at Rents amounting to **£40 per Annum.**

FREEHOLD.

Wheatsheaf Inn
Frome's Hill
Near Ledbury.

17. ALL THAT messuage and public-house known as the "Wheatsheaf" with the outbuildings yard and garden thereto belonging situate at Frome's Hill in the Parish of Bishop's Frome in the County of Hereford and also ALL THOSE the gardens orchard and two meadows thereto adjoining and containing in all 7 acres 2 roods 24 perches or thereabouts.

Sale of the Wheatsheaf
Top: From the Hereford Imperial Brewery to the Tredegar Brewery in 1898
Bottom: From the Tredegar and Hereford Brewery to
the Cheltenham and Hereford Brewery in 1948

The Wheatsheaf in 2001

172

the origins of the building. As with many country establishments, the main business is now in the well-established restaurant, so much so that it advertises as the Five Bridges Inn, Public House and Restaurant.

The straightening of the road past the Five Bridges gives the motorist a good run at Frome's Hill, which is certainly needed. At the top is the settlement of Frome's Hill itself, mostly in Bishop's Frome parish but at the top of the hill it borders onto the parish of Castle Frome. To the right is a road that cuts across to the B4214 road to Ledbury, and somewhere about here was a short-lived beer house at **Half Hide**. In 1851 the name of William Fincher appeared in a directory as a beer retailer, and in 1858 he added the trade of stone mason. He seems to have been succeeded by James Barrett, described in 1867 as a beer retailer and carpenter, but the establishment closed soon after.

The most noticeable establishment in Frome's Hill is the **Wheatsheaf Inn.** Described by the Royal Commission on Historical Monuments as being of 17th-century origin, the Commissioners recorded that it had been recently almost entirely modernized, a process of alteration and extension that has continued to the present day. It has been a licensed establishment for many years, and an early reference is an advertisement in the *Hereford Journal* of 10 January 1821 for a farm to be sold by auction at the **Wheat Sheaf Inn**, Frome's Hill. William Henry Hopkinson, landlord for the last quarter of the 19th century, was also the assistant overseer for the parish. It was a Hereford Imperial Brewery pub and is recorded in the 1898 sales details. Described by CAMRA in 1985 as 'An old coaching pub-cum-petrol station, run by a very friendly landlord. The pub once belonged to the Hereford and Tredegar Brewery and is full of old-fashioned charm.' However, as a result of a recent planning dispute the pub is now closed and the car-park is barricaded off by beer kegs. The Frome's Hill Brewery, based at the **Wheatsheaf**, is not at present in production. At the time of writing (April 2003) news comes that the **Wheatsheaf** has been sold and it is to be hoped that it will reopen in the very near future.

Opposite the **Wheatsheaf** was the **Half-way House Inn**, first mentioned in the 1861 census when it was held by 57-year-old William Sheppard. In directories of 1858 and 1867 he was described as a farmer of Halfway Head on the strength of the 6 acres that he farmed, but it would seem most likely that the licensed trade was a useful addition to his income. In 1891 the **Half-way House Inn** was held by Edward Chater, aged 77; he was succeeded in that year by William Cole, and then, at the beginning of the 20th century, by his widow Mrs. Alice Cole. The inn seems to have survived into the 1920s but no longer.

Documentary references show that somewhere in the vicinity of Frome's Hill was a pub called the **New Inn**. In 1851 it was held by Agnes Hodges, then described as a widow aged 54, and a farmer of 27 acres, but the 1861 census gave her age as 70, having apparently aged 16 years in a 10 year period! The **New Inn** was last mentioned in a directory of 1867 and closed soon after.

From Frome's Hill the road drops down a long incline and at the bottom crosses the River Leadon, only a brook at this point, entering the scattered parish of Cradley. A mile-and-a-half further on, the B4220 from Bromyard joins on the left, and a short distance in the direction of Bromyard were two former establishments. The first, on the left, is now called the Quiet Woman, but was formerly **Mockhall**. In 1851 it was run by Timothy Hill, a master shoemaker who employed six people as well as running the beer house. It does not seem to have

The Crown at Cradley looking somewhat worse for wear in 2002

been a beer house for many years for by 1858 he was simply described as a shoemaker. Further up the road, on the right-hand side is Ridgeway House, which was called the **New Inn** in 1834 when it was occupied by William Edwards. By the 1850s it had acquired its present name and had stopped serving liquid refreshment.

The central part of Cradley is to the south of the main road, with another settlement along the road at Stifford's Bridge. Taking the road to the south, the **Crown Inn** is about a mile along on the right-hand side, just past the left turn to King's Bridge and the settlement around the parish church. It had its origins in the late 19th century, when John Griffiths was a farmer, beer retailer and horse dealer at a farm called Little Westfields. By 1902 the name had been changed to the **Crown Inn** and the publican was William Lawrence. Memories of the **Crown Inn** at the time of the Second World War were recorded by the late Mr. Leslie Adams and quoted by Wynnell Hunt:

> His memories of the village include some of the old Crown pub, with its beer off the wood and its spittoons. His grandfather took part in competitions there which involved pitching heavy metal rings on to a post in a pit. These quoits are still in the possession of his widow.

In 1931 the Royal Commission on Historical Monuments described the **Crown Inn** as timber-framed and of 17th-century date, but noted that it had been heightened and extended to the west.

In modern times it was a popular venue for the rock band Black Sabbath, one member of which had a house along the road to Bromyard. Although still licensed, it has been under repair and renovation for some considerable time. A planning application to redevelope the site for housing, which was reported in the *Malvern Gazette and Ledbury Reporter* on 8 November 2002, was opposed by local residents and by CAMRA, and a Crown action group — The Crown Crusaders — was formed to fight the proposal. In January 2003 a 758 signature petition was handed in to Herefordshire planners, together with 200 letters of objection and the planning application was withdrawn. A new planning application was submitted in April 2003 to develop and reopen the **Crown**. It includes the building of four houses and conversion of a barn into holiday accommodation. The application, if approved, will mean that the Crown will open its doors for the first time in 15 years.

Opposite the **Crown Inn** is the road to King's Bridge, and down there, just past the house called St. Katherine's, there was a beer house that originally had the fascinating name Mobbledeplecks, but in the 19th century was changed to the simple Westfields. In 1867 John Stonehouse, a shoemaker, lived at Westfield, but later in the century Alexander Woodhouse was here and the name had been changed to the even simpler **New Inn**. At one time the **New Inn** was closed on Sundays, the reason being given in the reminiscences of two local ladies who wrote:

> The most notable change has been at The New Inn which had belonged to the Woodhouse family for a great number of years and Mr. Alec Woodhouse was the last of the family to be the landlord there. He owned the New Inn and other property in the vicinity. A staunch churchman, he did not open his public house on Sundays but was to be seen in his dark Sunday suit in his pew on Sunday mornings. He was a very straight man, some said he was a miser. He kept a good house and the New Inn was the place for a quiet drink and a gossip. Mr. Woodhouse was a school manager and a District Councillor. He drove his old white pony to Bromyard for Council meetings, but at all other times she grazed peacefully in the meadow behind the New Inn. On the death of Mr. Woodhouse the properties were sold. The New Inn is now open on Sundays. Mr. Bill Wood was landlord for a time but the present one is Mr. Speak.

For most of its licensed history the **New Inn** was a beer house, but a full licence was granted in 1960. It later became known as the **Stable**, the story of which is best told in the words of Wynnell Hunt:

> In more recent times the name New Inn was changed in a rather forceful way. Friends of the owners removed the old inn-sign one dark night, repainted it with a picture of a horse and gave it a name more in keeping, they felt, with the owners' interest in horses! The brewery played along with this and agreed to keep the new name and so it became known as The Stable. The old name 'New Inn' could still be seen on the wall before the building was demolished in 1999.

A new house has been built on the site of the **New Inn** and there is now no sign that there was ever a pub here.

There were also two beer houses in the old centre of the village. The present Post Office and stores, to the north of the church, was a

The Bull's Head, now the post office and stores in Cradley in 2002

beer house in the 1830s and although it does not seem to have lasted long, it acquired the name of the **Bull's Head**. This splendid 17th-century building was described in 1931 by the Royal Commission on Historical Monuments as being:

> of T-shaped plan, the S. cross-wing being of earlier date than the N. wing. The upper storey projects slightly at the W. end of the cross-wing, on a moulded bressumer and shaped brackets. The central chimney stack of the cross-wing has four grouped shafts, set diagonally.

Bull's Head Cottage, a 17th-century building just over the road from the stores, was also a short-lived beer house. When the

Bull's Head Cottage in 2002

Commissioners of the Royal Commission on Historical Monuments visited it had a thatched roof.

The oldest established of the Cradley pubs were at Stifford's Bridge on the main Worcester road. The first of these, on the right-hand side travelling

177

THE VALUABLE OLD ESTABLISHED FREE AND FULL-LICENSED INN AND PREMISES

KNOWN AS

"THE RED LION"

situate at Stifford's Bridge, on the main road from Worcester to Hereford, together with two Cottages and

15A.   3R.   17P.

of fertile Meadow and Pasture Orchard Land adjoining thereto.

SCHEDULE.

ORD. No.	DESCRIPTION.	CULTURE.	A.	R.	P.
693	The Red Lion Public House and Outbuildings ...	... ...	0	1	14
482	The Old Timber Yard	Pasture Orchard ...	0	2	23
694	Rickyard Meadow	Pasture	0	2	36
692	Waggonhouse Meadow	Pasture	3	3	5
695	Waggonhouse Orchard	Pasture	5	2	7
696	Stifford's Field	Arable	4	2	22
694a.	Two Cottages and Gardens		0	0	30
		TOTAL ACREAGE ...	15	3	17

THE INN contains : **On the First Floor**, Landing, Store Closet, Bedroom 20ft. 3in. by 18ft. 4in., Ditto 10ft. 9in. by 12ft. 3in., Ditto 15ft. 6in. by 14ft. 4in., Ditto 16ft. by 13ft. 8in., and one smaller ditto, and front and back Staircases.

On the Ground Floor are large Club Room 27ft. 6in. by 15ft. 10in. by 10ft. 5in. high with tiled grates., Sitting Room 13ft. 6in. by 11ft. 6in., Passage, Tap Room 18ft. 2in. by 16ft. 7in., Bar 12ft. by 11ft. 2in. with bay window, Kitchen 18ft. by 11ft. 8in., Pantry 15ft. by 8ft. 6in., with slate slabs and shelves, Cider Cellar, and Ale and Wine Cellar.

The other Premises comprise : Courtyard with pump and well of water, Brew-house with sink, and Out-offices, Stable-yard with stabling for nine horses, Coach-house, Hay Loft, Coal Place, Cider House with Press, Barn, Poultry House, Cowshed for four cows, Cart and Implement Sheds, and Pigstyes. There are also two capital brick and tiled Cottages with good Gardens, Pigstyes, and Sheds.

The Inn and Premises are let to MRS. ANNE M. WOODBRIDGE, at **£20** per annum, and the tenancy determines on the 29th September next. The Pasture and Arable Land is also in her occupation on a yearly Michaelmas tenancy at **£55** per annum.

One Cottage is let to LT.-COL. THURLOW at **£6** per annum, and the other to MISS WEAVER at **£5** per annum, Tenants paying rates.

Tithe Rent Charge paid by Tenant (value for 1906), £3 2s. 11d.   Land Tax, £2 13s. 2d.

Sale of the Red Lion in 1906

towards Worcester, is the **Red Lion**. In 1931 the Royal Commission described it as being of 17th-century origin, with 18th-century and later additions to the north-west side and both ends of the original block, the original fireplace having an oak lintel cut to a flat arch on the soffit. It has had a long history as licensed premises, and in the *Hereford Journal* of 10 March 1790 an advertisement gave notice of a farm that was to be sold there by auction. Similarly on 21 November 1821 an advertisement gave notice of timber that was to be sold by auction.

William Stokes, who was there in 1858, seems to have been succeeded by Henry Orgee, and in the early 1860s the Court Baron of the Manor of Cradley was held 'at the dwelling-house of Henry Orgee, called Red Lion Inn, situate

The Red Lion at Stifford's Bridge in 2001

at Stifford's Bridge...'. By 1867 James Woodbridge was licensee, and he later had farming interests at Old Workhouse farm, and then Wells farm. He was succeeded by his widow Ann Maria and in 1902 she is recorded as also farming at Brook House and Old Workhouse farms. In the Woodbridges' time, and later, the **Red Lion** was the meeting place of the Loyal Cradley Lodge No. 5874 of the Independent Order of Oddfellows, Manchester Unity. A painted board of officers covers the period 1872 to 1910, and the Lodge was still operating in the late 1920s.

The position of the pub near the Cradley Brook is vulnerable to the heavy storms that seem to have developed in recent years, and while it had been flooded in the past, on 9 April 1998 a disastrous flood caused serious damage, the floodwater reaching almost to the top of the bar. As a consequence the pub was closed for three months while it was being totally refurbished at a cost of about £120,000. This included replacing the wooden floor in the bar and dining areas with a slate flagstone floor to mitigate damage should flooding to that extent ever occur again. Like most inns with a roadside situation it is now mainly a food pub, particularly popular at weekends, and also for older citizens for lunch during the week. While enjoying its hospitality admire the four evocative photographs of the pub *c*.1900 hanging in the dining area

A little further down and on the opposite side of the road is the **Prancing Pony**, a new name for an historic pub, better known by its earlier name of the **Seven Stars**. Like the **Red Lion** it has a long

The Seven Stars in 2001

history, and an advertisement in the *Hereford Journal* of 1 September 1802 gives notice of an estate to be sold by auction at the **Seven Stars**. In the middle of the 19th century the pub was held successively by Matthew Boucher, who also worked as a cooper, and his widow Maria. In the first part of the 20th century the Friendly Society called the Pure Order of United Britons met in the **Seven Stars**. The present owners have been here for nine years, and soon after they came the old barn at the front of the pub was rebuilt as a restaurant, and in the summer of 2002, a few months after the name was changed, a new conservatory extension was built at the front, replacing a rectangular bay window. The 1985 CAMRA described it as a 'Roadside locals' pub', but noises have been heard in the pub, with doors slamming upstairs when there is no-one there — perhaps better explained by a gust of wind rather than a poltergeist. Ancient fishing rights on the adjoining Cradley brook are still enjoyed by the pub.

The Seven Stars has become a Prancing Pony by 2002

From Stifford's Bridge the road climbs up through Storridge, and at the top of the

The New Inn at Storridge in 2001

hill, opposite the church, is a turn to Birchwood, where, in the 1830s, one James Preece had a beer house. When the main road starts to drop down, there are one or two corners, and then a long straight, with the consequent temptation to build up speed, leaving Herefordshire for Worcestershire near the bottom of the hill. This temptation should be resisted, for just inside the county boundary is the **New Inn**, which seems to have been established as licensed premises about 1900. In 1941 H.B. Watkins, the then landlord, brewed his own beer. There are no neighbouring houses, and in 1985 CAMRA said that it was 'A friendly country pub relying on passing trade...' a situation that it still true. In recent years the **New Inn** was the home of the Malvern Darts League, with darts every night of the week, and the bar covered with trophies of all sorts. It is said that so seriously was the darts competition taken that the loss of a match was a matter for mourning! This has now changed, with a new licensee taking over at the beginning of March 2003, and darts are off the menu. However, the bonus is the longer opening hours, as previously the New Inn did not open at lunch time, and only later in the evening, but breakfast is now available from 8.30 a.m. and the bar opens at 10 a.m.

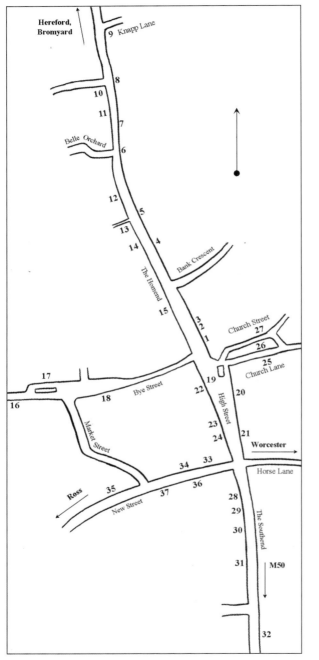

1 New Inn
2 Seven Stars
3 King's head
4 Horse Shoe
5 Ship & Castle
6 Railway
7 Plasterers Arms
8 Nag's Head
9 Pound House
10 Queen's Head
11 White Horse
12 Plough
13 Fox
14 Swan
15 Farriers
16 Bridge
17 Brewery
18 White Lion
19 Sun
20 Bull
21 King's Arms
22 Lion
23 Chequers
24 Feathers
25 Jolly Crispin
26 Prince of Wales
27 White Hart
28 Royal Oak
29 Bush
30 George
31 Unicorn
32 Bowling Green
33 Bell
34 Crown & Sceptre
35 Ring of Bells
36 Talbot
37 Vine Tap

The Pubs of Ledbury

182

CHAPTER TEN

Ledbury
THE HOMEND—EAST SIDE

Quite often, the most informative description of a town may be found in an old directory, and Ledbury is no exception. An 1830 *Road Book* describes it as:

> An ancient well built market town situated in a declivity near the south end of the Malvern Hills about 1 mile west from the river Leddon from whence it derives its name. ... In the principal street is the old Market House, which is raised on strong oak pillars, and composed of timber and lath, plastered and white washed; the beams being coloured black. This method of building predominates in the more ancient parts of the town; and many of the houses have projecting stories; the modern houses are chiefly of red brick.

At that time there were 618 houses with 3,058 inhabitants (1,513 male & 1,545 female).

The writer continues:

> Great quantities of cider are also manufactured in the neighbourhood, which constitute a considerable article of trade: the clothing trade was at one time very flourishing in this town, but it has greatly declined of late years.

In 1891, the town had an importance which has since been largely lost and this has had some effect on its hotels and public houses. Reflect on the description in Kelly's *Herefordshire Directory* for 1891: 'Ledbury is a market and union town, head of a county court district, parish and polling place, on the road from Hereford to Tewkesbury ...' The road to Malvern and Worcester is not even mentioned.

The description goes on:

> The Worcester and Hereford section of the Great Western railway passes through the town on the north side, and it is the junction of the line to Gloucester.

At that time:

> The streets are lighted with gas by a company from works in New Street, and supplied with water from a reservoir south-east of the town, fed by springs.

The directory gives an impression of the vibrancy of the town — the Post Office was open for the sale of stamps and other items on weekdays from 7 a.m. to 8 p.m. and on Sundays, Christmas Day and Good Friday from 7 to 10 a.m. There were four deliveries of letters, although it was admitted that the fourth was only partial (local letters only) at 7.15 p.m. However there was a Sunday delivery starting at 7 a.m.

The directory also gives full details of the transport from the railway station (Richard Roberts, Station Master). The railway was then an important carrier of goods and the Great Western and Midland Parcels Receiving Office was at the **Royal Oak** where E.H. Hopkins was the agent. Passengers were expected to arrive at the station from all over the area, and 'an omnibus from the **Feathers Hotel** and **Royal Oak** P.H. attends the arrival and departure of all trains'.

Goods that arrived at Ledbury were transported throughout the eastern part of the county and the carriers were all based at public houses in Ledbury. In 1891 they included:

> ASHPERTON—E. Newman, **New Inn**, Tues.
> BOSBURY—Mr. Cartwright, **Seven Stars**, Tues.
> BROMSBERROW—Henry Hardman, **Royal Oak**, Tues. & Fri.
> DYMOCK—Fencott, **Plough**, Tues.
> PENDOCK—Shaw, **New Inn**, Tues.
> MUCH MARCLE—W. Davis, **Seven Stars**, Tues.
> REDMARLEY—J. Bailey, **Seven Stars**, Tues.

It is evident that 100 or so years ago Ledbury had an important part to play in the administration of the county and the public houses and inns of the town played their part by providing an essential part of the infrastructure — places where people could meet in convivial circumstances, places to eat and places to stay for the night.

But Ledbury was not always a peaceful town:

During the reign of King Charles I, Ledbury often found itself close to the scene of war and was once hurled into the thick of the fighting when two of the leading protagonists, Prince Rupert and Col. Massey, led their respective armies into battle in the main street. The bloody encounter that ensued has found a little corner of history as the Battle of Ledbury.

Hereford and Worcester were loyal to the king, but both cities were captured and recaptured several times by the opposing armies. Gloucester, commanded by Col. Massey, was heavily garrisoned by the parliament. The roads from these three cities converged at Ledbury's Upper Cross. From all directions came troops marching behind the flying plumes of cavaliers or the bobbing helmets of Cromwell's officers.

In 1645 Prince Rupert was near Leominster when he heard that Col. Massey was marching on Ledbury with a large number of soldiers. The prince and his company marched all night and on the morning of 22 April they charged down the Homend, taking the Roundheads completely by surprise.

It was Tuesday, Market Day. Massey's men seized carts and wagons to block the road. The barricade was forced after desperate fighting and Lord Loughborough's troop of horse charged forward to the Market House where further severe fighting ensued.

A second charge was led by Prince Rupert from the direction of Church Street. A running fight developed as Massey's troops fell back towards the church. They were still furiously exchanging fire when they reached the churchyard and to this day their bullets are embedded in the church door while others are on display in the chantry. Also on view there is the sword of one of the parliamentarians' most spirited leaders, Major Backhouse, who died after being shot through the head in the High Street.

Prince Rupert and Col. Massey each had a horse killed under him. Massey was driven out of the town and his men dispersed. Prince Rupert and his weary soldiers rested in Ledbury that night before resuming their march to Ludlow.

Prince Rupert wrote: 'Massey was soundly beaten yesterday, his foot were quite lost and his horse beaten and pursued within six miles of Gloucester'. With the chivalry of his age he added 'He himself and some of his officers made a handsome retreat'. Of the rebels 120 were killed, many wounded and about 400 were taken prisoner.

A street scene looking eastwards in the Homend in 1830.
At this time The Homend was the home of many inns and beer houses

No doubt there were celebrations by the Cavaliers in the local pubs throughout that night and relief from the citizens that their houses were not to be pillaged by the Parliamentarians as would have occurred had the town been taken.

The main road through Ledbury runs from north to south. It is The Homend to the north; High Street in the centre; and The Southend, becoming Gloucester Road, to the south. There are two main crossroads; Lower Cross to the north and Upper Cross to the south. Lower Cross is the original main intersection and it is here that Bye Street (earlier Bishop Street) led in a westerly direction towards Ross, and Church Street (earlier Back Lane) went up the hill to the east, leaving the grounds of the minster church, Lower Hall, and Upper Hall on the right, as it ascended Dog Hill and then followed Green Lane on its way towards Worcester.

The Upper Cross is where the present main roads intersect. New Street leads off to the west towards Ross, whilst Worcester Road leads eastwards. On the south-eastern corner of this junction is Ledbury Park, possibly the Park that originally formed part of the Bishop's Palace. Ledbury Park, built by the Biddulph family in about 1600, was described by Pevsner as 'the grandest black-and-white house in the County'. The part of Worcester Road closest to the intersection was at one time known as Horse Lane. An entry in the *Woolhope Club Transactions* (the journal of the local society devoted to 'the practical study, in all its branches, of the Natural History and Archaeology of Herefordshire ...') notes that 'The New Road from the corner of the new water tank to the Crab-tree corner opposite Mr. Martin's Lodge, was made about the time of Charles II. At Crab-tree corner, on the left, is the old way into Ledbury.'

This chapter deals with the pubs, present and past, along the east side of The Homend, starting close to the centre of the town and heading northwards, on the road leading towards Leominster and the turning for Hereford opposite the railway station.

At No. 5 Homend was the **New Inn**, which was described in the early 1930s as being 'close to the lower cross roads, [this inn] together with the adjoining shop and houses were refronted in the 18th century. The rear wing has some exposed timber-framing and in the south wall there is an original window of four lights with moulded mullions'. The County Record Office has a collection of deeds and wills relating to the property covering the period from 1679 to 1852. In some of them it is described as being in High Street, but it is normally given as being in The Homend. In the latter part of the 17th century it was called the **Crown** or **Old Crown** and was in the hands of the Buckenhill family, but passed through the Amphlett, the Berrow and the Jenkins families before the Beddoe family bought it 1749.

Works were afoot in early 1778 when the *Hereford Journal* carried the following advertisement:

> JOHN HATTON, at the New Inn at Ledbury in this county, takes this method to inform the Nobility, Gentry, and others, that the additional new buildings, improvements, and alterations of the said inn are now completely finished, for the accommodation of all his Friends, and the Public in general, who may be assured that every attention in his power will be given to make it agreeable to those who choose to honour him with their commands.
> Neat Post-Chaises and careful Drivers.

Could it be that John Hatton was referring to the construction of the Assembly Room at the rear of the inn? They were all the vogue towards the end of the 18th century.

In 1782 the inn was for sale:

> To be Sold by Auction, on the Premises, on Monday the 29th of July instant, or in the mean time by private contract, The New Inn, in Ledbury: Also two pieces of pasture land, containing about two acres, within a mile of Ledbury to be sold at the same time. The Inn is a new brick-house, sashed, with new stabling, and good yard and garden, situated in the middle of the town of Ledbury.
> For further particulars inquire at the Said Inn.

This may not have been successful for in 1783 the inn was advertised to be let, and again in 1784 when it was described as being:

> lately rebuilt in the modern taste at a considerable expense, with a sashed front, and now called THE NEW INN; consisting of two large parlours, and a dining-room in front; several good bedchambers ... a coach-house, stables and other necessary detached buildings for a large Inn.

The advertisement was repeated several times in the following year and the inn was clearly not as good an investment as the proprietor thought. However it was sufficiently important in 1787 to be the venue for a meeting of a proposed association for the Prosecution of Felons.

The inn must have had some problems, which culminated in March 1788 when the following advertisement was placed in the *Hereford Journal*:

> To be sold by Auction, at the New Inn, in Ledbury, on Saturday next the 29th day of March instant, all the HOUSEHOLD FURNTURE, LINEN, and Effects of John Richards, at the New Inn aforesaid, consisting of four post and other bedsteads, with stuff and other furniture, Feather Beds, Bed Quilts, Sheets, Blankets, Mahogany and other Tables, Chairs, Chest of Drawers, Pier and Swing Glasses, a Clock, Kitchen Furniture, and Brewing Utensils, some Red Port and other Wines, Brandy, Rum, Gin, and Cyder in bottles and cask, some Beer and Ale in cask, some Hogsheads and other Casks; also an exceeding good One Horse Chaise and Harness.
> N.B. The Sale to begin at ten o'clock in the morning, and continue till all is sold.

Ledbury, Herefordshire.

TO be Let, and entered upon immediately, at Midsummer, or Lammas next, All that capital Messuage, formerly THE CROWN INN, but lately rebuilt in the modern taste at a considerable expence, with a sashed front, and now called THE NEW INN; consisting of two large parlours, and a dining-room, in front; several good bedchambers, a kitchen, back kitchen, brewhouse, and two excellent cellars; a coach-house, stables, and other necessary detached buildings for a large Inn.

The above has, for time immemorial, been used as an INN, or PUBLICK-HOUSE, and always esteemed a good accustomed house; for which, on account of its eligibility of situation, it is most admirably well adapted, being near the centre of the town of Ledbury, in a very spacious street, where the markets and fairs (for which Ledbury is not inferior to any town in the county) are chiefly kept; and is also equally convenient, if not preferable, for the Post-chaise business, to any Inn in the town, the late occupier having had employment for several chaises.

Ledbury lies between Worcester, Gloucester, and Hereford, and about an equal distance from each, by means of which, it has a very great thoroughfare to those cities; and is also the great road from Wales to London, Bath, and Bristol.

N. B. Should it be thought necessary, the Proprietor will have no objection to make any reasonable alteration, or improvement, to accommodate an eligible tenant; and there is great reason to expect, that a person properly qualified for the business will meet with due encouragement.

☞ For further particulars, and a view of the premises, apply to Mr. Richard Hill; or to Mr. Thomas Nott, Attorney at Law, Ledbury.

May 5, 1784.

The 1784 sale of the New Inn

By the early 19th century the problems appear to have been resolved and in 1802 T. Merrick:

Respectfully informs Gentlemen Travellers, and others that he has entered upon the above Inn, which, with the Stabling, he has fitted up in a very comfortable style for their accommodation; and having laid in the choicest LIQUORS, &c. he hopes, by unremitting attention, civility, and keeping a good Larder, to participate of the favours of his Friends and the Public at large.

Messers. Harris and Co.'s Waggons leave the New Inn every Tuesday and Friday, for Worcester, Oxford, and London; and return on Thursday and Sunday, for Hereford, Hay, Brecon, and all parts of South Wales.

A Friendly Society was re-established there in 1803, although it had probably started as early as 1791. However, there was a potential disaster in 1817 when a labourer named Underwood murdered a groom at the inn. The murder was a news item in the *Hereford Journal*:

Murder. – Last Thursday morning, between the hours of four and five o'clock, a most cowardly and savage murder was perpetrated at Ledbury, in this county, of which, W. Harris, ostler at the New Inn, in that town, a most civil and industrious man, was the victim. It appears Harris rose at four on the Thursday morning for the purpose of brewing, and whilst he was engaged in lighting a fire under the furnace, his inhuman murderer who was previously concealed on the premises, taking advantage of his defenceless position, completely cut his head asunder with an axe, which he found in an out-house, and by repeated blows, completed his remorseless purpose. He then took a watch belonging to the sufferer and his smock-frock, and was doubtless proceeding to further plunder, when the arrival of the Worcester Wagon, caused him to fly from the scene of his cruel atrocity. The body of the deceased was discovered on the brewhouse floor a little past five o'clock, and he immediately afterwards expired. He had the preceding day paid the rent of his mother's house, and was a most respectable man in his situation in life. On Friday a man who states his name to be R. Underwood, was apprehended at Worcester, and conveyed to Ledbury, where he fully confessed the perpetration of the murder, and in consequence has been committed to our County Gaol, to take his trial. The murderer we understand was lately discharged from the army. The Coroner's Inquest is not yet closed, but we hope to give the result next week. It since appears that Underwood had concealed himself during the preceding day in the hay-loft of the New Inn, for the purpose of committing the robbery, and that in the course of the night he formed the horrid plan which he afterwards effected. The watch belonging to the deceased, and a smock worn by Underwood as a disguise were found by his directions, concealed on the bank of a rivulet near Malvern. Since his confession he has acknowledged, that his mind has been much relieved by the disclosure, and he awaits his fate with resignation. Lord Somers and the neighbouring Magistrates were most active and persevering in the necessary investigations, and too much praise cannot be given to the Inhabitants of Ledbury in general, for the zeal they have manifested on the occasion. On application to the Office in Bow-street, Mr. Bishop, the officer, was sent to assist in discovering the murderer, and materially contributed to the result which has followed. Underwood was fully committed on the oath of Mr. Bishop, and on his own confession, under a warrant signed by Mr. Barratt, Mr. Kearney, and Mr. Higgins, the Magistrates.

The list of executions carried out in Hereford since 1770, printed by W.H. Vale in 1856, has the following to say:

RICHARD UNDERWOOD
Executed March 31, 1817, for the Murder of William Harris,
ostler and brewer at the New Inn, Ledbury.

He was a native of Ledbury, and confessed to the murder. He appears to have had no other object than robbery. Harris had kindly permitted him to sleep in the stable on account of his poverty, and Underwood fell upon him with a coal-axe and killed him, stole his watch and some little money; but though he changed his appearance, by cutting off his whiskers, he was soon apprehended in a public-house at Worcester.

Underwood was executed on the flat roof above the entry to the the County Gaol in Commercial Road, Hereford. It was so arranged that:

executions may be fully exposed to the general view of all spectators without the walls, and of all the prisoners within, who should be arranged around the general court for that purpose, and in the hope of preventing crime by making a due impression on all who witness these melancholy examples.

The New Inn in the early years of the 20th century

By the second quarter of the 19th century the New Inn was a centre for carriers, with transport to Cheltenham, Gloucester, Tewkesbury and Worcester and points east, leaving most days. This may well have been due to the influence of the Bosley family who were running the establishment in the 1820s and 1830s. It could well have been the same family who then moved to Hereford to run both the Green Dragon and the City Arms.

Willam Butt seems to have taken over from John Bosley at the New Inn, at least in the carriage business. In the 1831 book *Hints of Ledbury* there is the comment:

> The chief carriage conveyance for goods by way of Worcester and Gloucester, are Mr. Butt's wagons to and from these cities, which go three times a week to Worcester, and once to Gloucester. The invariable care and attention which Mr. Butt pays to the business, added to the moderation of the charges, has procured for him the principal part of the carriage between Ledbury and Worcester, and will doubtless do so with Gloucester. Tuesdays, Thursdays, and Saturdays are the days for Worcester; Thursday for Gloucester. Put up — Pack Horse, Worcester; Duke Island, Gloucester.

The New Inn assembly rooms

By 1847, William Butt was certainly the landlord, to be followed by Mrs. Hannah Butt in 1867 — probably his widow. She died on 15 August 1879, but the carrier's trade continued to be an important part of the business of the inn to the extent that in 1881 there was a resident carrier's agent, one Joseph Fawke who, poor man, lived with his three unmarried sisters! At that time the inn had Elizabeth Symonds as manageress. She was a 59-year-old widow, one of the three daughters of Hannah Butt, and ran the place with three 'live-in' servants.

George Wargent, writing in a series of articles in the *Ledbury Free Press and Hereford Advertiser* recollected that during the mid-19th century:

Election times in Ledbury were of immense excitement. It might be mentioned in passing that Ledbury formerly possessed the privilege of returning two members of parliament but the inhabitants petitioned to be relieved from the franchise on the grounds of their poverty and inability to support the members. What I remember first about the Hustings — of course it was open voting then — they were at the bottom of Butcher's Row and were open for a week. This was when the voting was for a County Member. There were two compartments for the voting and each voter as he went up was asked by an official 'Who do you vote for?' After declaring for whom he wished to vote. whether for the Tory or Liberal, the vote was recorded by polling clerks and those who voted Tory received a ticket for refreshment at

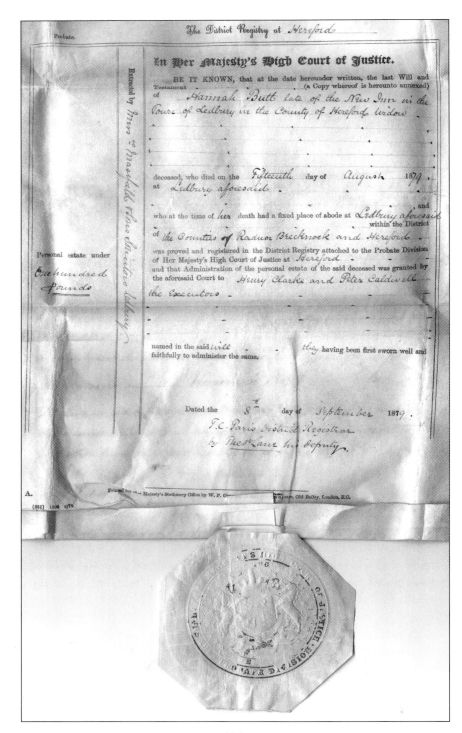

Probate.

In Her Majesty's High Court of Justice.

BE IT KNOWN, that at the date hereunder written, the last Will and Testament .... (a Copy whereof is hereunto annexed)

of *Hannah Butt late of the New Inn in the Town of Ledbury in the County of Hereford Widow*

deceased, who died on the *Fifteenth* day of *August* 1879, at *Ledbury aforesaid*.

who at the time of *her* death had a fixed place of abode at *Ledbury aforesaid*, and within the District

of *the Counties of Radnor Brecknock and Hereford*

was proved and registered in the District Registry attached to the Probate Division of Her Majesty's High Court of Justice at *Hereford*.

and that Administration of the personal estate of the said deceased was granted by the aforesaid Court to *Henry Clarke and Peter Caldwell*

the Executors

named in the said *will* *they* having been first sworn well and faithfully to administer the same.

Dated the *8th* day of *September* 1879.

T.C. Paris District Registrar
by Theo Lane his Deputy.

Personal estate under

One hundred Pounds

Extracted by Piper & Mansfields Solicitors Ledbury

A.

[251] 1000 6/79

Printed for Her Majesty's Stationery Office by W. P. C——— Square, Old Bailey, London, E.C.

194

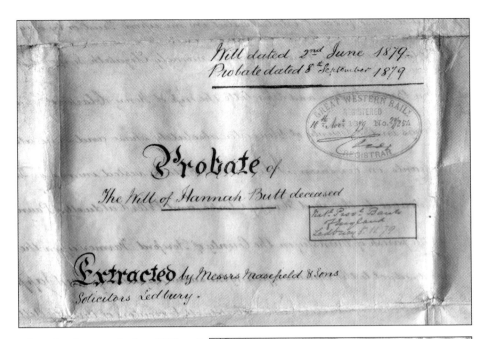

The Probate of the Will of Hannah Butt came into the hands of the authors of this volume shortly before it was completed. There is the last will and testament of Hannah Butt and the Probate from the District Registry at Hereford complete with its seal.

Mrs. Butt died on 15 August 1879 and the cover of the Probate shows that she had shares in the Great Western Railway and that she banked with the Ledbury branch of the National Provincial Bank of England.

She left her real and personal estate, which was less that £100, to be shared equally between her three daughters.

the Feathers Hotel, and those who voted Liberal were given a ticket for refreshment at the New Inn. This was a questionable proceeding as was also the free distribution of beer and cider during the time of polling. Free fights were the rule rather than the exception and generally the affair ended in a Mêlée from which perhaps half a dozen would emerge with black eyes and broken noses. Two bands used to play in the street nearly all the week in the election and the bells rang during the day. Business became dislocated whilst the election was in progress, but thanks to the Ballot Act, the semi-barbarous scenes are things of the past.

---

107. LEDBURY.—THE NEW INN.

ALL THAT messuage or Inn known as The New Inn situate in Homend Street in the Town of Ledbury in the County of Hereford with the stables buildings and all other outbuildings and appurtenances thereunto belonging, TOGETHER with the site thereof and the land occupied therewith.

A detail of the sale from Arnold Perrett to the
Cheltenham Original Brewery in 1937

The inn continued to serve customers throughout the first half of the 20th century, eventually with John E. Edmunds as proprietor during the Second World War. It closed in the mid-1970s and has since been converted into several shops. The rear yard is approached through a

The New Inn in 2001

typical inn passageway; on the left is a jettied overhang that may have included the timber-framing mentioned in the 1930s, but is now rendered. It originally contained the **New Inn** assembly rooms, but is now used for retail purposes.

Separated from the **New Inn** by a couple of shops was the **Seven Stars** at 11 Homend. This pub suffered a disastrous fire in 2001, leaving little but the façade. It was described by the Royal Commission in the early 1930s as being of:

> late 16th century date [with] exposed timber-framing at the rear. The upper storey formerly projected on the front, but has been underbuilt. One post and part of the moulded bressummer are exposed in the passage. The main doorway has a moulded frame and scrolled brackets at the head. A room on the first floor has a plaster ceiling with fleurs-de-lis and rosettes, now papered over.

An earlier building is said to have been a private residence during the medieval period, becoming an inn in 1526, although no firm evidence has so far been found. The *Universal British Directory* of 1793 records Richard Evans as the victualler there. By 1813 William Barrett, who 'rode to hounds in scarlet', had become the licensee and continued there for many years. At that time the weekly market was held in the streets of Ledbury: 'Sheep were penned in High Street near St. Katherine's Chapel, pigs opposite the "Seven Stars" and cattle further up the Homend'. By 1850 the inn had been taken over by Elizabeth Fawkes. It is highly unlikely that she is a descendant of the infamous Guy who, inspired by religious zeal, attempted to blow up King James I and both Houses of Parliament in 1605, but could she possibly be related to the less well-known Francis Fawkes, vicar of Orpington in the third quarter of the 18th century, who is best known for his comic drinking song 'Little Brown Jug'?

Yo, Ho, Ho,
You and Me,
Little Brown Jug
Don't I love thee!

Perhaps the Fawkes family, living at the **New Inn** in the early 1880s, were her descendants. The inn must have been successful, for Elizabeth eventually took in Mrs. Elizabeth Roberts as partner, and by 1867 she had taken over. She was still there and working as innkeeper in 1881, when she was aged 72. Her daughter Jane was the barmaid, and her two unmarried sons, William and Robert, were a grocer and a butcher respectively.

Towards the end of the 19th century the **Seven Stars** was the base for several carriers, including those to Bosbury, Much Marcle and

Redmarley. Harry Tarbath, who was landlord in the early years of the 20th century, used to drive a four-in-hand stage coach between Ledbury and Gloucester before the railway was built in 1885. The younger brother of James Tarbath of the **Lion Hotel** in Bromyard, he died in 1932.

During recent renovations workmen found a 'strange metal contraption' lodged in a chimney, which turned out to be a roasting spit, still in good condition. The article goes on to say:

> The big chimney had another surprise in store — a bake oven set over the fire where the mistress of the house could cook cakes and bread. ... Old oak beams are also being revealed as the workmen strip away hardboard and plaster to bring the pub back to its original half-timbered condition. And as the back of a cupboard was removed one of the most unexpected sights appeared. The original front of the pub could be seen in the gap, complete with carved beams ... when the work of restoration is finished ... one of the most historic corners of the pub will not be open to the public. This is the priest's hole — a secret nook among the beams at the top of the building where the good Catholic publican of the 17th century sheltered fleeing clergymen.

The Seven Stars shortly before the fire

A few years earlier there had been a proposal to convert three buildings — the **Seven Stars**, the **New Inn**, and the former Gas Showrooms — into one large pub, but the plan was subsequently dropped.

Seven Stars is a common pub name with at least one other example still operating in Herefordshire. It was originally a religious symbol referring either to the star of Bethlehem or to the Virgin Mary's crown. It is usually shown on pub signs as the constellation of the Plough or Great Bear, but earlier often referred to the seven major planets. Shakespeare refers to the seven stars in King Lear:

> *Fool:* The reason why the seven stars are no more than seven is a pretty reason.
> *Lear:* Because they are not eight?
> *Fool:* Yes, indeed: thou wouldst make a good fool.

whilst the *Dilly Song* has

> Seven for the seven stars in the sky,
> Six for the six proud walkers, etc.

The façade of the Seven Stars after the fire

The inn continued to serve customers till the night of Sunday 23 July 2001. A few days later the *Hereford Times* reported:

> The historic black and white timbered pub was burned to a shell. The fire also spread along the terrace, claiming the two and three storey buildings either side. Practically all of the grade II listed coaching inn will now have to be taken down.
>
> 'There are two dangerous gables and a couple of dangerous floors. Virtually the whole of the pub has to be demolished apart from the façade,' said Herefordshire Council building control officer, Chris Massey. The building was well alight at 2 a.m. when 70 fire-fighters arrived, including all crew members from Hereford, teams from Ledbury, Bromyard and Leominster and watches from as far as Malvern, Upton on Severn, Droitwich, Pershore and Evesham.
>
> All occupants of the pub were accounted for and nearby residents were evacuated as a precautionary measure by police and fire-fighters. There were no injuries. Fire-fighters say the blaze is the biggest they have dealt with in the town in living memory. The last of 10 pumps left the scene after a 19-hour battle.
>
> The group of buildings, including the 19th-century Treacle Boutique building and the modified 18th-century Co-op Travel either side of the pub ... were fenced off from the public as emergency building services moved in to deal with the chaos.

A footnote at the end of the article recorded that 'a Ledbury woman ... of the Homend, appeared at Hereford Magistrate's Court on Monday and was remanded in custody to appear at Worcester Crown Court next Tuesday, charged with arson, being reckless as to whether life will be in danger'.

In July 2002 the landlady, Janet Kaye, was cleared by a jury at Hereford Crown Court of starting the fire and recklessly endangering human life.

The restoration of the **Seven Stars** was well under way in October 2001 when there was considerable concern that further disruption would be caused, leading to a downturn in trade for local shops. The *Ledbury Reporter* observed that during the summer, temporary traffic lights outside the burnt-out pub made the Homend one-way for two months. The owners, the Punch Pub Company, appointed Ledbury architects Stainburn Taylor to supervise the restoration, but could not forecast a completion date because of the extensive damage and the difficulty of restoring the building in a sympathetic manner. However, they were granted planning permission to rebuild the Grade II listed building and stated that the idea was to 'restore the pub to its original glory'.

Next door to the **Seven Stars** was the **King's Head**, which was operational during the first half of the 19th century. George Wargent remembered it as a butcher's shop, but commented that as a pub it was kept by a Mr. Cook 'so that out of four houses in succession, three were licensed — all seemed to thrive and there was a skittle alley in each'. The inn probably closed before 1850.

The King's Head in 2002

Continuing down the east side of the Homend, the **Horse Shoe** is still a thriving pub. It is a 17th-century building with an approach up several steps, in part reflecting the rising ground directly behind the inn. William Paine, the licensee in the late 18th century, was also a house-carpenter. He was there for many years, but by 1830 his wife, Mary had taken over, followed by Miss Elizabeth Paine, presumably his daughter. After one or two changes around the middle of the century, Francis Matthews became licensee some time before 1867. He may have stayed as long as 20 years and in 1879, at the age of 55, had a second daughter Edith. At that time his eldest daughter, Alice, who worked as barmaid, was 25 years old, and his wife, Jane, only 38, so it would seem that he lost his first wife and married for a second time. At the time of the 1881 census, they had a young live-in domestic

The Horse Shoe Inn in 2001

The Ship and Castle in 2001

servant, Ada Dark, aged 12, and two lodgers.

A Friendly Society, which had been formed there by 1794, had a new set of rules in 1832. It was still operating when George Wargent was young, for he recollected that the members had a church parade each year. The inn was then a flourishing public house doing a big trade and 'when the cattle were sold in the street outside the inn, buyers and sellers transacted a good deal of business inside the house'. When the cattle were being sold, the auctioneer stood at the top of the inn steps.

The **Horse Shoe Inn** and the neighbouring Powell Cycles shop apparently suffered a regular ghost. Pip Powell recalled the noise of mysterious footsteps on the stairs in the 1930s and, when his daughter was a child in the 1960s, she 'was always aware of a presence outside the bathroom door'.

Often the name is given as **Horseshoe**, but more correctly it is two words. Pubs with this name have the advantage of a simple visual sign, made more significant by the long-standing belief that a horse-shoe brings luck. Originally a horse-shoe hung correctly — with the two ends pointing upwards — was said to be a protection against witchcraft. They must never be allowed to become inverted or the luck will 'run out'. An alternative story has been applied to the Horseshoe Inn in Tottenham Court Road, London. Many years ago, the first landlord, one Kelsey from Lincolnshire, brought with him a horseshoe, not just for luck, but because in Lincolnshire folk lore it was regarded as a safeguard against *delirium tremens*! He named his inn after the celebrated horseshoe.

No. 123 The Homend was a beerhouse run by John Haines for a relatively short period in the mid-19th century, named the **Ship and Castle**. It is now part of Isaacs Stores.

The **Railway Inn**, a little further out from the town centre, had several changes of names, the earliest apparently being the **Drovers Arms**. Towards the end of the 18th century it had become the **Red Lion** and a Friendly Society was in existence there in 1794. According to Wargent:

> It was a recognised house for Welshmen because, before the railway was made to Ledbury, hundreds of little black Welsh cattle were taken by road, and the drovers invariably put up for the night at this inn and the cattle were put out to 'tack' at the New Mills and elsewhere; it was a common sight to see the drovers throw down the cattle on their backs to nail bits of iron to their hooves, which was considered necessary in consequence of the animals having to travel the road so much.

By the 1830s it was often referred to as simply the **Lion**, with Elizabeth Hooper as landlady. The 1841 census shows that John Fawkes, the landlord, was then aged 30 and that four drovers stayed at the inn for the census night.

In the later 1840s and early 1850s, the inn was run by various members of the Alford family

In 1857 the **Red Lion** was advertised in the *Hereford Journal* as being the closest inn to the new railway stationon the Hereford to Worcester line, then being built:

LEDBURY, HEREFORDSHIRE
TO INNKEEPERS
TO BE LET,

And entered upon the 10th of October, THE RED LION INN, situated in the principal thoroughfare of the Town of Ledbury, and the nearest Inn of any pretensions to the Hereford Worcester Railway, the Works of which are now being proceeded with. The House contains Ten good Bedrooms, Two Parlours, Bar, large Kitchen, Back-Kitchen, Brew-house, excellent Cellars, Stabling, Yard, with Carriage Entrance, and every accommodation requisite for carrying on a large Business. Rent and coming in moderate. An enterprising and persevering Tenant cannot fail to obtain a respectable Business.

For further particulars, address Mr. Dunn, Ledbury.

The faded sign for the Railway Inn

The Worcester and Hereford Railway took a considerable time to build and was not fully open until 17 September 1861. It must have been about this time that the name was changed to the more prosaic **Railway Inn**, in the hopes that its position close to the station would compensate for the loss of the drovers' trade. This caused some confusion in an 1867 directory, which included the **Red Lion** as well as the **Railway**, both with Mrs. Elizabeth Dixon as landlady!

The increased trade was not to last for long, for in 1871 a Committee of clergy and gentry from the Ledbury area was set up to provide a cottage

Once the Railway Inn

hospital in the town. In the first instance they needed a building to rent and in 1873 they took over the **Railway Inn**, then described as a well-built three-storey house. Charles Renton in his book, *The Story of Herefordshire's Hospitals*, described the building:

> On the ground floor there were two large rooms suitable for a dayroom and a boardroom, together with a kitchen and an adjacent pantry. Upstairs on the first floor a male and female ward were created accommodating two patients in each, an operating theatre and matron's room. Several other rooms were available on the second floor.

It was eventually replaced by a purpose-built hospital, which opened in 1892 on a site opposite the old **Railway Inn**. The old hospital cost £230 a year to run and in an attempt to obtain extra funds for the running of the new, larger building, collecting tins were placed outside the **Feathers Hotel**, the **New Inn**, the **White Hart**, the **Plough**, the **Ring of Bells** and inside and outside the hospital. The old building still survives with the **Railway Inn** sign still dimly visible high on the gable end.

The next drinking establishment on the east side of The Homend was a cider house called the **Plasterer's Arms**. Little is known about this establishment, but it may have been the premises of a beer retailer called William Jones, who occupied part of plot No. 99 on the 1841 tithe map, just past the **Red Lion**, but not quite as far as the Baptist chapel.

A plan of Ledbury included in the 1824 *Ledbury Guide* shows a turning on the east side of the Homend with **Nag's Head** inscribed next to it. A 'Nag's Head Yard' is entered in the 1881 census with three families resident — those of Thomas Bridges, a groom; Richard Cox, a carpenter; and James Davies, a butcher; whilst Ann Cook, a charwoman, lived by herself. The census details suggest that it was next to the National School House and it is almost certainly the surviving cruck house, now an important visual feature of this part of The Homend. The following description is in the *Woolhope Club Transactions* for 1966:

> There are three bays with the original chimney in the middle bay. Three of the trusses are box frame with only the one cruck truss which happens to be the one exposed. The timber work as a whole appears to be about 1600. It may be that what is left is the late

extension along the street of an earlier cruck house most of which has disappeared. All that can be safely said is that it is an early seventeenth century house incorporating an earlier cruck truss.

Wargent commented:

From **Nag's Head Inn** to the Pound House was an orchard, on a corner of which was built a school and a school house. The **Pound House** was as it is now, and the reason it was called the **Pound House**, was because a 'pound' [an enclosure to impound stray animals] was situated on the lower side of the house and it is to be seen to this day behind the posting station. In those days a man named Farley lived at the 'pound' and sold cider.

He continued: 'Knapp Lane is a very old thoroughfare and was used more in bygone days than now'. The use has again changed somewhat and Knapp Lane is used by many people as a means of avoiding the traffic in the centre of Ledbury. The **Pound** is now Turnpike Cottage.

The Hereford Road leads off The Homend almost opposite the railway station. It was down here that the **Express**, colloquially known as the **Bull and Boar**, stood, apparently on the north side of the road. Had it been the **Bull and Boar** this inn may well have been the scene of the 'barbarous and unmanly' practice of bull-baiting. Ludlow is still famous for its 'Bull Ring', where, as Tony Hobbs describes in his *Pubs of Ludlow and Neighbourhood:*

The cruck-framed Nag's Head in 2001

A ferocious bull (or bear) was tethered by a stout steel chain to a strong post in a ring or inn-yard. Our 'rude forefathers' then gathered round to watch and bet as bull-dogs, one at a time, were set to bait the bull. The skill of the dogs, which in those days were long in the jaw and leg, was measured by their ability to pin the bull by the nose. It was quite a profitable business for the bull's keeper. He received two or three pence for three runs from each dog-owner and took a collection from the spectators. He usually had about him a piece of wood to lever open a dog's jaws which fastened too tightly on the bull. The animal could be baited three or four times a day, a collection being made each time. The landlord of the local inn [in Ledbury's case the **Bull and Boar**] would hire the keeper and the bull or bear for three days for about ten shillings, in the hopeful expectation of increased trade. People of all classes watched the 'amusement', even on occasion members of the Corporation, dressed in their robes. Bull-baiting was a popular sport at wakes, while bear-baiting was sometimes held in celebration of a marriage.

In Ludlow bull-baiting was practised until the latter end of the 18th century although it was not stopped nationally until 1835. As the writer of a Ludlow guide said in 1822 'it is much to the credit of the inhabitants that this relic of barbarism, adopted by our ancestors, and calculated to corrupt the heart and harden it against every tender feeling of humanity, is now discontinued here'.

However this may be, it is most likely that the inn was opened to serve railway construction workers and the 1861 census records that James Hamblett was a railway contractor and public house keeper in Hereford Road — doubtless making money from both enterprises at the time that the Hereford to Worcester railway was being built. By 1871 Hamblett had moved on and the **Express** was run by James Greenway, the son of the landlord at the **Bridge Inn,** who was also a coal merchant. By 1881 he had been replaced by Thomas Bibbs who was there for some time. The inn was adjacent to the skew bridge that once carried the

The Pound House

Ledbury to Gloucester railway over the road. This railway was opened in 1885 and closed in 1959. The inn was still operating in 1910 when it belonged to the Great Western Railway with John A. Carpenter as a beer and cider retailer. It probably closed shorly afterwards and the site is now occupied by a building supplies merchant.

Alfred Watkins' photograph of the Express with the railway embankment on the right

Masefield's *The Widow in the Bye Street* written in 1912, is a low-life story in verse, described as being set in a little Shropshire town [?Bridgnorth], but generally believed to be actually in Masefield's home town of Ledbury. The story is of a decent lad, his mother's support, led by a worthless strumpet into jealousy and murder. It is a tragedy in which young Jim Gurney worked as a navvy on the making of the new railway line in the old canal bed. According to Alfred Watkins, there is no mistaking the little inn where the lad drank himself into a murder frenzy. In 1930 Watkins wrote

It is there, near the station, but without its former licence.
An inn so hidden it is out of sight
To anyone not coming from the west,
The high embankment hides it with its crest.
Canal men used it when the barges came,
The navvies used it when the line was making.

Then Plaisters End, the scene of the murder, has its position exactly described by the short cut across the fields taken from the inn, and the longer way 'by the mills'.

CHAPTER ELEVEN

Ledbury
THE HOMEND—WEST SIDE, & BYE ST.

In the previous chapter the eastern side of The Homend was described from the Lower Cross to the outskirts of the town. In this chapter the reverse course is taken, starting with the **Queen's Head**, the most distant pub from the town centre on the west side of The Homend. It functioned as a beer house in the middle of the 19th century being next to the old route to Belle Orchard. The 1841 tithe map shows the property (No. 124 on the Tithe apportionment) as being partly occupied by Richard Edwards, a beer retailer, but by 1851 he had been replaced by James Barton. Wargent in his *Recollections of Ledbury* published in 1905 wrote that 'Mr. Harrington's house was a licensed premises called the **Queen's Head** at which there was a bowling alley'. It probably closed during the third quarter of the 19th century.

The one time Queen's Head has been a private house for over 100 years

At the Belle Orchard, two houses were merged into one and a cider and perry factory was established by 1851. Edna Dickinson in her notes on licensed premises in Ledbury suggests that it may have been known as the **Bell Inn**. The 1881 census mentions the **Bell**, Orchards House, in the Homend where Charles T.

The White Horse in the 1920s and in 2001.
Although the building has been tidied up the windows are still recognisable

Jones was a cider merchant. He lived with his three grown-up sisters
— all domestic servants. The building was demolished in 1891 to
make way for housing, whilst the remaining part of Belle Orchard was
used as the site for the new Cottage Hospital, replacing the earlier one
in the **Railway Inn** opposite.

A few doors south-wards at No. 122 was the **Pack Horse Inn**, a
beer house run by Benjamin Bennett between 1835 and 1851. Shortly
afterwards it was renamed — the **Pack Horse** becoming a slightly
more dignified **White Horse**. However, it may have been little more
than a beer house. Mrs. Elizabeth Banks was shown as being the
innkeeper at the **White Horse** in the 1881 census and again in the 1902
Jakeman and Carver's *Directory*. In the earlier record her husband,
William, was described as a gardener. Some 10 years later, in 1891,

William Banks, was shown in the Kelly's *Directory* as a beer retailer, with no mention either of gardening or of the inn's name. The **White Horse** continued to serve beer well into the 20th century, finally closing its doors in 1930 when it became a private residence. Had it stayed open for a few years longer it may well have survived till after the Second World War, for between 1937 and 1943 the adjoining alley led to an old bakery that was converted to become the Employment Exchange during the years of the depression.

A longer-lasting pub was the **Plough** at No. 74 The Homend. The building is grade II listed where it is described as 'of 17th-century date,

this inn has exposed timber-framing in the upper parts of the south front and the west end'. Little can now be seen and the building appears to be mainly of mid-19th century date. An earlier building is shown on a lithograph of *c*.1830 when Thomas Andrews was landlord (see chapter 10). Being a little way out of the centre of the town, the various landlords often had another job in addition to running the pub. Thus in 1793, William Morris also ran a shop, and for the last two

The Plough finally closed its doors as an inn in the late 1990s

Pursuant to 10 Edw. & Geo.5 G 24 S 55. These Premises are permitted to be open for the sale of Intoxicating Liquors between the hours of 10 & 10·30am and 2·30 & 4pm on Tuesdays for the accomodation of persons attending the Market.

Licensed in pursuance of act of Parliament for Public(b) Music & Dancing. Or other Public Entertainment of the like kind

The Plough had a Market Licence allowing it to stay open in the afternoon

THE FOX LANE LEADING TO HILLS YARD 1993

The Fox Inn early in 2001. It has since been converted to an Indian restaurant

decades of the 19th century, Thomas Harry Howard was also a horse dealer. His wife's first baby daughter was born just before the 1881 census and at that time had not even been given a name although she was then two weeks old. At the beginning of the 20th century the inn was the base for the Independent Order of Odd Fellows, Loyal St. Katherine Lodge No. 6315. The **Plough** finally closed in the late 1990s; it is now a shop selling imported goods.

The **Fox Inn** has been closed for many years, but its name is commemorated in the adjoining passageway where there is a small plaque, which was provided by the Ledbury and District Society Trust in 1993. The inn was originally called the **Fox**, then apparently there was a name change to the **Crown** or **Little Crown** for a time in the 19th century, but it had reverted to the **Fox** well before the end of the century. Thus in the 1793 *Directory* it was the **Fox** with Joseph Smith as victualler, and in the 1822 Pigott's *Directory* both the **Fox** and the **Crown** appear with John Jones as landlord. However, the Davis lithograph of *c.*1830 appears to show the **Crown** in the same position as the **Fox** is later known to be. From 1831 to 1867 only the **Crown** (or occasionally the **Little Crown**) is mentioned in directories, but by 1881 the **Fox** had returned, with Elizabeth Drayton as innkeeper, and the **Crown** had finally disappeared. By 1891 the inn had been taken over by John Hollings and it continued to be entered in the directories under the same family for well over 50 years, with James Hollings in 1929 and Edwin in 1941, apart from 1902, when Charles George Curnock was shown as being at the **Fox**. It closed in 1967 and for a time the building housed a firm selling motor accessories. At the end of 2001 it reverted to being a licensed establishment — this time as an Indian restaurant.

The **Swan Inn** was almost opposite the **Horse Shoe**. It was a low building that stood next to a black and white building with a projecting porch. An inn called the **White Lion** is shown in approximately the same position as the later **Swan** on a 1788 plan of Ledbury. This inn may have been host to one of the earliest Friendly Societies in England. A statement on a broadsheet giving the rules of the society (now in Hereford Library) states that it had been 'held regularly ever since the 31st day of May, 1753, and has raised a fund of about £200'. The broadsheet was printed by C. Pugh in 1785.

It was during the 1780s that the **White Lion** was a regular venue for auction sales advertised in the *Hereford Journal.* Typically, in 1781 there was an advertisement involving the sale of two farms by auction 'at the dwelling-house of Elizabeth Grundy, Widow, called the White-Lion, in the town of Ledbury'. Elizabeth died early in 1789 and the *Journal* carried an advertisement:

WHITE-LION INN,
LEDBURY, Herefordshire.
John Grundy respectfully informs the public, that he carries on the business of his late aunt Grundy, at the above inn, where he humbly hopes for the continuance of the favors (*sic*) of her customers and the public in general, his utmost endeavors (*sic*) will be used to render the house comfortable, and to provide good entertainment and excellent liquors.

John was not a successful landlord and less than 18 months later, in August 1791, he announced that the **White Lion** was closing as a public house:

WHITE-LION, LEDBURY
JOHN GRUNDY

Begs leave to inform his friends and the public, that he has discontinued the business of the above house; and he takes this opportunity of returning his sincere thanks for the many favours conferred on him, and assures them he shall always retain a grateful remembrance thereof.

By 2001 the Swan had become the Olive Tree

Apart from an auction sale at the **White Lion** in 1795, there appears to be a gap of a few years before the **Swan** emerged at the beginning of the 19th century. This was when the Barnes family ran it for at least 28 years — first James and then Elizabeth, presumably his widow. By 1867 they had been followed by the Webb family — first William, followed in 1876 by Sarah, presumably another widow. She may also have died relatively young, for in 1881 the inn was being run by 32-year-old George Webb and his wife Ann. Although it has been closed for nearly a century, the wrought iron bracket for its hanging sign is still there. Even the name survived for some time in the Swan cycle shop. Now the bracket provides a similar service, for the sign of the 'Olive Tree' Italian restaurant hangs from it.

Little is known of the **Farrier's Arms**, a licensed premises at No. 32 The Homend, now the premises of Eager's Electricals. This now incorporates two dwellings, one of which was the house of a blacksmith. Earlier, according to Wargent, 'the two dwellings were a public house called "The Farrier's Arms", there being a blacksmith's shop behind'.

214

There were other pubs in The Homend from time to time, one possibly called the **Glaziers' Arms**, although the identification is entirely dependent on a late 17th-century trade token which may refer entirely to William Browne's profession rather than a public house. Similar tokens were issued by William Hooper (the Weaver's Arms) who was certainly a weaver, William Berrow (the Grocer's Arms in High Street) who is listed as a mercer, and Reighinald Randolph (the Blacksmith's Arms in High Street) who could well have been no more than a blacksmith. In addition there were many beer and cider retailers in the Homend during the 19th century that only occasionally appeared in directories.

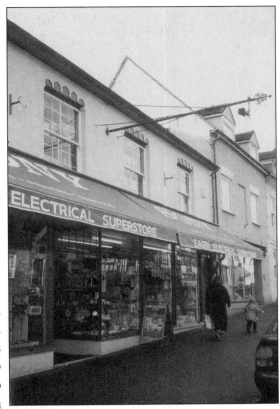

Eager's Electricals was at one time the Farrier's Arms

Although the main crossroads has moved to Upper Cross, Lower Cross is still the central point in Ledbury, with Bye Street leading off to the west, eventually becoming Bridge Street as it crosses the line of the long-since closed Ledbury to Gloucester railway. Bye Street was at one time the main street leading westwards from Ledbury taking a rambling route towards Little Marcle and Ross-on-Wye. As with the Bye Street in Hereford, the name may be a contraction from Bishop Street, alternatively it may reflect its later status. Bye Street in Hereford was even less fortunate — its name was eventually changed to the mundane Commercial Street! In Ledbury, this was at one time the second largest street in the town in terms of trade, but it lost much of its importance as New Street developed. It started as a narrow road close to the Lower Cross and then widened out. Typically, there was a Shop Row in the middle of the wide part of the street, forming a series of islands. At one time a stream ran down the middle of the street; it started from Upper Hall and was culverted in 1830. There were several inns in Bridge Street and Bye Street, one of which — the **Brewery Inn** — is still open.

Bridge Street is so named because the road originally crossed the Gloucester to Hereford canal. The area around Bridge Street was formerly known as Happy Land and was not a residential district until after the completion of the canal when an estate was opened up by the Ledbury Land Society. The canal had a somewhat chequered history — the section from Gloucester to the Wharf near New Street in Ledbury was opened in 1798, but it took almost another 50 years before the scheme was completed to Hereford in 1845.

In 1930, Alfred Watkins wrote about the demise of the canal:

Early in 1881, hearing it was about to be closed (the embankment at the Ledbury station end of the new Ledbury-Dymock railway having already started), I persuaded another young boating spark (Ted George, whose father had founded a timber business at the Canal Wharf at Hereford) to come with me on a two days final water-trip by canoe along the whole length to Gloucester. A very jolly trip it was, chasing down ducks who flew and flapped in terror at the strange invaders, diving through tunnels, with a small boat's lamp to give light carefully balanced on the bow, and shouting songs to keep our spirits up in the case of that long weird tunnel (1 1/4 miles) at Oxenhall, where we could not see the other end, and were paddling into the blackness of night, with the water washing the walls on both sides, for in this one, the tow-path went over the top of the hill, and the canal-men had to 'leg' their barges through by pushing with their feet against the roof. This, however, was on the second day's trip after passing Dymock and the belt of daffodil country about Boyce Court, where, as I wrote in my half-century-ago account of the trip [not found] 'they spangle the hedgerows and literally carpet the meadows, and even on the bank their graceful flowers bend over and look down into the natural mirror of the water'.

At Ledbury the dusk was falling when we landed at the wharf, left our canoes in a warehouse there, and walked up Bye Street for a night at the Feathers.

Where the canal used to be crossed at the bottom of Bye Street by a bridge with the lock below, now stands the railway bridge with the line in the old canal bed.

The passing of the Ledbury to Gloucester canal through Ledbury seemed to me to give it a touch of romance. Canals may not seem romantic to present day people, but when they came as a new idea at the end of the eighteenth century they were called by the general term of Inland Navigation, and looked upon as bringing up goods from the sea to inland pastures, meadows and villages. A new race of men evolved to dig them, and they were called navigators, or later on navvies. I have heard the full name used in Ledbury half a century ago. 'Just then two navigators slightly inebriated came rolling down the street'. Great burly men, with a slow rolling walk something like a sailor's, wearing short jacket, characteristic neck cloth, and spacious corduroy trousers, hitched to the body by three tight straps, one round the waist, the others below the knees, leaving the upper part bagged up a little, the forerunners of plus-fours. They have changed to another type now but lingered on for a time to make the earlier railways, which came so soon after to supercede the waterways. The early name the 'cut' clung to our local canal. To me as a small boy, walking down along a bit of it on my way to school [about 1865] there was romance in the canal people and all their trappings. The touch of jazz decoration about the boats and fittings, that checkers pattern we used to see on the posts of inn-doors being a favourite, the buckets and boat-poles and hooks all a bit different to such things elsewhere, and all gaudily decorated if at all possible; the loud-voiced women, the only women at that time working on equal terms at the same jobs as the men, steering, swearing, shoving, working the locks. The children, taking their turn at the tiller, or walking alongside the old draught-horse, the wonder how there was room for all to sleep in the tiny cabin.

There was a need for a public house near the canal bridge and Wargent describes what must have been the original one:

The houses all the way down to the bridge on the same side were similar in style to their present appearance but 'The Brewery Inn' was then unknown. There was a small thatched house occupied by Mr. T. Brookes at the corner of the lane known as 'Dirty Hole' which was known as 'The Quiet Woman' kept by a man named Hardwick.

This was most probably on the north side of the road and at the time of the 1841 tithe survey, a John Hardwick was in a house which was part of No. 160 on the tithe apportionment. His name was at the end of the list, so presumably he was at the west end of the row and hence on a corner site. Presumably this was the **Quiet Woman** which shortly afterwards lost its licence.

The tale is taken up by Dickinson who stated that:

> Brace's lodging house, a Ballard building at the far end of the island site in the centre of the road, was licensed. It did a big trade among canal people but some time later it ceased to be a public house, and after this closure the Boat Inn [now the **Brewery Inn**] was licensed. The lodging house later became the Golden Crown Chinese restaurant and was destroyed by a gas explosion on 23 January 1983. A new building erected on the site is currently the Paradise Tandoori Indian take-away.

This was not the whole story for Wargent noted:

> Directly after the canal to Hereford was made Mr. Thomas Edy had Bridge House built, and it was known for some years as 'The Bridge Inn' kept by James Greenway and subsequently by Mr. Goode during whose tenancy the licence was lost. A bowling alley was attached to this inn as to many others in the town. It is now a private residence called Bridge House.

The one time Bridge Inn still stands next to what was the bridge over the canal and later the railway

218

The Brewery Inn about 1880

The Brewery Inn in 2001

The **Bridge Inn**, also called the **Canal Inn**, was a simple beer house that probably lost its licence in the 1870s. The building survives today, close to the cutting that once took the canal and later the railway.

Somewhere opposite the **Bridge Inn** was the short-lived **Pointer's Tavern**, which was run in 1861 by Maria Morvan, a widow, and her son Alfred, a brewer. Ten years previously Maria and her husband John kept a lodging house in the Homend.

The **Brewery Inn** is an attractive building of 17th-century date on the northern side of Bye Street. Wargent suggests that the **Brewery Inn** replaced the lodging house mentioned above and was originally called the **Boat Inn.** This may well have been the **Boatman's Arms** mentioned in an 1851 directory with Francis Heath as a beer retailer. He was also a boat builder, strongly suggesting that the inn did not open until after the canal was completed to Hereford in 1845. It was called the **Brewery Inn** in the 1881 census, but without any

The White Lion in 2001

indication of an innkeeper, for the head of the house, Richard Hickman, was described as a corn miller. Howwever, the 1891 Kelly's *Directory* mentions Benjamin James as a beer retailer in Bye Street and the family continued to run the **Brewery Inn** till at least 1940.

There is now no trace of any brewery although the building next to the inn on the west, which is shown on many photographs with its first-floor hoist, could well have had such a use.

On the opposite side of Bye Street to the **Brewery Inn**, and closer to the centre of the town was the **White Lion**. It was of sufficient importance for an estate to be sold by auction there in June 1795. Throughout the middle of the 19th century Edward Lissiman was the landlord and also the agent to Holloway, a general carrier. The inn closed during the latter part of the 19th century.

The **Green Dragon** may have been an earlier, or even alternative name for the **White Lion**. In 1830 John Barnes is listed as the licensee of the **White Lion**, whilst in the following year he is in the same profession at the **Green Dragon**, both in Bye Street. This is the latest mention of any Dragon in Bye Street, but the **Green Dragon** was apparently of some importance and was well patronised during the 18th century.

It was the Ledbury Turnpike Act of 1721 that established a town-based trust covering all roads entering the town and appointed a total of 39 trustees. The Act empowered the 'several trustees or any three of them to meet together at the sign of the **Green Dragon** in Ledbury ... on or before 24th Day of July 1721'. Later in the century it appears to

This building, with its typical hanger for a pub sign, may have been the Blue Boar

have been a base for Samuel Partridge, an ironmonger from Ross, who arranged for his printed catalogues to be available at the inn.

Also in Bye Street was the **Horse and Groom**, but its precise position is uncertain. According to Wargent 'Mr. Summers place was a butcher's shop kept by James Cale and approached up a flight of stone steps. It afterwards became a public house called the **Horse and Groom**, being kept by a Mr. Benjamin, cooper, and afterwards by Mr. George Ellsmore'. The various 1850s directories correct Wargent in detail, the publican being called Benjamin Cooper. Edna Dickinson suggests that an earlier name for this short-lived pub may have been the **Blue Boar**, an otherwise unlocated pub. She goes on to propose that it was on the south side of Bye Street, on the site of the Job Centre and adjacent to the northern side of the entrance to St. Katherine's car park.

CHAPTER TWELVE

Ledbury
THE CENTRAL AREA

High Street, which joins Lower and Upper Cross, has as its centre-piece the early 17th-century Market Hall with its open ground floor and its herringbone bracing on the south side of the first floor facing down High Street. The street is wide enough to accommodate stalls on market day and still allow the traffic to flow, but in the early 19th century it was a different story. Then, running from the Lower Cross parallel to the Market Hall as far as St. Katherine's Chapel was the Butchers' Row. Wargent, in his 1904 *Recollections of Ledbury,* noted that:

> There were about eight shops in the row including several butchers. The first was a straw bonnet makers and a bookbinder's shop on the same premises, the proprietor being a Mr. Tranter. Mr. John Cale, butcher, was next door, and then came an open space where 'tumbling shows' were erected, a great attraction in those days. The next building was a butcher's shop, the last to carry the business on being a man called Daniel Webb. Adjoining this was a public house called the Rising Sun. There was hardly a block of houses without a pub. Another blank space separated the inn from a fish shop and a small bakery kept by a Mrs. Bayliss. Next door was the indispensable barber's shop where basket making was also carried on. ... Then came the end house with frontage facing up High Street. This was a butcher's shop kept by Mr. John Webb.

The **Rising Sun** was kept by Bartholomew Green in the 1820s with John Johnson taking over in 1831 and renaming it the **Sun Tavern**. By 1835 Elizabeth Johnson was the landlady. The Butcher's Row survived until an 'Act for the improvement of the High Street' was passed in

223

1835, and by 1840 all the shops including the **Rising Sun** had disappeared and High Street once again became the broad market place of the original 12th-century design.

This chapter deals with the inns in the central part of Ledbury; in High Street, between the Upper and Lower Cross, and to the east of Lower Cross in Church Street and Church Lane.

On the east side of High Street at No. 7 the **Bull** is still serving customers as it has for many years. However, this is not an old-established inn in Ledbury terms, for the building has had a confusion of uses and names during both the 19th and 20th centuries. In the 1840s, it was owned by Robert Baggott, a breeches maker. Wargent suggests that it was then the 7th stop of the London to Hereford Mail Coach, but this is questionable as the mail coaches used the **Feathers**, the **New Inn** and the **George**. It was probably a local 'tale' based on the number of the house.

After Mr. Baggott left it became a licensed house called the **Malakoff**, but only for a short time. This must have been shortly after 1855, for the Malakoff Tower was one of the principal defences of Sebastopol. In early September 1855, during the Crimean War, there was an unsuccessful British attack on the southern defences of Sebastopol, but shortly afterwards the siege of Sebastopol ended with its capture. The French, who were our allies in this war, were sufficiently proud of the victory to re-name one of the suburbs of Paris Malakoff. The **Malakoff Inn** only lasted for a few years and by 1861 the building had become a fishmonger's shop.

During the later 1860s and '70s it once again became an

In the 1960s and early '70s the Hereford Bull was remowned for its steaks inn, run by the Harris family under the rather unwieldy name of **No. 7 Wine and Spirit Vaults**. By the time of the 1881 census the head of the household was William Armell Cotterell Gabb and the inn became simply **No. 7** or **No. 7 Inn**. He was described as a wine and spirit merchant, whilst his wife, Mary, was the landlady and his 17-year-old daughter, Anne, was described as 'assistant in bar'. During the mid-20th century it became the **Hereford Bull**, but once again the name has been shortened and it is now a simple **Bull**.

The Bull in 2001

The **King's Arms**, which was a few yards further south down High Street at Nos. 16 and 17, was an important town inn of the 18th century. However, by 1773 it had fallen from grace and on 10 June the *Hereford Journal* advertised:

> To be sold to the best BIDDER, On Wednesday the 30th instant, at the King's Arms, Ledbury, between the hours of two and six in the afternoon, according to conditions to be then produced, unless sold in the meantime by private trade, THAT well-accustomed INN the said KING'S ARMS, together with a garden coach-house, assembly-room, stables, granaries, wool lofts, and all other buildings thereto belonging, now in the possession of John Yarnold, the proprietor thereof.
>
> Likewise to be sold two post-chaises, six horses, the stock of liquor, household goods and furniture belonging to the said inn.
>
> For particulars apply to Mr. John Homes, attorney at law, in the Town's End, near Ledbury aforesaid.
>
> N.B. All the creditors of the said John Yarnold are desired immediately to send an account of their respective demands to the said John Homes.

2001. This was once the King's Arms

This was very obviously a bankruptcy sale with creditors attempting to get some of their money back. The inn was bought by Luke Morris of the **Plume of Feathers**, just across the road, who advertised that 'the same will be instantly fitted up in a decent manner, and continue open as well as the Plume of Feathers'.

Although the inn had a banqueting hall and stables for the use of guests who arrived on horseback, the approach was too narrow to admit carriages and in 1778 the hostelry succumbed to the competition of the town's coaching inns and closed. In 1885, the building became the shop premises of L. Tilley and Son, printers, stationers and booksellers. The historic part is No. 17 which is of 16th-century date and was at one time plastered over. By 1930 the plaster had been removed and the front exposed with close-set timber framing to the two upper stories. The top storey projects on a moulded bressumer and there are moulded beams within the shop.

There were three inns on the opposite side of High Street, but only the **Feathers** has survived. The **Lion** was nearest to the Lower Cross and was active in the late 18th and early 19th centuries. It was the home of a Friendly Society founded on 2 November 1791, when the **Lion Inn** was described as being 'in the Cathol' (see p.227) and was kept by Richard Jones. The rules of the society are of some interest. One stated that no one was to be admitted as a member unless he had had the small-pox. Another required the members to promise to prefer and employ each other in their trades and employments before any other that is not of the society except for a reason approved by the members. Finally, 'if any member of the society leads an idle or scandalous life, or gets the venereal disease, he shall receive no benefit from the box'.

The 'Cathol' was the alley between Butchers' Row and St. Katherine's Hospital. The name is assumed to be a contraction of St. Katherine's Alley and it appears on maps of 1788 and 1824. As the pub was stated to be in the Cathol, it was clearly not in Butchers' Row and hence must have been on the St. Katherine's side of the alleyway. An 1817 plan of St. Katherine's indicates a building on that side of the alley, more or less where the central tower of the present almshouses now stands, marked 'Premises on Lease to J. Bosley / Expires 24 March 1817'. Since John Bosley was later at the **New Inn,** where he took over from Ann Bosley about 1830 or 1831, this would seem to locate the **Lion Inn**. It also suggests that the pub probably closed in 1817. The building was demolished by 1822, when the first part of the present almshouses, including the central tower, was built.

The **Chequers** was at No. 26 High Street, but had closed probably before the middle of the 19th century when the premises became a fishmonger's run by a Mr. MacDonald. More recently it was a branch office of the Birmingham Midshires Building Society.

A few doors down from the Chequers is the **Feathers**, which was a celebrated posting house during the 18th and early 19th centuries and continues in the tradition of providing good food and

Once the Chequers Inn

accommodation. In the early 18th century it belonged to the Biddulph family as there is an inventory of furniture belonging to the inn in the Biddulph collection in the Herefordshire County Record Office. However, it was not always praised. On Saturday 11 August 1787 the **Plume of Feathers** (as it was then called) was visited by the Hon. John Byng. He noted in his diary 'Dined there, in haste, on some tough mutton chops, a sad inn; and well that I had not made it my night stop'! Even so, it was sufficiently successful in the latter part of the 18th century for Luke Morris of the **Plume of Feathers** to take over the **King's Arms** across the road. There were many auction sales held at the **Plume of Feathers** during the 1780s and 1790s, but in 1797 it changed hands:

FEATHERS INN, LEDBURY,
HEREFORDSHIRE
G. TAYLOR (*Many Years Waiter*
at the NEW INN, HEREFORD,)

begs leave respectfully to inform the Nobility, Gentlemen Travellers, and Others, That he has taken and entered on the above Inn: where he humbly solicits a continuance of the favours of those Gentlemen who frequented the house in his predecessor's time (Mr. LUKE MORRIS); and hopes to merit the patronage of the PUBLIC in general, by the most assiduous attention to their comfortable accommodation.

G.T. has laid in a Stock of OLD WINES and other LIQUORS; and also keeps Neat POST-CHAISES, with able Horses, and careful Drivers.

The New Inn in Hereford was one of the principal inns of the city, but it, together with the Redstreak Tree, was bought by the Corporation in 1809 to provide land on which to build a Council Chamber. In the event this project did not go ahead and part of the two sites eventually became the Butter Market. Perhaps Giles Taylor could read the writing on the wall and thought it best to abandon Hereford in favour of Ledbury.

The **Plume of Feathers** is a reference to the plume of three ostrich feathers, first adopted as a crest by the Black Prince, and is the badge of the heir apparent to the throne of England. The **Feathers** is thus one of many inn signs like 'The Crown', 'The Lion', 'The Unicorn', 'The King's Arms' and 'The Queen's Head' that were used to suggest loyalty to royalty.

Auction sales continued into the 19th century including the Advowson of Castle Frome, and various tithes, woodland, estates and cottages. In October 1810, a Public Dinner was held at the inn to celebrate the 'Anniversary of His Majesty's Accession to the Throne'. This was, of course, George III — Farmer George — who had ascended to the throne in 1760 and was to reign for 59 years.

The inn was at the heart of Ledbury's social life and in January 1820 hosted the Ledbury Card and Dancing Assembly. Later in the year there was the half-yearly meeting of the Proprietors of the Herefordshire and Gloucestershire Canal Company, still striving to complete the project as far as Hereford.

By 1822 Giles Taylor was the postmaster with the Post Office in the **Feathers Hotel**; he was still there in 1835 when the hotel was described as including within its facilities 'commercial, posting and excise office'. Giles apparently died around that time and for the next few years the inn was run by Eliza Taylor, presumably his wife.

In an 1830 Guide the **Feathers** was described as:

The principal inn, and from its excellent and ample accommodations, it is exceedingly well accustomed. Chaises and horses are let, and the several coaches stop here. Annual assemblies are held, and the ball-room is spacious and convenient. The uniform attention gentlemen meet with here makes the bar-room a resort for elect society.

The **George**, and the **New Inn**, are the next, at each of which wines, spirits, and good general accommodation may be obtained. At the **George** a billiard-room is established. There are many other respectable inns, as the **Oak**, **Unicorn**, &c., where the traveller will meet with every attention and civility.

It was at this time that Wargent described events associated with the **Feathers**:

Horse dealers did a big trade outside the **Feathers**, the horses being trotted up and down High Street ... The Royal Mail (four horse) from London came via Cheltenham arriving at the **Feathers** at 10.00 a.m. and then proceeded, after changing horses, to Hereford, where another coach proceeded to Aberystwyth. The letters were not numerous and the guard had collected his letter bags, was off his box and across into the post office run by Mr. Taylor, opposite the **Feathers**, in a minute, and in about the same time had returned with the few outgoing mail bags.

The Gloucester mail coach ran up to 1885 starting from the **Feathers** at 8.00 a.m. and calling at Dymock, Newent and Gloucester, returning to Ledbury at 6.00 p.m. The first proprietor of this coach was Mr. Ben Roberts. There were several stage coaches and at the **Feathers**, six post boys were kept and others at the **George Hotel** in the Southend. The post boys looked quite spick and span in their breeches, yellow jackets and white top hats, also top boots, spurs and whips.

By the 1840s the inn had been taken over by Francis Henry Deakins who again spent many years in service. He was still there in 1858 when the following coaches left the inn each day:

The Gloucester Mail at 8 a.m.
The Hereford Mail at 1 p.m. and 6 p.m.
The Monmouth Mail at 1 p.m. and 6 p.m.
The Worcester (Queen) at 9.30 a.m. and The Mail at 5.20 p.m

By 1867 the **Feathers** was described as being a 'Family and Commercial' Hotel with James Stevens as landlord, and the Inland Revenue Office was still stationed there. By 1891 there was an

The Feathers about 1890 when the whole front was rendered.
Outside is the coach which met all trains at Ledbury station

230

'assembly room with a large platform and capable of holding 500 people; a smaller room in the hotel serves as a Corn Exchange'; William Manton was the proprietor.

The **Feathers Hotel** was included in Volume 2 of the *Inventory of the Historical Monuments in Herefordshire,* published in 1932, and became a Grade 2* listed building in 1953. The accounts taken from these two sources provide the following description:

The Feathers Hotel was formerly two houses, the left-hand (south) block was originally three stories high and was built about 1560-70. It has close-set timber framing and each of the upper stories project. In the early 17th century the roof was removed and an additional story consisting of five gables with moulded barge-boards and pendants was added. There is a coach entrance on the left with panelled double doors.

The right-hand block is three stories high and was built at the beginning of the 17th century, probably about the time that the roof was raised on the earlier part. It is again of close-set timber studding.

The Feathers about 1910 after the render had been removed

A 1962 advertisement for the Feathers Hotel

The Feathers in 2001

Only the upper floor projects; the one below formerly projected but has been underbuilt. The back wing and the staircase wing were added later in the 17th century.

As can be expected, the interior has been much altered, but much timber framing is exposed. The staircase, of late 17th century date has been altered and partly re-arranged; it has twisted balusters and heavily moulded strings.

The hotel successfully survived the transformation from stagecoach to train and eventually motor vehicles, and is now the most prominent inn in the town.

Church Lane leads off the Lower Cross in an easterly direction towards the parish church. Confusingly it was called Church Street until the adjoining Back Lane became Church Street. So as

The Jolly Crispin in 2001

not to add to the confusion, only the modern names are used in the following descriptions.

Church Lane is an attractive cobbled way, a mecca for the tourists, with all the requirements — museums, a pub, and the Ledbury public conveniences! At one time there were two inns in this short street; the **Jolly Crispin** on the south side and the **Prince of Wales** on the north. Now only the **Prince of Wales** survives.

In the mid-19th century the **Jolly Crispin** was run by Samuel Pedlingham, a shoe-maker as well as beer house keeper.

Pedlingham was quite a character and was apparently the ringleader in a bell-ringing scandal. This was when the Rev. Jackson, vicar of Ledbury, was inhibited from performing his duties while a court action was pending in the Court of Arches, London, and the curate, the Rev. Charles Augustus Solbé, was in charge. Because of this the accustomed parish ringers had ceased to ring as a body before Christmas 1869, so other ringers were appointed. These new ringers included the Rev. Solbé, and beer and 'bacca' were not then allowed in the belfry as had been the case before.

On 14 April 1870 a false rumour that the Rev. Jackson had been acquitted swept through the town and the old ringers went and rang to celebrate without asking permission. The Rev. Solbé being fetched, he attempted to enter the belfry but the door was locked on the inside. He left the churchyard for about five minutes and on his return found Samuel Pedlingham pacing up and down outside the belfry. Pedlingham was abusive and, in a provocative gesture, drank beer from a jug in front of Rev. Solbé. While this was going on the bells were being set down and the ringers slunk out, averting their faces, but a list of names was taken.

The sequel came a few days later when ten ringers appeared in the Ledbury Petty Sessions, charged 'For that they, on the 14th day of April, were severally guilty of riotous, violent, and indecent behaviour in a certain churchyard and belfry, to wit, the churchyard and belfry belonging respectively to the parish church of the said parish of Ledbury'.

The charge was brought by Rev. Solbé against nine people including Samuel Pedlingham and John Fleetwood. After the facts were brought out in court, the charges against all but Fleetwood and Pedlingham were dropped — Pedlingham as ringleader and Fleetwood because he was a parish constable and should have known better! In the event the Bench dismissed the charge against Fleetwood, but they fined Pedlingham 20s. and costs for indecent behaviour.

This was not the end of the trouble for Pedlingham. A second incident happened nearly 18 months later, and it was no doubt the ringers that had been associated with the above incident who were once again involved.

On 30 August 1871 Ledbury magistrates refused to renew the licence for the beer house in Church Street kept by Pedlingham. As it had been his livelihood for 30 years, he appealed against the decision at the Quarter Sessions held in Hereford on 16 October 1871. A number of people spoke in support of the way in which he ran his beer house, and a petition was produced signed by a number of people including the Rev. Jackson. However, the fact that he had been convicted for assault on at least three occasions, the bell-ringing conviction recounted above, and the fact that he had been seen drunk on a number of occasions all told against him and his appeal was dismissed.

This obviously upset his friends the Ledbury ringers and they decided to express their support. The *Hereford Journal* of 21 October 1871 described what happened:

A NOVELTY. — A muffled peal was played on the Ledbury bells, on Tuesday night last, as an expression of sympathy, we presume, on the part of the ringers with one of their number who had on the previous day sustained a defeat in an appeal case prosecuted by him at the Quarter Sessions for the county on the previous day. This performance is, we imagine, quite unique.

This local incident was taken up by the church paper *Church Bells* on 25 November 1871. The tone was in marked contrast to the light-hearted way in which the incident was treated by the *Hereford Journal;* also the length of time which Pedlingham had kept his beer house was given incorrectly:

> At the quarter sessions held in Hereford on Monday the 16th of October last, one Pedlingham, a ringer, and keeper of a beer house in Ledbury, appealed against the decision of the magistrates at a petty sessions, who had refused his certificate to enable him to continue his beer house, which he had kept for nearly ten years. After a long enquiry, the court decided in support of the decision of the magistrates. On the following evening the ringers expressed their sympathy by ringing, during the whole of the evening, muffled peals on the eight bells of the parish church.
>
> This is the grossest belfry outrage we ever heard of. It would be well if legal steps could be taken to censure the parish authorities and punish the ringers, who never ought to be allowed to enter the belfry.

According to Wargent it was the custom in the belfry at that time to have 'the ringers' jar or barrel, which consisted of 4½ gallons of beer or cider, which was trammed on one of the steps in the ringing chamber. After a peal, a horn of beer or cider was handed round to each ringer. It was supposed in those days that the ringing went better if intoxicating liquors were handed round.

The **Crispin, Jolly** or otherwise, must have closed more or less immediately following the refusal of the licence.

Dickinson writes:

> The present owner, Mr. Alan Lloyd, believes that Crispin House and the adjoining Ivy Cottage were at one time connected, as there is a blocked-up doorway in the hall of Crispin House which must have led into Ivy Cottage, and the two properties seemed to have been owned by the same person. Possibly at some time Ivy Cottage may have been the ale-house, as the brew-house is directly behind it and the Prince of Wales directly opposite.

The **Prince of Wales** has the advantage of frontages on two streets — Church Lane and Church Street. It is a late 16th-century building that probably became a beer house some time in the second quarter of the 19th century. At that time it was kept by a Richard

Tyler who eked out a living as a shoe, patten and clog maker as well as running the beer house. By the 1881 census the landlord was the 60-year-old John Tomkins and his wife Eliza. They ran the establishment by themselves without any live-in servants, and had two young lodgers, both railway labourers. The **Prince of Wales** has its main entry in Church Lane, with a rear access in Church Street which was until recently directly opposite yet another inn, the **White Hart**.

Describing his early visits to the small pubs in Ledbury, Alfred Watkins remembered:

The Prince of Wales had a prominent sign to attract tourists during the early part of the 20th century

I knew well the inside of all these back-street inns and their landlords (almost all of them kindly and decent folk) as I was going to them to sell the ... stout from my father's brewery.

Most of the inns brewed their own ordinary ale in those early days, and bought 'stout' and 'bitter'. Only the other day I came on an old ex-innkeeper of my acquaintance in a disused brew-house in the Church Lane, and secured for our museum an old style bailing-pail used in the home-brewing days. A bright clean-faced little old man he is, and ... the chief bookie of the town when he kept the adjoining inn [presumably the **Prince of Wales**]. ... In the old days he always boasted that he never would drink his own brewed beer; but in contrast, the innkeeper at the **Brewery Inn** always boasted that he never drunk anything but his own brew.

ALL THAT messuage or Inn known as The Prince of Wales Inn situate in Church Lane and Church Street in the Town of Ledbury in the County of Hereford with the buildings and yards and all outbuildings and appurtenances thereunto belonging TOGETHER with the site thereof and the land occupied therewith AND ALSO ALL THAT building and the land whereon the same was erected situate in Church Lane aforesaid bounded on the north and east sides thereof by the said Inn on the west by premises belonging to the Parish of Ledbury and on the south by Church Lane aforesaid as the same is now used as a beer and cider cellar.

The Prince of Wales was included in the sale of Arnold Perrett Ltd. to the Cheltenham Original Brewery in 1937

Front and rear views of the Prince of Wales in 2001

Watkins remembered a man coming up to him after he gave a talk in Ledbury who said, 'I was living in Ledbury when a drunkard broke out of Sam Bowlers at the **White Hart**, and ran, quite naked to climb the steeple'. Watkins continued: 'This seems to be the story in verse used by Masefield in *The Everlasting Mercy,* the epic of the conversion to a clean life of a foul-mouthed country-town poacher'. In the poem:

From '61 to '67
I lived in disbelief of heaven
I drunk, I fought, I poached, I whored,
I did despite unto the lord,
I cursed, 'twould make a man look pale,
And nineteen times I went to jail.

He quarrelled and had a set fight with another poacher, organised by 'Silas Jones, that bookie wide', keeper of the back-lane inn where the sots meet. There, in an upstairs room, Saul spends his winnings with his pals:

Hot Hollands punch on top of stout
Puts madness in and wisdom out.
From drunken man to drunken man
The drunken madness raged and ran.
'I'm climber Joe who climbed the spire'
'You're climber Joe the bloody liar'
'Who says I lie?'
'I do'
'You lie.
I climbed the spire and had a fly'
'I'm French Suzanne the Circus dancer,
I'm going to dance a bloody Lancer'.

From three long hours of gin and smokes,
And two girls' breath and fifteen blokes',
A warmish night and windows shut,
The room stank like a fox's gut.
The heat and smell and drinking deep
Began to stun the gang to sleep.
Some fell downstairs to sleep on the mat,
Some snored it sodden where they sat.
Dick Twot had lost a tooth and wept,
But all the drunken others slept.
Jane slept besides me in the chair,
And I got up; I wanted air.
I opened window wide and leaned,
Out of that pigstye of the fiend
And felt a cool wind go like grace
About the sleeping market-place.
The clock struck three, and sweetly, slowly,
The bells chimed Holy, Holy, Holy,

And in a seconds pause there fell
The cold note of the chapel bell,
And then a cock crew, flapping wings,
And summat made me think of things.

The poem goes on when Saul rings the fire-bell at St Katherine's in the market-place and 'shouted fire at doors of parson, lawyer, squire', and smashed their windows.

Later the parson finished:

Meanwhile my friend, 'twould be no sin
To mix more water in your gin.
We're neither saints nor Phillip Sidneys,
But mortal men with mortal kidneys'.
He took his snuff, and wheezed a greeting,
And waddled off to mothers' meeting.

Watkins' friend, who remembered the naked man, continued 'It was not he, but another, who ran a-muck after pulling the fire-bell'.

Until relatively recently drinkers could stagger out of the back door of the **Prince of Wales**, weave their way across the quiet Church Street, and climb the three steps into the **White Hart**. This early 19th-century building looks more like a private house than a pub, but the large trap-door in the pavement provided a typical pub access for large barrels of beer to be rolled into the cellar. The worn sign that hung over the door for many years demonstrated the family nature of the business with 'Roger George' painted over the

The White Hart, shortly after it closed in 2001

239

Christian names of an earlier member of the Baker family. Very much a back-street pub, the **White Hart** was a simple beer house for many years, under the management of Francis Matthews in 1851, Samuel Bowler took over in 1856 and is remembered by the adjoining Bowler's Yard. Mrs. Elizabeth Gurney was in charge around the end of the 19th century followed by Mrs. Annie Elizabeth Lewis from the 1920s to the Second World War.

Roger Baker took over as licensee at the **White Hart** around 1988. He was described as being 'of impeccable character', but in July 2001 everything changed. The *Ledbury Reporter* provided the tale under the headline 'Axe attack landlord is jailed'. Baker thought that his wife of 39 years was having an affair with a regular customer, Trevor Hughes. On Sunday, July 16, he followed Hughes into the toilets and struck him on the back of the head with an axe and punched him several times in the face. Fortunately Hughes' injuries only amounted to cuts, grazes and bruises, but he was covered in blood. When arrested, Baker said in mitigation 'I only hit him with the blunt end'. At the Worcester Crown Court, Roger Baker pleaded guilty to assault causing actual bodily harm and possessing an offensive weapon. He was jailed for 15 months.

Following this event the pub closed its doors and later in the year Baker's wife, Dorothy, applied for planning permission for a change of use to a private house by converting the ground floor bar into three separate rooms. Although Ledbury's town council regretted 'the loss of a pub in the town', they gave their support to the application.

In the 18th century the **Fish Inn** was a drinking establishment on the north side of Church Street. Deeds in the Herefordshire Record Office show that it was bought in 1701 by Edward Jones and then passed to his son, Richard Jones. It was bought by Thomas Edy in 1792 for £100, but by this time it had ceased to be a licensed premises.

CHAPTER THIRTEEN

Ledbury
THE SOUTHEND & NEW ST.

The Upper Cross is the 'new' main road junction for Ledbury with the aptly named Southend continuing the line of High Street to the south, the Worcester Road leading off to the east, and New Street replacing the earlier Bye Street (from Lower Cross) as the road goes westwards towards the Marcles and Ross-on-Wye. This is the junction now controlled by traffic lights and marks the southern limit of the shopping area of the town although a straggle of shops continue down New Street. When markets were held in the streets of Ledbury, The Southend was the home of the cheese market and, according to Wargent in his *Recollections of Ledbury*, it was not uncommon to see 'hugh stacks of cheese ... on the pavement from Upper Cross down as far as the George Hotel'.

Surprisingly there does not appear to have been any inns in Horse Lane, now Worcester Road — the main highway leading towards Worcester and Tewkesbury from the Upper Cross. This may be because on the south-east corner stands Ledbury Park, built by the Biddulph family about 1600 and described by Pevsner in his *Herefordshire* volume as 'the grandest black and white house in the county and the only one to vie with the houses of Shrewsbury'. The boundary of the Park follows along the Worcester Road and also along The Southend with a garden wall — a rare fusion of town and country house. However, some distance along the Worcester road, near the junction with what was called 'Cut Throat Lane' in the mid-19th century, was a building once called the **Retreat**, now a house called Pomona Cottage. In an 1867 directory Joseph Shephard is shown as a beer retailer at Pomona Cottage.

Some distance along the east side of The Southend there was an inn, which was used as a convenient meeting place during the late 18th century. In July 1774, the *Hereford Journal* carried an advertisement to the effect that 'Notice is hereby given, that a meeting of the Trustees of the Ledbury Turnpike, will be held at the Bowling-Green in Ledbury aforesaid, on Wednesday the third day of August next; at which the Gentlemen are desired to attend upon particular business'. During the 1780s and '90s several other meetings were held at the **Bowling Green**, including the letting of the various turnpike tolls and meetings concerning the proposed canal.

Bowling Green Cottage with its sundial

When the licence was renewed in 1790 the publican was Timothy Stark, but the inn apparently closed soon afterwards. This is probably the house that is now called Bowling Green Cottage and was doubtless associated with the Biddulph family. In the south wall of the cottage is a fine sundial dated 1783.

Returning to the Upper Cross, the first inn on the western side of The Southend is a magnificent five-bay building called the **Royal Oak**. It was described by the Royal Commission in the early 1930s as being:

> ... built probably late in the 16th century on an L-shape with the wings extending to north and west. The front [to the Southend] has been refaced in brick. The timber-framing is exposed in the back wing and in the covered entrance to the yard. Inside the building, the dining room is lined with original panelling, with an enriched cornice; the overmantle is made up and has enriched pilasters between the bays. The roofs are of queen-post type. The cellars have rubble walling.

The **Royal Oak** was certainly operating as an inn in the latter part of the 18th century, and is considered to have been a coaching inn since 1645, whilst the rear part is reputed to have been a cider house in 1420. The Amey family ran the establishment in the late 18th and early 19th

The Royal Oak in 2001, and, below, a plaque with its basic history

THE ROYAL OAK

1420 - REAR PART OF BUILDING CONSTRUCTED, USED AS A CIDER HOUSE.

1520 - FRONT PART BUILT AS SEPARATE HOUSE, USED AS ACCOMMODATION.

1645 - THE BUILDINGS JOINED TOGETHER AND USED AS A COACHING INN.

1856 - BRICK FACADE ADDED TO THE FRONT AND ALL EXPOSED INTERIOR BEAMS COVERED IN.

1995 - RESTORED AS NEAR AS POSSIBLE TO ITS ORIGINAL STATE.

centuries, first Richard Amey in 1793 and then Mrs. Mary Amey, presumably his widow, at least until 1841 when she was 75 years old. Her son, Benjamin, then 45 years old, was also resident and presumably helped with the running of the inn. Odd things happen at most inns, but the idle reader must have wondered at one advertisement in the *Hereford Journal* of 9 April 1800: 'Black gelding left at the Oak Inn, Ledbury on 25 February — take it away or it will be sold to pay expenses'. By 1816 a Friendly Society had been founded at the inn.

Towards the end of the 19th century the landlord, Ernest Hambler Hopkins, was also the parcels agent for both the Great Western Railway and the Midland Railway Companies and advertised that an omnibus from the inn 'attends the arrival and departure of all trains'.

In 1902 the Royal Hall, adjoining the **Royal Oak Hotel** seated about 500 people and was licensed for stage plays, concerts, meetings, dances etc. In 1934 the Hall was bought by the Eastnor Lodge of Freemasons.

The **Royal Oak** continues to flourish and is still one of the principal inns of the town.

The one time Bush Tavern in 2001

A few doors south of the **Royal Oak** was the **Bush Tavern** — a beer house during the mid-19th century. Wargent commented 'The **Royal Oak** stood as now, but where the driving way is to the yard was a shop kept by Mr. Juckes as a cabinet maker's. Mrs. Amery (*sic*) was landlady then. Mr. W. Preece's paint shop was a public house kept by a Mr. Chadd. Henry Chadd was a beer retailer in 1835, but by 1851 he was a cordwainer with two employees and the pub side of the business had probably closed.

Some two doors away from the **Bush** was another licensed house — the **George Hotel** and posting establishment. This has led to a degree of uncertainty concerning the precise building that housed the **Bush,** but it was probably the one in the photograph. This was a time when landlords were brewers and after mentioning the **Bush**, Wargent went on:

> Every landlord brewed his own beer and nearly every public house had a skittle alley. At one time there was no stated hour observed for the closing of the public houses and many scenes of disorderliness were enacted at midnight and in the early hours of the morning. On Sunday the public houses were closed during the hours of Divine Service.

The **George** played an important part in the social life of Ledbury during the latter part of the 18th century, with its Assembly Room in regular use. William Hatton was the licensee from the 1770s until his death late in 1789. In 1775 he was issuing tickets for the Ledbury First

Assembly and Ball and must have survived the September 1781 advertisement in the *Hereford Journal:*

> To be let, and entered upon at Candlemas next, That large, commodious, and well accustomed Inn, called The GEORGE, in Ledbury, with or without twenty acres of meadow ground, eight of which are orcharding.
>
> Inquire of Mrs. Powles, at the Nether-Hall, Ledbury.

The grand Ledbury Ball was held at the end of both 1783 and 1784 (the latter included a Card Assembly; the admission being 2s. 6d). The following year Hatton again advertised the Ball in the *Hereford Journal:*

> LEDBURY ASSEMBLY BALL
>
> will be at the George Inn, on Wednesday the 4th day of January next. William Hatton, of the above Inn, begs leave to express his obligations to the public, for the encouragement he has received, and to inform the Nobility, Gentry, Travellers and others, that the said Inn is completely and genteely (*sic*) furnished, that he has laid in a large stock of the best Old Wines, and other Liquors, and humbly hopes by every attention in his power, to merit the future favours of the public, which will be most gratefully acknowledged, by
>
> Their most obedient servant
WILLIAM HATTON.
>
> *Dec. 28th 1785.*

Like many landlords William Hatton died in post, in December 1789, and an advertisement in the *Hereford Journal* laid out the details:

> Notices to debtors and creditors of Mr. William Hatton, late of Ledbury, Cooper and Innholder, deceased.
>
> To be let, and entered upon immediately, All that large, commodious, and well accustomed INN, called THE GEORGE, in Ledbury aforesaid, now in full and respectable business, and where the Hereford DILIGENCE, to and from London, stops six times in the week: late in the possession of William Hatton deceased; with or without 20 acres of exceeding good meadow and pasture ground, near to the town of Ledbury, eight acres of which is orcharding, now in perfection.
>
> For further particulars apply to the Rev. Michael Fowles, of the Netherhall; or to the said Thomas Nott.

N.B. A tenant may be accommodated with the Furniture and Fixtures in the said house; together with a large quantity of good Hay, Stock of Wine; Ale, Cyder, and other Liquors; but also, with the Chaises, and Horses, at a fair appraisement.

William Thomas took over the inn and the responsibility for the Assembly Room and for the regular auction sales and lettings that were held at the inn as it progressed into the 19th century. A Friendly Society had been set up at the inn some time before 1794.

An important event took place on 30 March 1798 when the canal from Gloucester to Ledbury was finally completed. The proprietors came to Ledbury by boat and the *Hereford Journal* recorded that 'A

No 10 The Southend in 2003, once the George Inn

dinner was provided at the **George Inn**, where the greatest conviviality prevailed and many appropriate toasts were drunk ... Coals of the first quality are now delivered at the Wharf [at the end of New Street] at 13s. 6d. ... the former price was 24s. per ton'.

The tithe apportionment for 1841 shows that the **George Inn** was then owned by Eliza Taylor of the **Feathers**, and was occupied by James Nott and Thomas Williams. Joseph Antonio, who was born in Germany, took over in the late 1840s and the inn took on a new phase of life, being host to the County Court, which was held there with Benjamin Parham Esq., judge, Daniel Moore, clerk, and Benjamin Hodges, bailiff. The Court also had an office in Horse Lane.

The **George Inn** was at No. 10 The Southend which Joe Hillaby describes as being:

> ...conceived on a large scale. Built of brick with three pediments, and the central bays set back, it is an odd composition which has been seriously marred by the introduction of shop windows at the northern end and inappropriate replacement windows in the attics.

The whole of the late Georgian building was doubtless the **George Hotel**; it is now split into several parts.

Dickinson observed that the names of some of the soldiers who fought in the Battle of Ledbury were etched on the small windows at the back of the premises, but that these have long since disappeared. When Byng visited Ledbury for the first time on 30 June 1781, he noted in his diary:

> The streets of Ledbury are very slippery, being paved with a marble stone, brought from a neighbouring quarry, which furnishes chimney pieces etc.

Byng does not name the inn at which he stayed but observes that on the window of the inn the following lines were engraved:

> Yes, virgin window, I presume
> The first to scribble here,
> But with a wish to save thee from
> Each brother sonnetteer.
>
> Oh, never here may word obscene
> Offend the virtuous eye,
> Nor vicious passion crimson o'er
> The blush of modesty.
>
> Sure the abandon'd wretch was born
> Of Erebus and night,
> Who writes but with design to shock
> Those eyes that seek the light.

It is evident that visitors leaving graffiti, both obscene and sexual, in inns and hotels, has been a problem for several hundred years!

Dickinson also stated that the premises were later divided and the southern part served as the County Court whose Registrar was Mr. George Piper. It was later known as Old Court House and housed the Russell Endowed Middle Class Boys School which was opened in

1899 with Mr. F.W. Wade as Headmaster 'to provide a sound education for the sons of professional and business men'. It was well before this, by 1867 at the latest, that the **George** had closed its doors to the public.

Continuing down The Southend, a confirmed toper would not have been able to pass the **Unicorn** at No. 16. Monson-Fitzjohn explains that:

> The word unicorn comes from the Latin *unum cornu,* one horn, and is first mentioned in 400 B.C. by Ctisias. It is one of the present supporters of the Royal Arms. The supporters of the old arms of Scotland were two unicorns, and on the succession of James VI of Scotland to the throne of England in 1603 as James I, he substituted the Unicorn of Scotland for the Dragon of Queen Elizabeth, and the 'Lion and the Unicorn' have remained ever since 'fighting for the crown' as the nursery books inform us.

The Unicorn was represented by medieval writers as having the legs of a buck, the tail of a lion, the head and body of a horse and a single long pointed horn, white at the base, black in the middle and red at the tip, projecting from the middle of its forehead.

A 13th-century description comes from *Le Bestiaire Divin de Guillaume,* Clerc de Normandie:

> The unicorn has but one horn in the middle of its forehead. It is the only animal that ventures to attack the elephant, and so sharp is the nail of its foot, that with one blow it can rip the belly of the beast. Hunters can catch the unicorn only by placing a young virgin in his haunts. No sooner does he see the damsel, than he runs towards her, and lies down at her feet, and so suffers himself to be captured by the hunters. The unicorn represents Jesus Christ, who took on Him our nature in the virgin's womb, was betrayed by the Jews and delivered into the hands of Pontius Pilate. Its one horn signifies the Gospel of Truth.

There are many other references to this mythical animal in literature, perhaps the best known and loved being:

> 'Well, now that we have met,' said the Unicorn, 'if you'll believe in me I'll believe in you. Is that a bargain?'
>
>   (Lewis Carroll, *Through the Looking Glass and what Alice found there*)

The **Unicorn** was active by 1784, when a Friendly Society was founded there. The preamble to the Articles of Association reads:

Whereas it hath been an ancient custom in this kingdom, for persons of divers trades and callings to meet together to cultivate Amity and good Fellowship among themselves, and for Supporting and Relieving each other in Old Age, Sickness and Infirmity ... therefore T. Pritchard and John Hope of Ledbury and others covenanted that they would keep the Articles and Rules as agreed on.

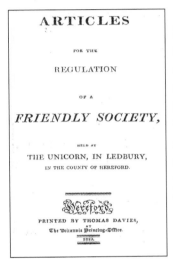

The 1810 Articles of Association

It was agreed that meetings were to be held on the first Wednesday in each month; the usual box with three keys to be provided, one key to be kept by the landlady Elizabeth Greenway. Payments were 10d. to the box and 2d. for spending at each meeting. After two years, sick pay was 5s. weekly for six months, with 3s. later. Old age or disability entitled members to 3s. 6d. weekly if payments had been made for 15 years, and the sum of £2 was allowed for burial. In addition, if £30 was in the box, £2 10s. was given to the widow and if £60 then £5 was given.

The **Unicorn**'s Friendly Society must have been successful as it was still active in 1847. In addition the Manchester Union of Oddfellows met on these premises, their lodge room apparently being built over the stables and entered from the **Unicorn** yard. The landlord in the 1830s was Isaac Gwinnett and he occupied no. 269 on the Tithe map apportionment. The inn probably closed about 1850.

Back to Upper Cross where New Street leads off to the west and, on the north side at No. 3 was once the **Bell Inn**. It was certainly in existence in the late

This private house was probably the Unicorn

New Street looking towards Upper Cross about 1910.
On the left is the Bell; on the right the Talbot

18th century and by 1830 had been bought by the Carwardine family. In 1841, when the tithe particulars were being put together, it was owned and occupied by Mary Carwardine, then 75 years old. Joseph Morgan followed her, but by 1858 it was run by Henry Traherne, who also had a wine and spirit merchant's shop in the High Street. The **Bell** closed about 1930 and the building is now occupied by an estate agent.

Only a few doors further along the street was the **Crown and Sceptre**. Now called Lanark House, this is yet another inn that became an estate agent's office, although it was empty in 2001. It adjoins the rear vehicular entry

The Bell in 2002

The Crown and Sceptre in 2001

to the **Feathers Hotel** yard and is opposite the **Talbot**. It operated as an inn for a relatively short period in the mid-19th century and is shown as no. 214 on the tithe apportionment. It was then owned by Joseph Allan Higgins and occupied by Richard Calloway who previously held the Talbot. By the time of the 1851 census Richard Calloway, then 71, described as 'late innkeeper' and wife Elizabeth, 72, were living in the St. Katherine's almshouses. After Calloway, the inn had several members of the Harris family as licensees. At that time it was the base for carriers travelling to Hereford and Gloucester and for an omnibus that went to Dymock every Tuesday. It probably closed as an inn well before the beginning of the 20th century, the last directory entry being 1876.

Further down, but still on the north side of the street, the **Ring of Bells** is the one survivor along this stretch of New Street. It was probably opened some time in the first half of the 19th century with Thomas Nott as beer retailer from at least 1835 to 1850. Apparently Nott had a hobby of hand bell ringing and kept a set of 10 hand bells, tuned to the scale of B major, behind the bar. Not surprisingly, the inn is said to have been named after his hobby.

A letter cover postmarked Worcester 19 April 1865 to the Ring of Bells

However, Alfred Watkins had different ideas, and, writing about his visit to Ledbury in 1880, observed that:

I have been curious, as one brought up in what is now a cider county, to know how that drink stood in those days [the 14th century], and here Langland [a poet of the period] clearly gives the information, when he classes it with scarce wines

No nectar and no cider
and no costly drink
Shall moisten me
or slake my thirst.

Watkins goes on:

It was not until much later that the local drinking of cider became general in our county, when Evelyn could write [in his *Pomona* of 1629] 'By the noble example of my Lord Scudamore and of some other public-spirited men in these parts, all Herefordshire is becoming in a manner but one entire orchard'. What a contrast between the 'costly drink' of Langland's time and its status in the nineteenth century, when here in Piers Plowman's land, the farmers made the 'men's cider' in great casks, and allowed to their workers seldom less than two quarts a day, and a gallon in harvest time. True it might be a bit 'peart' at times, as John Masefield's Nan remarks in handing some out to her sweetheart, but a cider drinker does not mind that, 'We like it to cut the phlegm of a morning' said one of them.

Probably the town man regarding (wrongly) cider as naturally a sweet drink would say to the men's cider 'Peart ist the word'. Many years ago when the old *Clarion* newspaper had several young journalists of outstanding ability — Robert Blatchford foremost, one of these (Neil Lyon, I think) gave his impressions in a series of articles, of a trip on foot across country which included Ledbury.

There he found himself in the evening in a decent little inn called the Ring o' Bells. Here, in a diversion, let me say that this does not mean a peal of bells used to call the parish to church, but a set of six (in a few cases two more are added on a bracket, to make the octave), hung in a hoop over the shoulders of the leading horse in a team drawing a wagon, so as to give warning in narrow lanes of their approach. Well, in the top room of this inn, the *Clarion* man found that many of the lads and lasses of Ledbury were having a dance. He was not loth to join in, and partook of the refreshments. The more solid of these he did not record, but the cider, contained in a bucket in one corner of the room to be dipped into with small mugs by the dancers, did seem to make an impression. He reported it as not unpleasant, but that later on he formed an idea that he had swallowed a spiral staircase, which as he noted, was not a nice experience to an unsuspecting Fleet Street man. But let me do justice to to-day's cider of commerce, and say that the spiral staircase is in this quite absent.

It was only in the years of cider scarcity that my father's brewery had a trade for 'Harvest beer at 6d. a gallon', reminding me of the comment I once heard on 'such tack' by a man who was asked by his master how he liked the drink. 'Well, sir, it be just right'. 'But what do you mean by "just right?"' 'Why, if it had bin a bit better we wouldn't a-had it, and if it had bin a bit wus we couldn't a-drunk it, and so it be just right'. This was in the last quarter of the last [19th] century, and now with a minimum wage act, the custom of drink allowance has ceased.

The **Ring of Bells**, whatever the origin of the name, continues to serve locals and visitors to Ledbury.

Back to Upper Cross again and taking the south side of New Street, the first inn is the **Talbot** or **Old Talbot** or even **Ye Olde Talbot Hotel**.

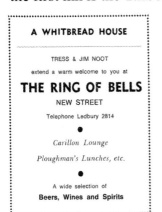

Until the beginning of the 20th century the whole of the roadside front was plastered. When this was removed it revealed fairly close-set and partly moulded timber framing.

Upper left: A 1960s advertisement
Left: The 2000 inn sign
Above: The Ring of Bells in 2001

253

In the middle of the façade at first-floor level is a large bay window. Below it, the doorway is flanked by fluted Ionic pilasters supporting an entablature with a strapwork frieze. The panelled door has a shaped and enriched panel at the top with the initials I.A.F. 1[6]00.

Inside the inn, the western room on the ground floor is lined with original panelling with entablature and carved frieze. The panelling on the west wall has a

The Talbot in the late 1880s before the render was removed; C. Wetson was the landlord

Ye Olde Talbot in the early 20th century after the render had been removed to expose the fine timber framing

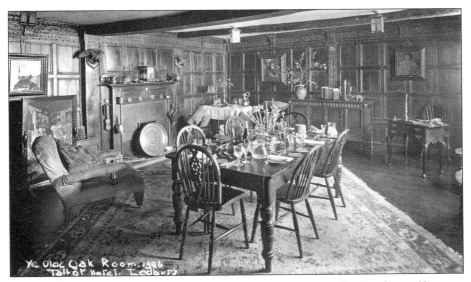

Ye Olde Oak Room. 1596
Talbot Hotel. Ledbury

central Ionic pilaster, fluted and carved and bearing the date and initials 1596, A.N. The original fireplace, in the east wall, is flanked by tapering Ionic pilasters; the overmantel is of three enriched arcaded bays divided and flanked by terminal figures and finished with an entablature with carved frieze and brackets. It is said that in the Civil War, during the battle of Ledbury, fighting took place here between Prince Rupert's men and the Parliamentarians, and that several bullets can still be seen in the panelling.

Upper: The Oak Room about 1920
Lower: The fireplace and overmantel of c.1596 about 1930

As with most inns in Ledbury, there was a Friendly Society based at the **Talbot**. Called simply the Talbot Society, it was founded in or about 1791. According to their 'Articles' meetings were to be held 'on the first Wednesday in the month at the **Talbot Inn** kept by John Brown'. The monthly sum payable was similar to that at the **Unicorn**, and the payments out were in the same proportion. They had two feast days—Midsummer Day and Boxing Day — when there was the usual procession to church, the members bearing wands. Absenteeism or indecent dress incurred a fine of 5s.

This is one of the few inns where a complete list of landlords is available and is therefore worth publishing. The framed list is in the rear passageway at the inn:

c.1782	Mary Gannesford	1912	Sidney Francis Allen
1793	John Brown	1917	Thomas Michael Pudge
1815	John Skip	1926	Edwin William Cushinn
1824	Richard Calloway	1929	James Summerfield
1834	William Norris	1933	John Allwood
1843	Thomas Norris	1944	Elsie L. Stead
1859	John Matthews	1948	Leslie W.C. Wrist
1867	Frederick May	1966	Carol Judge
1881	C.C. Wetson	1970	Darrel V. Hartshorne
1890	William Palmer	1977	Nicholas Guest
1901	Charlotte Palmer	1983	Ernest A. Harrison
1905	Alfred James Daw	1988	Pauline Jennifer Ryan
1905	Richard Drinkwater	24/8/89	Colin Geoffrey Price

The Norris family are mentioned in the 1841 census when William and Mary had a family of four. Two years later Thomas Norris was the landlord and was also a dealer in copper. He was presumably William's son and had a 34-year-old wife, Elizabeth, who came from Worcester.

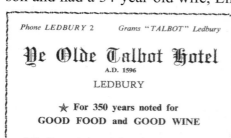

Phone LEDBURY 2   Grams "TALBOT" Ledbury

𝔜𝔢 𝔒𝔩𝔡𝔢 𝔗𝔞𝔩𝔟𝔬𝔱 ℌ𝔬𝔱𝔢𝔩
A.D. 1596

LEDBURY

★ For 350 years noted for
GOOD FOOD and GOOD WINE

Fully Licensed   A.A. and R.A.C. appointed
H. and C. in all bedrooms
Gas and Electric Fires   Garage

Left: A 1940s advertisement
Above: The 2001 inn sign

Resident with them on the census night were their nephew and niece, five Irish lodgers and three servants.

Leslie and Gwendoline Wrist held the licence of the **Talbot** for some 18 years between 1948 and 1966. During their time at the hotel, they were host amongst others to Boris Karloff, famous for his role as Frankenstein's monster. They also had a Labrador dog that was trained to ring time by holding a handbell in its teeth.

A few doors further down New Street at No. 26 was the **Vine Tap**, formerly the **Bunch of Corks**. In the yard behind the inn was the Vine Brewery. It may have had a yet earlier name as the licence of the **'Blew' Bell**, held by Ann Shinn, was renewed on 14 September 1791. As the **Bunch of Corks** it was held by a Mr. Shinn and by the 1841 census it was owned and occupied by Sarah Shinn, presumably his widow. Ten years later Richard Court had taken over — in 1841 he had been a 25-year-old cooper working at premises further down New Street. The 1851 census indicates that Richard had married Sarah, who had subsequently died, and that he was living there together with her 18-year-old son, William, an apprentice carpenter.

The Vine Tap and Brewery in the 1890s

257

Little is known about the brewery (see chapter 2), but the inn continued to serve customers until November 1974 when it closed its doors and became a private house. In 1984 it was sold and became the 'Tai Wah' Chinese Restaurant, eventually to be replaced by another called the 'Sun On'. Neither was successful and in 2001 the building was looking a little forlorn.

The last inn in Ledbury is a considerable distance further down New Street. Still open, and now called the **Full Pitcher**, it has apparently had a variety of names including the **Biddulph Arms**, the **Brick House**, and the **Red Bull**.

Upper : The Vine Tap in 1960 still sported its hanging sign
Lower : The only reminder of the Vine Tap in 1999 was the name painted over the door

The inn is close to what was the wharf on the Hereford to Gloucester Canal, opened as far as Ledbury in 1798. Of the event the *Gloucester Journal* reported:

We have the satisfaction to announce to the Public that the Herefordshire and Gloucestershire Canal is completed as far as Ledbury. The opening took place on Friday last [29 March 1798] on which day several of the Proprietors and Gentlemen of the Committee embarked at the junction of the coal branch near Newent, in the first vessel laden with merchandize which was followed by three others laden with Coal. They passed through the Tunnel at Oxenhall which is 2,192 yards in length in 52 minutes; at the further end they were met by several Gentlemen and entertained with a cold collation at the Boyce, the seat of Mr. Moggeridge.

Both ends of the Tunnel, as well as several Bridges on the Canal, were lined with spectators, who hailed the boats with reiterated acclamations; indeed the sight was very impressive and it is supposed that upwards of 2,000 people were present on their arrival at Ledbury.

John Biddulph of Ledbury Park came from an old-established family of bankers and had been interested in the canal, which passed through some of his family's lands, for some time. By the early 19th century he was on the committee, eventually becoming chairman, and was instrumental in the appointment of Stephen Ballard as manager and engineer — the man eventually responsible for the completion of the canal to Hereford.

The **Biddulph Arms** was owned by Lord Biddulph (hence the name) and was probably opened about the same time as the canal and by the 1840s had Joseph Antonio as landlord (he was also licensee of the **George** in The Southend). Wargent noted that 'Extensive business was carried on at the Old Wharf opposite the **Biddulph Arms** in timber, coal, stone and other trades ... there was once a lodge of the City of London Oddfellows here'. Antonio was followed by James Hill, who probably witnessed the demise of the canal and its replacement by the Hereford and Gloucester Railway in 1885, whilst Richard Drinkwater, who was also a farrier, took the inn into the 20th century. The inn survived the loss of its canal trade and during the 1920s, '30s and '40s it was operated by an organisation, formed in 1904, called the 'People's Refreshment House Association Ltd'. Now the **Full Pitcher**, the inn, almost in rural surroundings, continues to serve the public as, in the early 19th century, it served the bargees who brought

---

409. LEDBURY—THE FULL PITCHER INN.

ALL THAT piece of land at Ledbury containing altogether 8·422 acres or thereabouts delineated and edged pink on the plan annexed to a Conveyance dated 27th July 1955 and made between The Right Honourable Michael William John Baron Biddulph (1) John Alfred Inglis Jones and Archer Francis Laurence Clive (2) and the Company (3) TOGETHER with the messuage or Inn known as The Full Pitcher Inn and other buildings erected thereon.

Sale of the Full Pitcher to the Cheltenham Brewery in 1960

The Full Pitcher in 2001

thousands of tons of Forest of Dean stone up the canal for trans-shipment to Eastnor for the construction of Earl Somers' Gothic castle.

Past the **Full Pitcher,** the A449 crosses over the ring road and heads for Ross. Bryant's map of 1835 marks a pub called the **New Inn** about a mile after the **Full Pitcher**, but there is no other mention and it appears to have been short-lived. To the east is the parish of Donnington where the 1790 list of licensed premises in the Hundred of Radlow records an inn called the **Little London** in Donnington — almost certainly a mistake for **Little Loddon**, named after the local river — the Leadon. This is the only known mention.

Waifs and strays in Ledbury from the 1790 list include the **'Catharine' Wheel**, held by William Underwood; the **Bird in Hand**, held by Benjamin Hodges; the **Horse and Groom**, apparently not the one in Bye Street; and the **Harrow**, with William Tandy as licensee. Finally, the **New Crown** of 1790, held by John Bosley, seems, like the **Little Crown**, to have been cashing in on the name of the **Crown Inn** after it changed to the **New Inn** in the early 1780s. By 1831 the **Fox** was called the **Little Crown** and then just the **Crown**, so it is difficult to be sure which is which.

CHAPTER FOURTEEN

Towards the Malverns : Colwall

Ledbury nestles under the western flank of the Malvern Hills, with two roads crossing the ridge, one at Wynds Point and a more southerly one at Hollybush.

Colwall is an elongated village on the western side of the Malvern Hills. It comprises Colwall Green, Colwall Stone and Upper Colwall, the latter lying on the flanks of the Malverns, almost above the tunnel that takes the Hereford to Worcester railway through the hill. There is also Colwall village, almost a mile west of Colwall railway station, presumably the original settlement, but now with just the 13th-century parish church and half a dozen houses.

The 1891 Kelly's *Directory* notes that 'Soda and seltzer waters are manufactured here'. The Malvern Hills comprise extremely hard and fractured rocks which can hold a huge amount of water within the fractures and acts as a giant sponge. Because of the extreme hardness hardly anything dissolves into the water, keeping it very pure indeed.

Bottlers such as Cuffs, Burrows and, most recently, Coca-Cola Schweppes are the 19th- and 20th-century successors of the 17th-century pioneers in the marketing of Malvern Water. The Malvern Water bottling plant is in Colwall, but many people still bring their own bottles to collect water from the various gushing springs in the area.

At Chance's Pitch, on the main road from Ledbury to the Malverns, the **Wellington** is set back on the southern side of the road just before the turning to Colwall. It is named after Arthur Wellesley, 1st Duke of Wellington (1769-1852), who became a national hero after his defeat of Napoleon at Waterloo in 1815. Between 1828 and 1830 he was Prime Minister. His popularity can be judged from the fact that he is present on more English pub signs than anyone else except Nelson.

The **Wellington** was probably opened in the second quarter of the 19th century and was certainly in operation in 1850 with John Bray, then Thomas Bray by 1858, as landlord. Wives often seem to survive their husbands in the licensed trade and by 1867 Mrs. Esther Bray was the landlady.

The Wellington at Colwall in 2001

By 1881 Richard Dallow had taken over and used the rear part of his premises for his other trades — those of wheelwright and blacksmith. He was then 41 years old and he and his wife, Mary, had to support their four children and his 82-year-old mother-in-law. They had a young domestic servant to help with the household and the inn. By 1910 it was owned by the Royal Well Brewery Co. of Upper Colwall.

In December 1936, P.S. Lewis of Ledbury went to the **Wellington Inn**, to find Norah Loftus, the licensee, lying on her bed 'in a state of collapse'. A doctor was called and she became hysterical. She was clearly drunk, and even though she could hardly stand tried to make her way to the bar for another drink. In Court she agreed that when Lewis arrived there was no one responsible on the premises. She said she was suffering from the after-effects of shock for she had only purchased the inn and had the licence transferred to her three months earlier, having moved there from Warwickshire. She had brought her staff with her, but had found, for reasons which weren't stated, that she had had to dismiss two of them. Indeed, she was still so upset at the time the case was heard, that she was reported as being under medical care at the seaside. Nevertheless, she was fined the maximum of 10s.

The inn, which was described by CAMRA as 'a 17th-century pub consisting of three cottages knocked into one' still serves visitors who need refreshment before the long climb up the hill to Wynds Point and Herefordshire Beacon.

The British Camp Inn & the Malvern Hills at the beginning of the 20th century

Here is the **British Camp Inn,** on the border between Herefordshire and Worcestershire. It was functioning from the middle of the 19th century and in 1881 had Peter Pockett as licensed victualler. Then aged 62, he was still bringing up his four children, the youngest, Lucy, being

The Malvern Hills Hotel in 2002

only four years old. The inn was reasonably successful as the Pocketts could afford a domestic servant. By 1891 it had been taken over by Mrs. Annie Ingram who advertised that 'picnic parties, tourists &c. accommodated; C.T.C. house; good stabling'. The inn continued into the 20th century with Frederick Jones as landlord in 1902. It was, of course, named after one of the Iron Age hill forts that are prominent features of the Malvern ridge, the nearest being the Herefordshire Beacon. An attempt to improve trade was made in 1908 when the Colwall Park golf course was opened on adjacent land. However, the

The Yew Tree at Colwall Green in 2001

project was unsuccessful and the course closed in 1920. The inn has now become a little more up market and in 1975 changed its name to the **Malvern Hills Hotel**.

Returning to Chance's Pitch, the next turning on the left is the road leading towards Colwall — the rather winding B4218. The first inn along the way is the **Yew Tree**, on the right-hand side as the road enters Colwall Green. In 1881 Charles Pedlingham was the innkeeper. All his seven children were still at home, enjoying the benefits of the inn. The eldest, Thomas, was a butcher; next came Charles, a carpenter, and then Albert, a gardener. The remaining four ranging from 15 to 8 years old were either students or not employed. He was probably the same Charles Pedlingham who was recorded as a 'corn and flour dealer and beer retailer' at the **Terrace** in Colwall Green in 1867. The **Yew Tree** was probably a beer house in the 19th century as Thomas Orgee is listed as a beer seller rather than an inn keeper in an 1891 directory. It was evidently owned by the Pedlingham family as in 1910, when Mrs. Kate Jones was the tenant, Mrs. C. Pedlingham lived on the premises. The CAMRA guide suggests that it was once an old cider house called the **Snuff Takers Arms**.

Maybe the **Terrace** was the same as **No. 2, Pullens Row** where Elizabeth Lloyd was recorded in the 1881 census as an innkeeper. She lived there with her six children, ranging in age from two to 20, and

A 1950s advertisement for the Horse and Jockey

her mother who acted as housekeeper. However, there is no other mention of either the **Terrace** or **Pullens Row** in the records.

The road winds on through Colwall Green and towards Colwall Stone, and between the two is a large inn on the left-hand side, most recently called the **Horse and Jockey**. The present building was probably built in the first half of the 20th century, but the inn would seem to be much older and was described as a simple thatched cottage. The *Hereford Journal* for 12 February 1784 advertises a messuage to be sold 'at the dwelling house of Thomas Gilding, known by the sign of the Horse and Jockey, in the parish of Colwall'. By the 1820s it had become the **Horse and Groom** and in the 1850s and '60s Henry King was listed as the landlord, but he had many other interests, being a farmer and landowner at Colwall Park and Sly House Farm as well as being a shopkeeper. By 1881 Edmund Nash had taken over the inn, and some ten years later was listed as a 'shopkeeper and miller (water)', but it is not known whether the water mill was part of the inn or a separate building.

By 1902 the inn had come up in the world, for it was then called the **Horse and Groom Hotel** with Martin James Powell as licensee. It was opposite the old Colwall National Hunt race-course and was used to house the jockeys and grooms. However, by 1941, the 'groom' had been dropped in favour of the 'jockey', and somewhat later the inn became the **Oddfellows Arms** for a short while, before reverting to the **Horse and Jockey**. Recently it was the base for the Silurian Border Morrismen, but even with all these prodigious drinkers and the regular name changes, the inn was unsuccessful and towards the end of 2001 it closed its doors and all the ground-floor windows were boarded up.

The Horse and Jockey boarded up in 2001

The road continues into the middle of Colwall Stone and here, on the right-hand side, adjoining the turning to the railway station, is the **Colwall Park Hotel**, which may have originally been the Temperance Hotel and Lecture Hall advertised in various directories

The Colwall Park Hotel in the early 20th century

towards the end of the 19th century with William Hall as manager in 1891. However, by 1907 it was called the **Colwall Park Hotel** and on an early 20th-century postcard it is shown as offering 'garage, petrol, oil, cars for hire'. This was when hotels really did try to help early motorists in any way possible.

The hotel also has a place in sporting history. In 1926, Mrs. Scott-Bowden, who owned the hotel, joined the women's liberation movement in a big way by organising a festival of women's cricket. The event was so successful that it led to the formation of the National Women's Cricket Association. The hotel continues to be a base for the festival and provides accommodation, meals and drink for visitors, but petrol and oil are now doubtless off the menu!

The **Crown Inn** was without doubt another place that started its life as a beer house in the latter part of the

The Colwall Park Hotel shows little change in 2001

267

19th century and had George Paton as a beer retailer around the turn of the century. For many years at the beginning of the 20th century it belonged to John Pullen of The Mount, Colwall, and was tenanted by Mrs. Emily E. Horton. It still continues to serve the

The Crown in 2001

inhabitants of Colwall as well as the visitors who find their way to this side of the Malvern Hills. It has, after all, the distinction of being one of the several 'first and last pubs' in Herefordshire.

The village road continues to rise up the Malvern Hills to Upper Colwall, where once was the **Chase Inn**, shown in the 1881 census with Charles Bowers as a beer house keeper and William Thomas as his barman. In 1910 it was a Spreckley house tenanted by William Cooper and was still going strong in 1941 with Thomas Bridges as landlord. In 1960 it was sold to the Cheltenham and Hereford Brewery. and finally closed its doors some time after 1990.

---

14.   COLWALL—CHASE INN.

   ALL THAT messuage or dwellinghouse called The Chase Inn with the buildings yard garden easements and appurtenances thereto belonging containing in the whole by estimation a quarter of an acre or thereabouts situate in the Parish of Colwall in the County of Hereford on the west side of a road leading from Wynd's Point to the Wyche.

Sale of the Chase Inn to the Cheltenham and Hereford Brewery in 1960

The final inn on the road, close to the summit was the **Victoria Arms** at the Wytch where Mrs. Maria Davis was landlady and shopkeeper in 1867. Also at the Wytch in 1867 was Charles Bowers, a baker and beer retailer at an unnamed beer house.

Somewhere in Colwall was the **Royal Oak**, mentioned in the 1881 census with William Rogers, who also acted as local butcher, as innkeeper. There is no mention of the **Royal Oak** in the 1891 Kelly's

Directory, but the inn is mentioned in 1902 with Thomas Smith as landlord. However, the 1891 directory does show a Thomas Smith as a cooper at Colwall Stone.

Thomas Collis also apparently ran a beer house, perhaps at Aston Cottage, where he was living in 1881. He was then described as a 'ropemaker employing one man and two boys'. However, in an 1891 directory he had become a 'beer retailer' as well as a 'rope and twine manufacturer'.

There is also the **Herefordshire House Inn**, included in an 1858 Herefordshire directory with W. King as landlord. There is no later mention, for strictly this inn is in Worcestershire, being just across the county boundary.

One of the more interesting 'drinking houses' in the area is still called the **Ale House** at Colwall village. The phrase 'church-ale' indicated a former church festivity akin to 'wakes,' when specially-brewed ale was sold to the local people and money was collected for church purposes. The use of the suffix 'ale' indicates 'revelry' since ale was the chief liquor provided. The church ale house at Colwall has been dated by dendrochronology (tree-ring dating) to 1530, so had been in use for some time when there was an unsuccessful attempt to ban church-ales in 1603. The feast was to last a little longer, but it effectively came to an end during the Commonwealth (1649-1660).

The Ale House at Colwall

269

The church ale house at Colwall, which stands on the eastern side of the churchyard, is a rare survivor. It is recorded in an unpublished poem which is in the British Museum (an extract from 'The Newe Metamorphosis. or a Feaste of Fancie' written by J(ervis) M(arkham) gent. in 1600).

Colwall, the towne on th' other syde the Hill,
Such kyndnes shew'd me, I remember 't still.
My kinde Hoste Hartland, where so longe I lay,
If it were fit, much good of him I'de say.
Yet this I found, that they were ignorant
of that whereof they scarcely sawe the wante —
I meane the truth and imortallitie,
The waye to blisse, The sacred devoie.
Some such abuses as I here did see
I will relate: from untruth they bee free.
Neere to thou Hilles, I did one Sabote keep:
As good have bin in bed and fast asleepe.
Oh, howe they doe profane the Sabote here!
I doe protest it made me quake for feare.
For popish superstition they doe still imbrace,
Whereby Religion they doe quite deface.
They have their Church-ale and old popish guise,
Mother of errors and of monstrous lyes.
The neighboure townes, they on the Sabote feaste,
A Master of Misrule enterteynes the guest
With drums and Bagpipes and with warlike gunnes.
Thus as to May-games all the people runnes.
They great provission make to enterteyne
Ideoates, Asses, and Fooles, old and vaine
And all this revelling crue to Church must goe.
About Mid-ser-vice, they go in a Rowe
After the Priest, into the Church-ale house
(Which in the churchyard standeth) to carouse.
Not to carouse, say they, but breake their fast
Because then Calves-heads will not longer last.
Which being don, to Church they hye agate,
Their latter service serves for after grate.
Then from the Church the May-pole they doe bringe,
And set it up (tis sure a heath'nish thinge)
The rest of th' day in feasting and in dancinge

270

They spende, which should be in God's name advancinge.
Like priest, like people, passing ignorant,
Which, when I sawe it did me greatly dant.

Puritan disapproval such as this led to the closure of the Colwall ale house, but it survived as an alms-house until the early 1930s. About that time it had a thatched roof and was used as a simple cottage. In 1989 it was restored to become the church hall, a use perhaps not to far distant from its original purpose. With its long diagonal braces it has been described as a typical 17th-century building, but the tree-ring date puts it in the first half of the previous century.

The road leading past Colwall church heads in a westerly direction towards Coddington and eventually Bosbury. Coddington — 'Cota's homestead' at a time before the Domesday survey — is a small hamlet with a total population of only 141 in 1891, lost in the wooded hills of this remote part of Herefordshire

Here was the **Golden Cross Inn**, a beer house from the mid-19th century. By the 1860s Mrs. Millborough Rogers was landlady. She was described as a 53-year-old widow who farmed six acres as well as running the beer house. The inn stayed in the same family for many years, with Stephen Rogers combining the innkeeper's job with that as a wheelwright at the beginning of the 20th century. He was followed by Howard G. Bond as tenant, the inn, according to the 1910 Land Valuation, belonging to Henry Martindale Vale of Coddington Court.

It is no longer 'golden', for it closed some time after 1917. The building survives as Cross Cottage, appropriately set next to the crossroads.

The Plough was the second pub in this small settlement around the beginning of the 20th century, when Mrs. Emily Farmer and then Mrs. Emma Wood combined the small inn with the

Cross Cottage at Coddington was once the Golden Cross Inn

village shop. By 1905 Walter Vine, who may have moved from the New Inn in Bosbury, had taken over. This, like the Golden Cross, was owned by Henry Martindale Vale and tenanted by William Duggan. It closed around 1910. This may have been an inn for a considerable length of time and was previously called the **Red House** and may locally have been known as the **Dolphin**. Bryant's map of 1835 marks it as **Red House** and in the 1851 census it is shown as being occupied by Hannah Farmer, a 66-year-old widow, who was the publican. An 1858 directory describes her as a cider retailer. By 1867 James Farmer, presumably her son, had taken over and combined his duties as a landlord with those of a mason.

When the inspectors for the Royal Commission on Historic Buildings visited around 1930 they described it as being:

> ... of two storeys with attics. It was built early in the 18th century, of brick with a band between the storeys. The south front has a modillioned eaves-cornice of wood and original windows with solid frame, mullion and transom; the doorway is flanked by fluted pilasters supporting brackets and a hood with a pediment; the door is of eight panels.

Since then the house has been much altered and the windows at the front are now modern plastic ones, the front door is now a window and the door-frame has gone. Concrete lintels set under the original brick lintels support the window openings on the ground floor. The present owners hope to remedy some of this damage — obviously it was a very accomplished house when it was built. The main room was flagged and was apparently used as a reading room, for a very old local recollected that there was a sign in there that read '[B]osbury and [C]oddington [R]eading [R]oom'

The Plough in 2002, now a private house

272

— the initial capital letters being in a different paint, had presumably faded away.

A short distance outside Ledbury, the A438 branches off the main road to head for the crossing of the Malverns at Hollybush, close to the southern end of the range of hills. Eastnor is a small village at the bottom of the long climb, which would hardly be noticed by the traveller except for the presence of Eastnor Castle. This is described in the 1891 Kelly's *Directory* as:

> A noble castellated mansion of stone, built by the grandfather of the late Earl Somers in the year 1815. The structure, which occupies an elevated site, is rectangular in plan, with four circular embattled towers at the angles, and a central keep, commanding a magnificent view of the Malvern hills and the scenery for which the adjoining counties are celebrated.

The inn at Eastnor was named after the family becoming the **Somers Arms**, a public house during the third quarter of the 19th century with John Lane as farmer and innkeeper. By 1881 it was run by Richard and Mary Williams. It must have been reasonably profitable for they had three servants — a waitress, a general servant and an ostler. However, it had become a Temperance Hotel by 1891

The Somers Arms at Eastnor in the early 20th century

273

with Mrs. Fanny Hodges in charge. It continued as the Somers Arms Temperance Hotel, before changing its name to the Somers Arms Private Hotel by the 1940s. It is now a private house.

The Temperance Movement must have been very strong in Eastnor, for it even has a Temperance Fountain. It is covered over with a structure something like a church lych gate and was intended to direct Eastnor people away from the evils of drink and towards the delights of 'Walms Well water' flowing from British Camp. On one wall under the canopy is a temperance message extolling the delights of a teetotal life. Perhaps the Temperance Movement is still strong in Eastnor — the village's Millennium project was to restore the fountain to working order, but with mains water from Dwr Cymru (Welsh Water) rather than Walms Well!

CHAPTER FIFTEEN

Ledbury to Hereford

The modern road from Ledbury to Hereford (the A438) looks like an accident — a second thought — for it doesn't go straight ahead from the main road through Ledbury, it bends to the left off the direct road leading towards Bosbury. Indeed, its total insignificance was even more apparent until the beginning of the 21st century when the traffic arriving in Ledbury from Hereford had to give way to the traffic arriving from the Bosbury direction.

Ledbury was the first town in Herefordshire to turnpike its roads as a result of the Turnpike Act of 1721, passed so as to help improve the diabolical state of the clay roads in Ledbury parish. One route led to 'Stokes-Court in the Parish of Stoke Edith', the remainder of the road to Hereford being turnpiked by the Hereford Trust in 1730. The new roads were popular with the gentry, but highly unpopular for all those who were used to free, if awkward, travel, especially when going to and from market. Not only did they have to pay for themselves, but for each head of livestock, for each horse pulling a cart or carriage and a further amount dependent upon the width of the wheel rim of their conveyance.

In the early 18th century a local disturbance occurred which concerned the toll gates; by that time nine had been erected around Ledbury. Gates were frequently damaged throughout the country and the government brought in draconian measures against any offenders caught. For the first offence the punishment was whipping, for the second transportation to the colonies. When this proved ineffective, the death penalty was added for those convicted of 'cutting down turnpikes'.

On the evening of 21 September 1735, a crowd of about 100, some with blackened faces and dressed as women (after whom the Rebecca Riots were so named) assembled to destroy the toll gates. When an attack was launched on the Hereford gate, Justice Skippe of Upper Hall arrived with his servants and neighbours. He took a number of prisoners before returning to his home. Nevertheless, most of the gates were destroyed during the night.

During the course of their destructive riot, the mob marched to Upper Hall to demand the release of the prisoners, otherwise they threatened to burn down the barns and stables. Guns were fired by both parties, and three men were killed and several wounded before the rioters retired, without having rescued the prisoners. These were sent to Hereford and thence to Worcester, where seven were released for lack of evidence and two were hanged.

Two others, James Bayliss and Thomas Reynolds, were sent on to London for trial before Lord Chief Justice Hardwick. Bayliss turned King's evidence whilst Reynolds was convicted and hanged at Tyburn. Whilst his grave was being dug someone noticed that he was still breathing. The crowd stole his body away and took it to a surgeon where he was bled and given some brandy. However, Reynolds had meanwhile become soaked in a rainstorm, and because of the generally debilitated state of his health, the cold and the wet succeeded where the hangman had failed.

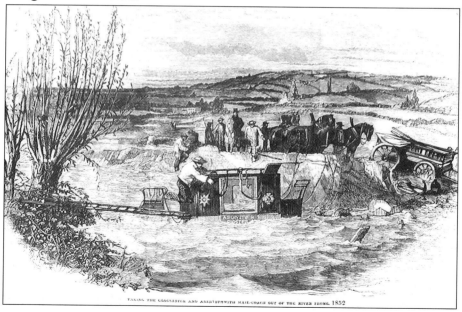

The coach accident at Frome Bridge in 1852

When the Ledbury Turnpike Act came up for renewal in 1742, the tolls were reduced in an attempt to overcome some of the resentment, but riots still occurred. Troops sent to quell the rioters were refused food and quarters by the townspeople and doubtless by the landlords of all the local hostelries.

The A438 road from Ledbury passes through the villages of Tarrington, Stoke Edith, Dormington, Bartestree and Lugwardine. The road crosses the river Frome between Dormington and Bartestree and the river Lugg at Lugwardine bridge before passing over the Lugg flats and climbing Tupsley pitch to arrive at Hereford where the **Cock of Tupsley** provides refreshment just inside the city boundary. This route was the new turnpike road, but even that had its problems as described by Mr. Nobbs, a guard on the Cheltenham to Aberystwyth Mail:

> At the time of the great floods in November, 1852, a bad accident befell this coach. Leaving Gloucester about midnight, travelling via Ledbury, it was crossing the Frome Bridge about 4 miles from Hereford when it was precipitated into the swollen river, the bridge having been washed away. Three horses were drowned, but the fourth, and the guard, driver and one passenger escaped. Not so the unfortunate inside passenger, a Hereford solicitor named Hardwick.

The earlier road took a different route. From Ledbury the main road to the west originally started with Bye Street. Well outside the built-up area of Ledbury at Flights Farm, a southern branch headed for Little Marcle whilst a north-westerly road circled around the western side of Walls Hill to join the present A438 at Waller's Green. After a few miles, the old road again left the A438 at Tarrington, staying on the higher ground to the south and passing close to Stoke Edith church and through Perton. A green lane still continues the alignment, eventually joining the winding village road by Upper Dormington and through Prior's Frome. Here in the 19th century was a 'comfortable little Wayside Inn licensed for Beer, Cider and Tobacco'. This was the **Yew Tree Inn**, which although it lost its main road position many years ago, survived as a village inn, and has recently been extended and a new entry built from the main road leading from Dormington to Mordiford. It was towards Mordiford that the old road from Ledbury led, for it was aiming for the crossing of the Lugg by the ancient Mordiford bridge, and thence through Hampton Bishop to Hereford.

277

The Verzons in 2001

The present A438 between Ledbury and Hereford still has its fair share of inns and hotels, increasing in density as Hereford is approached. There was also the occasional inn in the villages a short distance away from the main road.

On the right-hand side of the main road, about 3 miles out of Ledbury is the **Verzons**, a country house in Munsley parish. It is a seven-bay, three-storey brick building of handsome proportions set end on to the main road and it is only really appreciated when seen from the present car park. It was built around 1790 as a private house with some 18 bedrooms, but by December 1797 the contents were advertised for sale in the *Hereford Journal*:

HEREFORDSHIRE.
TO BE SOLD BY AUCTION,
BY WILLIAM CRUMP,
On Thursday, the Fourteenth instant, and the two following days, ALL the Elegant HOUSEHOLD FURNITURE and Plate, belonging to Mr. VAUGHAN, at Verzon-House, near Ledbury, consisting of mahogany four-post and other Bedsteads, with new elegant chintz and cotton Hangings, and Window Curtains; best goose Feather-beds, Mattresses, Blankets, Counter-panes, and a large quantity of Bed and Table Linen; mahogany and painted Chairs; Dining, Pembroke, and Dressing Tables; Chests and Drawers, Commodes; Looking Glasses;

and elegant mahogany Side-board, with vases and cellaret drawers; Sopha (*sic*); Carpets; China, Glass, Plate; and a large assortment of kitchen and other Furniture. Two handsome single Horse Chaises, and a good seasoned, useful Horse, only five years old.

The above furniture is modern, and having been but little used, is as good as new.

The furniture may be viewed the day preceding the Sale, between the hours of Ten and Two; and particulars may be had of the Auctioneer, at Ledbury.

The Sale begins each day at Nine o'clock in the forenoon.

By 1891 the Verzons was the residence of Rev. Arthur Henry Knapp, Rector of Aylton and curate of Pixley, Munsley being a rectory annexed to that of Canon Frome. In 1902 William Porter was living there. It became the Verzons Private Hotel, with the telephone number Trumpet 26, some time between the two World Wars.

The **Verzons Country House Hotel** was on the market at the end of the 20th century with an asking price of £395,000. It was sold in December 2000 to David Barnet Roberts and continues to attract a mixture of commercial and leisure interests. It is the base for several local society meetings including those of the Herefordshire and Gloucestershire Canal Trust.

The **Trumpet Inn** is half a mile beyond the **Verzons** on the south side of the A438 adjoining the junction with a long straight section of the A417 Leominster to Newent road. This must have been an important junction for many years — indeed, the A417 at this point is on the line of the Roman road which originally joined the legionary fortresses of Chester and Gloucester. The inn is of late 17th-century date, with later extensions. There is a 19th-century sandstone-rubble extension to the left with a catslide roof, but the main building is L-shaped and has much exposed timber-framing with brick and plaster infill. It consists of two storeys and attics. The principal room of the south-east wing has beams with run-out lambs tongue chamfer-stops.

The *Hereford Journal* of 18 July 1798 mentions some tenements to be sold at auction 'At the Dwelling-house of Mr. Richard Harris, called the **Trumpet Inn**, in the parish of Pixley'. Harris must have been unsuccessful as a landlord, for in 1819 the *Hereford Journal* included a 'Notice to creditors and debtors of Richard Harris of the

279

Sale of Household furniture in 1857.
The various items give a vivid picture of the
many activities taking place at an inn such
as the Trumpet in the mid-19th century

Trumpet ... Victualler and Huckster ...' who had then been declared bankrupt.

In the late 1850s and 1860s Hannah Taylor was described as beer retailer and shopkeeper — the **Trumpet** being a simple beer house, like many others in the country areas. She must have taken over after the sale of the household furniture advertised in the *Hereford Times* on 26 September 1857. The sale details provide a fascinating view of the general household goods in a mid-19th century country beer

Some of the words used above have gone out of general use:

Dimity—A stout cotton fabric, woven with raised stripes or fancy figures; usually employed undyed for beds and bedroom hangings, and sometimes for garments.

Moreen—A stout woollen or woollen and cotton material either plain or watered, used for curtains etc.

Skeet—A wooden bucket, pail, tub, or similar vessel used for some domestic purpose, chiefly for holding milk or water, and usually having a handle or handles formed by staves rising above the rims. Now a dialect word, chiefly in the north and west midlands.

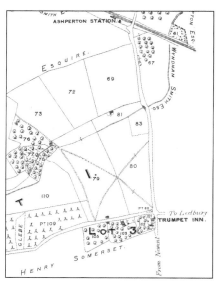

The plan accompanying the sale details (opposite) in 1890

Re WILLIAM HOMES, Deceased, HOMES v. HOMES.

HEREFORDSHIRE and GLOUCESTERSHIRE.

PARTICULARS, PLANS, AND CONDITIONS OF SALE

OF VALUABLE

FREEHOLD AND LEASEHOLD ESTATES,

PUBLIC HOUSES,

COTTAGES, &c., AND WOODLANDS,

KNOWN AS

THE POOLEND, CASTLE & CINDERS, TIPSGROVE, HURSTANS, AND

THE HILL FARMS, THE TRUMPET INN, MAJOR'S ARMS,

"The Trumpet Inn" is situated at the corner of four Cross Roads, and about 500 yards from the Ashperton Railway Station, and contains Bar, Bar Parlour combined, Tap Room, Bakehouse and Shop, Kitchen, underground Cellar and Four Bedrooms. The Out-buildings are Brewhouse, Fowls' House, Stable, Pigstye, Gig House, Cider Mill, Large Warehouse, and small Shed, and the following Enclosures:—

No. ON PLAN.	NAME.		STATE.					A.	QUANTITY. R.	P.
101	Trumpet Inn, Buildings and Garden	...		...	...	...	...	0	2	4
103	Two Cottages, Warehouse, and Orchard	...	Pasture Orchard, &c.	...	...	...	...	2	1	18
105	Trumpet Orchard	... ...	Pasture Orchard	...	...	...	...	2	0	21
102	Ditto	... ...	Ditto	...	...	...	...	0	2	39
							TOTAL	A5	3	2

The above, with the exception of the Two Cottages and Gardens, are in the occupation of Mr. Charles Hodges, at £43 per annum. Tenant paying all out-goings, except Tithe Rent Charge, apportioned at £1 7s. 0d. Land Tax 6s.

The Two Cottages, part 103, one brick-built and tiled, containing Four Rooms and Back Kitchen, and the other timber and brick-built and thatched, containing Two Rooms, each having a good Garden, are let to Mr. Charles Dutson and Mr. John Gibbons at the Rent of £8 per annum. Landlord paying Rates and Taxes.

Total Rental of Lot 3, £51.

This Lot is bounded on the north and east by Main Roads and on the south and west by Lands belonging to Lady Henry Somerset.

Sale of the Trumpet and the Major's Arms in 1890 after the owner,
William Homes, died and his will was contested

The Trumpet Inn in 1998

house, where the beer was still being manufactured by the innkeeper.

The **Trumpet** was up for sale again in 1890 together with over 5 acres of ground and two nearby cottages. The inn included a bakehouse and shop, whilst the outbuildings provided the landlord with the opportunity to brew his own beer and make cider.

At the beginning of the 20th century the beer house was rather splendidly described as **The Original Trumpet Inn** with James Townsend as shopkeeper and beer retailer. By 1941 George Rock was licensee.

The use of 'original' is a reminder that there is no copyright law relating to pub names. It may suggest that there had been an argument concerning seniority with another pub of the same name. Dunkling and Wright suggest that it was 'formerly a London sign as well, and possibly a synonym, in a loosest sense, of Bugle Horn, connected with the delivery of the mail'. The 'post-horn', used by the guard on the coach to announce the imminent arrival of the mail, was somewhat smaller that the trumpet and was usually made of brass rather than copper or German silver. The trumpet or bugle was used for military purposes before being included in the orchestra. Although the link is somewhat tenuous, it has some interest, for the 'bugle' was a wild ox, whose horn was used as a drinking vessel up to the 16th century and possibly later. The horn, suitably adjusted, could also be used as a hunting horn.

The small village of Ashperton lies a short distance north of the Trumpet crossroads and straddles the A417. Besides being on the Roman road from Gloucester to Chester and a one-time station on the railway from Worcester to Hereford, Ashperton was also a village on the Gloucester to Hereford canal. Although the section of the canal from Gloucester to Ledbury opened in 1797, it was not until 1845 that the course was completed to Hereford. The canal was still operating in 1858 with Jeremiah Cale as the agent, but its life was limited as the railway was completed in 1861. The construction of both canal and railway must have provided much needed trade for the local pubs. Although very much a rural area, Ashperton station boasted a station master — Evan Griffiths — and two coal merchants operated from the railway yard. The station closed in 1965.

In November 1797 the *Hereford Journal* advertised the sale of a property (including 'Black Lands') [see below] 'At the Dwelling-house of John Hill, called the **Three-Horse-Shoes Inn**, in the village of Ashperton'. Other house and property sales took place there on a reasonably regular basis especially towards the end of the 18th century. The reference to 'black lands' is interesting — the Blacklands is a crossroads settlement on the northern fringe of Ashperton, probably close to the original crossing of the south/north Roman road with another one leading from the direction of Wales towards Worcester. Field and road names often have a Roman connection and the use of 'black' is reasonably common. In Herefordshire alone there are some 75 cases of 'black' plus another name, often suggestive of a marshy, peaty pool or a wood. There are also some 84 instances of the use of 'black lands' for a field (including one in Lugwardine between Hagley and Sheepcot). It is suggested that black land could well refer to a patch of ground where the soil is much darker than the surrounding area — a likely indication of early settlement. The suffix '-wardine', meaning an enclosure or yard around a house, can also have Roman connections — Blackwardine being a typical example. Thus Lugwardine can be interpreted as 'settlement by the river Lugg'.

The Box Bush Inn in 2000

There is a single mention of an inn called the **Fleece**, with W. Wilks Jnr. as landlord in 1856, but by the beginning of the third quarter of the 19th century the only licensed premises mentioned in Ashperton was the **Box Bush Inn**. For much of the latter part of the 19th century it was run by the Burgwyn or Burgwin family. George was the innkeeper in 1867, but by 1881 his position had been taken over by Jane, then a 59-year-old widow, and her unmarried son Frank, a carpenter and joiner. It was sufficiently viable for them to have a 16-year-old general servant, Mary Elsmore, who came from Withington. Like many small public houses it was also the village shop. By the turn of the century George M. Watkins had taken over and besides running a grocery store he advertised 'accommodation for travellers. Charges moderate. Good stabling'.

In the *Herefordshire Village Book* one writer recorded:

> Until 1988 there was one village pub — **The Box Bush** — but it closed down, having been in the licensee's family for over 80 years. During the Second World War this pub ran the 'corner' shop and at one time dealt with 1,000 ration books — many of these belonged to gypsies who were working for local farmers. This shop closed in the 1960s and since then there has not been one. Sadly there is now no pub, but the **Hopton Arms**, just further down the road although just over the border into Munsley village, is considered the 'local'.

The **Hopton Arms**, somewhat closer to the Trumpet crossroads than the **Box Bush** and opposite Ashperton Park, is indeed in Munsley parish although well away from the centre of the village. It was originally called the **Royal Oak**, but was renamed by Mrs. Hopton in the 1930s when she renovated the pub. The Hopton family of Canon Frome owned much of the land in the area until the estates were sold in the 1950s.

The **Royal Oak** served a dual purpose in the second half of the 19th century, when the landlord, Richard Spencer, was variously a butcher

Above: the Hopton Arms in 2001
Right: The inn sign showing
Colonel Hopton

and a farmer — the inn also serving as the local abattoir! Belonging to the Hoptons' Canon Frome estate, the inn also served as a hunting lodge for parties staying at the Court.

Some 60 years after its name change to the **Hopton Arms**, the inn was closed and put up for sale with an asking price of £275,000. The selling agents were obviously not too confident of its future as a pub, for they included a comment that 'it may well have potential for other alternative commercial uses subject to Planning Permission'.

However, it was successfully sold as an inn and in October 1999 it reopened with a father and son partnership — John and Peter Groutage. They found a painting of Colonel Hopton and Mrs. Cibil Hopton at Canon Frome Court and copies of these now form the two sides of the sign outside the inn. Colonel Hopton was actually Lt. Col. John Dutton Hunt, captain of the British Army shooting team and a Director of the Royal Academy of Music. He took the name Hopton when he married Cibil Baskerville of Clyro. The Hoptons had a problem producing male offspring so Cibil took her mother's maiden name to keep the family lineage going. Colonel Hopton died

Sale of timber from the Stoke Edith Estate at the Foley Arms in 1862

in the mid-1930s; his wife died in her villa in the south of France following the Italian invasion.

The 1999 renovation has given the inn a Victorian image with an old bank counter forming a centrepiece bar.

Back to the A438 and turning towards Hereford, the **Tarrington Arms** is an imposing building on the left-hand side adjoining a minor crossroads. It is another inn with a relatively long history and several names. When the Hon. John Byng, travelled out of Hereford on Saturday, 11 August 1787, he decided 'To recruit my spirits I stop'd at the village of Tarrington and eat bread and cheese; and drank brandy and water, which forced me along with more alacrity'. The inn was obviously providing the right kind of service!

During the latter part of the 18th century there were several advertisements in the *Hereford Journal* for land, timber and property to be sold at the **New Inn**, Tarrington, doubtless a reference to the then new building. Early in the 19th century it became the **Foley Arms**, recognising the fact that all the land and virtually all the houses in Tarrington and the adjoining parishes belonged to the Foley family of Stoke Edith.

The *Hereford Journal* vividly describes an extraordinary escape at the **Foley Arms**:

The Foley Arms about 1900

On the night of 28 February 1832 Levi Parker, a pig dealer residing at Ledbury, who had arrived at the Foley Arms, Tarrington, where he slept, arose in his sleep, opened the window of his bedroom at the top of the house and fell over the parapet into the garden plot in front of the Inn, a height of more than thirty feet, which of course had the immediate effect of rousing the somnambulist to a serious view of his situation, and to thankfulness for his extraordinary escape, for he was not injured, and attended the market in this city where he transacted his business.

In the mid-19th century Mrs. Hannah Davies was the publican and also acted as sub-postmistress, but by 1867 John Jones had taken over, combining the jobs of beer retailer and blacksmith. Changes continued with the 36-year-old Frederick Bromfield as landlord in 1881. The business was sufficiently good for Frederick and his wife Mary Ann to employ two domestic servants and one ostler. The Bromfields were followed a decade later by George Sutherland. Shortly afterwards an attempt was made to improve the image and it became the **Foley Arms Hotel** under the management of Henry George Huntley.

For much of the 20th century it continued as a minor hotel, a convenient half-way point between Ledbury and Hereford. Towards the end of the century it suffered a rather unfortunate name change, becoming the **Glass Pig**! It was given the name when a number of Herefordshire properties, including the inn, were acquired to provide residential homes for people with learning disabilities. The inn was run as both a hostelry and a setting for providing day activity, and the name was chosen, presumably, to try and span the two activities. Of course there is always the rhyming slang 'pig's ear' meaning 'beer'.

The 1960s inn sign. The motto means 'That I may be of use'

In 1998 Richard Gannon took over the inn and once again the name was changed — this time a little more appropriately to the **Tarrington Arms**. History repeated itself in May 2000 when the village post office once again moved to the pub with Angela Davies as the new postmistress, continuing the over 100-year-old institution of a post office in Tarrington village.

The inn was up for sale again in February 2001, when it was described as having 'a large bar, snug, restaurant, five letting bedrooms, two self-contained flats, a beer garden and a car park'. Offers for the freehold, grade II listed building were invited around £300,000.

The Foley Arms as the Glass Pig

There has never been a pub in either of the next two villages — Stoke Edith and Dormington — although the latter was home to the **Dormington Court Hotel** for many years. Although licensed, this establishment did not really welcome locals coming in for a drink and concentrated on meals and residential use.

288

Dormington changes to Bartestree where the road crosses the river Frome — the site of the fatal accident back in 1852 and still called 'five bridges' giving some indication of the difficulty of crossing the river at this point. The road then rises past the now closed Roman Catholic Convent of our Lady of Charity and Refuge, built in 1863 as a refuge and as a Kelly's *Directory* delightfully describes 'for the reformation of fallen women and the preservation of those who are in danger of falling into bad courses'. It is perhaps as well that there were no licensed premises in the immediate neighbourhood!

The **New Inn** at Bartestree, or more correctly at Hagley, is not the original inn in this village. There was an earlier **New Inn**, on the same side of the road and a short distance to the east, when the present building was a private house called the Ferns. This is a high-Victorian house built for William Henry Godwin in 1880. His father, William Godwin, was the founder of the Godwin Brick and Tile Works at Lugwardine. With help from his younger brother, Henry, he developed the encaustic wall and tile business into a nationally recognised company. They produced tiles which were used in churches and cathedrals throughout the country and in such diverse places as Istanbul and New South Wales. Eventually the brick works was transferred to a new site in Tupsley and the decorative tile manufacture moved to a new site adjoining the railway at Withington. William died in 1883 and his son William Henry inherited the firm. By the turn of the century both Henry and William Henry had sold out; Henry at the age of 68 went on to pastures new, for he set up as a cider maker in Holmer, eventually selling the business in 1905. William Henry sold the Withington works in 1907, but this was quite a while after he had built the Ferns as his family residence.

The spiky, highly-decorated Gothic exterior exhibits some Godwin wall tiles, but internally the building contains excellent examples of sumptuous wood and plaster work and many more decorative tiles. There are even tiles in the cellars where the floors are made of seconds and now make a splendid display of the variety of tiles that were produced in the local factory.

Hilo Williams was landlord at the original **New Inn**, for he is shown as a beer house keeper in the 1881 census when he was 39 years old. His wife, Maria, was then 45 and there is no mention of children. He is

The New Inn at Bartestree in 2003

mentioned in the 1891 directory, but by 1902 George Cole had taken over. The Williams family had returned by 1905 when Mrs. Selina Williams was licensee. She stayed for at least 12 years, but by 1926 yet another Hilo Williams had taken over. The fore-name Hilo is not too unusual in the area; the Handley family of Bromyard (undertakers) use it as a middle name.

In this immediate area there was apparently a **Traveller's Rest** situated on the Hagley Pitch. The story goes that it, and the **Railway Inn** at Withington, were both closed by William Godwin before he

---

THE "CROWN AND ANCHOR" INN PUBLIC HOUSE,

Lugwardine,

Together with GARDEN and ORCHARD, situate about Three Miles from Hereford.

Let to Mrs. Ruth Hyde at Rents amounting to **£39 per Annum.**

LEASEHOLD – For a Term of 14 Years from the 3rd August, 1894, at £45 per Annum.

The Crown and Anchor was one of the many local inns belonging to the Hereford based Watkins' Imperial Brewery, and was included in the sale of the Brewery and some '35 Hotels, Public and Beer Houses' in 1898

opened the Tile Works at Withington in order to prevent his workmen from drinking away their wages! Perhaps the reason was associated with the way that Mrs. Martha Pember ran the beer house in the 1850s and '60s. On 9 January 1858 she was charged with allowing drunkenness in the **Traveller's Rest** and was fined 5s.

The new **New Inn** has survived all the prejudices and is now an integral part of the developing urban suburb of Hereford that is growing between Bartestree and Lugwardine.

There is another inn in Lugwardine — the **Crown and Anchor** — situated just off the main road, but once on the road that led around the New Court estate to join the Worcester to Hereford

1931 advertisement for the Crown and Anchor

road a short distance before the Lugg bridge. The **Crown and Anchor** is a 17th-century building with large 18th-century and modern additions. In 1813 Mr. Bowen, who was the licensee, augmented his earnings by tailoring. For many years it was an inn where the licensee was a woman — Mrs. Mary Ann Pymble in the 1850 and '60s, Mrs. Ruth Hyde around the turn of the century, and Mrs. Gertrude Matthews in 1931. By 1941 Mrs. Gertrude Southall was landlady — maybe Mrs. Matthews had re-married. There was the occasional man! Benjamin Martin was innkeeper at the time of the 1881 census and William Hyde in 1913.

35. ALL THAT cottage or dwellinghouse garden and orchard with the appurtenances containing in the whole one acre (be the same more or less) lying in Lugwardine and formerly within the Manor of Lugwardine in the County of Hereford and formerly known by the name of The Anchor Inn but now called and known as The Crown and Anchor Inn Lugwardine. *Crown & Anchor Lugwardine.*

At a much later date the Crown and Anchor was included in the Sale of the Hereford and Tredegar Brewery to the Cheltenham and Hereford group

The Crown and Anchor in 2003

The inn is still a thriving establishment, which for many years has been the meeting place for the Lugg Commoners. It is well known for its home-cooked food, and is a convenient 3 miles out from the centre of Hereford.

The A438 passes over the river Lugg by a bridge aligned at right-angles to the general lie of the land and then crosses the Lugg flats, an area which regularly floods on each side of the road, but leaves the slightly raised thoroughfare clear. At the end of the flats is the Tupsley Pitch with the **Cock of Tupsley** on its summit. The old **Cock Inn** was established well before 1800, but on a different site. An advertisement in the *Hereford Journal* of 17 September 1786 publicised a main of cocks between the gentlemen of Herefordshire and Breconshire that was to be fought '…at the Cock-Inn, within one mile of Hereford, (on the Ledbury road)' and this strongly suggests that the name of the establishment was derived from the inn hosting cock-fighting. It has also been suggested that it derived its name from the 'cock horse' that was needed to pull laden wagons heading for market up the adjoining hill from the Lugg flats as its

The Cock of Tupsley in 1994

present sign indicates. Dunkling and Wright provide a third alternative based on 'cock-ale'. This was apparently ale mixed with the jelly of a boiled cock and other ingredients. The authors do not make it obvious whether this drink was for pleasure or as a medicine!

Two years after the match between the gentlemen of Herefordshire and Breconshire the **Cock** was advertised as being for sale by auction, but the result was, as usual, not recorded. The **Cock** continued as licensed premises well into the 19th century, and the *Hereford Journal* of 4 September 1819 advertises wheat to be sold by auction at the **Cock**. The premises were offered for sale in 1835:

> All that old-established and desirable Inn called the Cock at Tupsley, with garden, malthouse, cider mill, cider house, stable, shed, piggeries, fold and about 3 acres of superior pasture land and orcharding adjoining, now in the occupation of William Teague.

It seems that the licensed use of the premises may have ceased not long after this, as the name does not appear in the more detailed trade directories that were published from the middle of the century onwards. Despite this the name continued to be used, and the 1888 six-inch Ordnance Survey map still includes the Cock of Tupsley on a site opposite the entrance to the present car park.

The present **Cock** was built in the 1960s by the side of the new road that had been built straight up Tupsley Pitch. As part of this the Tupsley Court estate was cleared away, and the **Cock** was built in a position that was marked on the 1888 Ordnance Survey map as a large pond, which was later filled in. The section of the old road that was superseded still survives as the narrow lane that winds up the hill past Lower House Farm, now the home of the Herefordshire Nature Trust, and joins the main road at Tupsley House at the top of the pitch.

The present **Cock of Tupsley** is just outside the city boundary and is the last pub in our tour of the pubs of East Herefordshire. The pubs of Hereford City were dealt with in the first volume in this series, and the remaining part of the county — the south-western quadrant — will be included in a forthcoming volume describing the pubs of Hay-on-Wye, the Black Mountains and the Golden Valley.

Sources & References

GENERAL WORKS

A Tour through the Whole Island of Great Britain, (Daniel Defoe), ed. P.N. Furbank
    & W.R. Owens, 1991
The Itinerary of John Leland, ed. L. Toulmin Smith, 5 vols., 1908 (reprint 1964)
The Life of Samuel Johnson, James Boswell, 1791
The Torrington Diaries, Hon. J. Byng, 1781 – 87

THE COUNTY

A Pocketful of Hops, Bromyard Local History Society, 1988
Alfred Watkins, A Herefordshire Man, R. Shoesmith, 1990
An Inventory of the Historical Monuments in Herefordshire, Vol.2, Royal
    Commission on Historical Monuments, 1931
Beer and Britannia. An Inebriated History of Britain, Peter Haydon, 2001
Bromyard: A Local History, Bromyard Local History Society, 1970
Bromyard round and about, Bromyard Local History Society, 1991
Bromyard, Minster, Manor and Town, P. Williams, 1987
Domesday Book, Herefordshire, F. & C. Thorn (eds), 1983
Castles and Moated Sites of Herefordshire, R. Shoesmith, 1996
Cradley. A Village History, Wynnell M. Hunt, 2002
Hereford and Worcester Railways Remembered, L. Oppitz, 1990
Hereford in 1892, Hereford Times, 1892
Herefordshire in Old Photographs, A. Sandford, 1992
Herefordshire on Old Postcards (Vols 1 & 2), T. Ward, 1986 & 1989
Herefordshire Place-Names, B. Coplestone-Crow, 1989
Hops and Hop Picking, R. Filmer, 1982
A Glimpse of Old Ledbury, David Postle
Ledbury in 'The Archive Photographs Series', T. Ward, 1996
Ledbury, A Medieval Borough, J. Hillaby, 1997
The Leominster Guide, Rev. Jonathan Williams, 1808
Little Cowarne, A Herefordshire Village, J. Hopkinson, 1983
Lugwardine in the Nineteenth Century. Lugwardine Historical Society, 1988.
Masefield Country, A. Watkins, Ms.
Memorials of the Civil War in Herefordshire, Two Vols., J. Webb, 1879
    (Reprint 2002)
Memories of Stoke Lacy 1952-2002, ed. John R. Davies, 2002

Nooks and Corners of Herefordshire, H.Thornhill Timmins, 1892 (Reprint 1974)
Portrait of Wellington Heath, P. Garnett, 2002.
Real Ale & Cider in Herefordshire (CAMRA), I. Wraight and M. Dyer, 1985
Recollections of Ledbury, George Wargent – Ten articles that appeared in *The
    Ledbury Free Press and Hereford Advertiser* in 1905, reprinted by Ledbury
    and District Society Trust in 1998.
The 1675 Thomas Blount Manuscript, N.C. Reeves (ed.) nd.
The Book of Ledbury, J. Hillaby, 1982
The Buildings of England: Herefordshire, N. Pevsner, 1963
The Folklore of Hereford and Worcester, R. Palmer, 1992
The Folklore of Herefordshire, E.M. Leather, 1912
The Herefordshire Village Book, W.I., 1989
The Story of Herefordshire's Hospitals, Charles Renton, 1999
This is Ledbury, Ledbury Chamber of Commerce, nd
Whitbourne: a Bishop's Manor, P. Williams, 1979
A Survey of Historic Parks & Gardens in Herefordshire, D. Whitehead, 2001
*A Parishioner's Account of Cradley in 1913, with a further glimpse into the life of
    the Parish between the years 1914 and 1929,* Miss Edwards, 1994

JOURNALS AND NEWSPAPERS ETC.
Transactions of the Woolhope Naturalists' Field Club, 1851 to date
Directories as quoted
Hereford Journal
Hereford Times
Bromyard News
Bromyard News and Record
Malvern Gazette and Ledbury Reporter
Ledbury Free Press and Hereford Advertiser

INNS, TAVERNS & BREWERIES
Arnold Perrett Sale, 1937
Hereford & Tredegar Brewery Sale, 1948
A Taste of Ale, R. Palmer, 2000
The Old Inns of England, A. Richardson, 1952
British Inn Signs, E. Delderfield, 1965
100 Herefordshire Pubs, J. Hurley, 1984
Pub Names, L. Dunkling & G. Wright, 1987
Brewing Industry, L. Richmond & A. Turton, 1990
Historic Inns and Taverns of the Welsh Marches, P. Davies, 1993
Paths & Pubs of the Wye Valley, H. & J. Hurley, 1998
The Pubs of Hereford City, R. Shoesmith, 1998
The Pubs of Leominster, Kington & north-west Herefordshire, R. Shoesmith &
    R. Barrett, 2000
The Pubs of Ludlow & Neighbouring Villages, T. Hobbs, 2002
The Pubs of Ross & South Herefordshire, H. Hurley, 2001

Index

LIST OF INNS

LIST OF OWNERS & LANDLORDS

Also from Logaston Press

Herefordshire's Postcard Past
by Tim Ward ISBN 1 904396 00 3 £9.95

In this collection of just under 200 postcards of Herefordshire places and life, largely made in the early 1900s, Tim Ward manages not only to provide interesting insights to the view or activity shown, but to bring out some of the history of postcard production in the county.

Sir Samuel Meyrick & Goodrich Court
by Rosalind Lowe ISBN 1 873827 88 1
320 pages with over 130 black and white and 30 colour illustrations £17.50

Sir Samuel Rush Meyrick was the founding father of the systematic study of arms and armour. His last days were spent in Herefordshire, where his magnificent collection of arms, armour and antiquities could be visited in his mock Gothic castle of Goodrich Court. The collection is now largely dispersed, with some of the choicest pieces at the Wallace Collection and at the British Museum.

When the Meyrick family moved on, Goodrich Court enjoyed 70 years as a grand house until its idyll was brought to an end by the Second World War. After sheltering Felsted School during the war, it remained empty and forlorn until demolished in 1950. Its exotic gatehouse still remains alongside the A40 trunk road between Ross and Monmouth.

Sir Samuel's story, and that of Goodrich Court and its treasures is no dry antiquarian tale, but often full-blooded and sometimes humourous.

Tewkesbury Abbey: History, Art & Architecture
edited by Richard K. Morris & Ron Shoesmith
ISBN 1 904396 02 X (hardback) £25 1 904396 03 8 (paperback) £17.50
Almost 300 pages, with colour plates

This is the first major book to appear on Tewkesbury Abbey for over a century and the most wide-ranging ever to be written on the subject. It brings together 18 authors, all of them acknowledged experts in their respective fields and in their acquaintance with the abbey. They shed new light on many aspects of the abbey's history, life and art, for the abbey is an internationally famous example of a Benedictine monastic church, outstanding for its medieval architecture and stained glass, and with a collection of tombs and chantries second only to Westminster Abbey.